في ذكرى

مارك لينز

NAGUIB MAHFOUZ

Essays of His Later Years

The Non-Fiction Writing of Naguib Mahfouz: Volume IV

Translated by R. Neil Hewison
Introduction by Rasheed El-Enany

First published in English in 2020 by
GINGKO
4 Molasses Row
London SW11 3UX

This first paperback edition published in 2026.

Originally published in Arabic.
© 2015 *Al Dar Al Masriah Al Lubnaniah, Cairo*

Translation Copyright © 2026 R. Neil Hewison
Introduction Copyright © 2026 Rasheed El-Enany

The moral right of the authors, and of the translator to be identified as the authors and the translator of this book has been asserted in accordance with the Copyright, Designs and Patents Act, 1988.

A CIP catalogue record for this book is available from the British Library.

All rights reserved. All rights reserved. Except for brief quotations in a review, no part of this publication may be reproduced or transmitted in any form or by any means, electronic or mechanical, including photocopy, recording, or any information storage and retrieval system, without permission in writing from the publisher.

The authorised representative in the EEA is:
Haus Publishing
Casella Postale 32
50037 San Piero a Sieve (Fi)
Italy
(gpsr@gingko.org.uk)

Paperback: ISBN 978-1-914983-44-3
ebook: ISBN 978-1-909942-14-1

Typeset in Optima by MacGuru Ltd

Front Cover: Creswell, K.A.C. The Citadel. K.A.C. Creswell Photograph Collection of Islamic Architecture, Photograph Collections, Rare Books and Special Collections Library, The American University in Cairo, Egypt.

Printed in the United Kingdom by CPI Group (UK) Ltd, Croydon CR0 4YY

www.gingko.org.uk

تمت ترجمة هذا الكتاب بمساعدة صندوق منحة الترجمة
المقدمة من معرض الشارقة الدولي للكتاب

This book has been translated with the assistance of the Sharjah International Book Fair Translation Grant Fund

Contents

Introduction

by Rasheed El-Enany

On 14 October 1994, an impoverished young man, under the influence of fanatic religious instigation, tried to assassinate Naguib Mahfouz by stabbing him in the neck as he was about to be driven by a friend to a gathering somewhere in Cairo; hence the cut-off date of the essays assembled in this volume. Following the attack, which he miraculously survived, Mahfouz was left unable to use his writing hand and his weekly column in *Al-Ahram* newspaper, of which this is a collection, stopped for a while, to be continued later in a different format. As I was getting closer to the end of the articles, a growing feeling of uneasiness gradually took hold of me. Turning to the article dated 12 October 1994, a cold shiver ran down my spine, as if I were living through a countdown to the stabbing incident. Two days after the publication of that article a knife was going to make its way to the neck of the great man, who would have been smiling affably and raising his hand in a greeting motion at the young man he thought was approaching to greet him, as strangers often did when they saw Mahfouz. In my horror, I cannot help but think that at that moment the knife must have resented its inanimate state which made impossible an opposition to the action it was being directed to do. Like the rest of us, Mahfouz, being no privy to the future, had no idea that two days after publishing an article titled 'Good Morning to the World' a terrorist attempt would be made on his life.

I continued reading the articles of October 1994 with mounting anxiety and trepidation. How could he go on writing, week after week, as if nothing was going to happen? He must be warned! The imminent doom must be intercepted! Someone must scream in alarm in the face of the unknown! On 12 October, he writes that we live in 'a world replete with offensive things, and it is rare to come across something pleasing', yet he concludes his article with characteristic stoicism, calling to his readers to 'open your newspaper, and do not despair of taking in what is better and brighter'. How ironic! Two days later those same readers were going to open their newspapers to read the news of the attempted murder of their beloved author. During the rest of the month and while Mahfouz was fighting for his life, *Al-Ahram* published two more articles penned by him, dated 20 and 27 October: he had written and submitted them ahead of schedule, as he often did.

In the first, titled 'From Enlightenment to Comprehensive Reform', he writes of terrorism as a symptom of the absence of social justice: 'extremist ideas and calls to terrorism may find an echo in souls that are exhausted by poverty, despair, and feelings of injustice.' This is an argument he repeats ad infinitum throughout the essays of this book and elsewhere in his fiction and non-fiction writing. For him, terrorism is a social phenomenon with underlying causes which could not be resolved through security measures but through democracy, education and social justice. In the second article, titled 'Pathological Tensions', he points out that all discussions in society are 'marked by the overwhelming stamp of vehemence and violence'. He further laments that people 'cannot bear other opinions' and have become lacking in 'any kind of understanding or tolerance', and that 'the climate of terrorism has gained ground in literature, thought, and debate'. He concludes by blaming all these serious faults in society on the damage caused by living far too long under 'totalitarian regimes'. It was as if Mahfouz, in writing these articles, immediately before the incident, was prophetically running ahead of everyone in trying to explain and place in context the terrorist attempt on his life that was about to happen. In fact, this entire volume with its scores of essays written over a five-year period strangely leads up to a state of mind with which the assassination attempt does not come as a shock.

Mahfouz writes about a polarised society: one bereft of its old values; one where democratic government is a sham and an emergency law giving the state huge freedom-curbing powers has been habitually renewed since the assassination of Sadat in 1981; where social inequality is paramount; corruption is rife; and where fundamentalist intolerance has taken root and adopted armed struggle as the means to resist an unjust authoritarian state. If we look at the first essay in this volume, dated 19 January 1989, we find that its title alone says it all and paves the way to 14 October 1994: 'Towards a Society Not Based on Violence.' If anything, Egyptian society five years on was even more deeply mired in violence, such that one of its greatest writers and a lifelong defender of the rights of the underprivileged was not safe from assassination in his old age.

The period covered by the essays in this volume, 1989–1994, was eventful both in a regional and international sense. This is the period that witnessed the end of Communism and the Cold War, marked by the fall of many totalitarian regimes in Eastern Europe and the emergence of democracy. In the MENA region, Saddam Hussein invaded Kuwait in 1990, followed by a war to liberate Kuwait led by the USA. There was also the start of the Algerian civil war in 1992 following the cancellation of election results that would have brought to power the Islamic party of FIS (Islamic Salvation Front). Mahfouz engages with all these events with vigour and clarity of vision, but above all with the constancy of thought and principle that characterised his writing from start to finish. Freedom, democracy and social justice are recurrent words in his vocabulary; they are like keys that open the door to his thought and the positions he takes in relation to public events.

A committed socialist all his life, on 26 September 1991, shortly before the official dissolution of the Soviet Union, he writes an article titled 'The Russian People', in which he extols the Russian people for 'having written a shining history for themselves in the experiment of human civilisation'. He sees them as having undertaken 'the realisation of the dream of millions of people to create the desired paradise in this life'. For this end they 'had to endure persistent hardship, suffer immense sacrifices [...] and do without human freedoms, and human rights'. According to Mahfouz, the failure of the Communist experiment can be ascribed to the totalitarian methods of the regime that applied it: 'If the Communist project had been founded on a democratic system, it would have been established in an atmosphere of liberty and would have benefited from the successive criticisms of its economic and philosophical systems and followed a beneficial development, cleansing it of all the negative aspects that brought it down.' For him, totalitarianism is an abhorrence, as he expounds in an earlier article tellingly titled

'A Disease Called Dictatorship', where again he laments the failure of the great project of Communism because of the repressive regime that put it in practice, allowing cruelty, rampant corruption and the crushing of individual dignity. He describes dictatorship as 'the first foe of humanity', and in a language untypical of him but which reflects the intensity of his feelings on the issue, he writes: 'A curse on dictatorship and dictators! They have tainted history with blood and shame, and there is not one fool among them who has not left behind him a nation stripped and torn apart, its hopes destroyed.' By contrast, he sees democracy as 'a way of life that cannot be matched [...] by any other'. However, he entertains no illusion that democracy is immune from failings and problems; the difference he points out is that under autocracy problems 'become excessive when they are secure from scrutiny and beyond hope of change'.

Mahfouz paints the conflict between democracy and autocracy in the stark terms of one 'between good and evil'.[1] It is no wonder then that a few months later, at the beginning of 1990, he lists the prime world achievement of 1989 as the 'tempestuous revolution for freedom set off by the people of the [Eastern Bloc] that laid the foundation of totalitarian rule and sanctified it... [demonstrating] that there could be no justice without freedom and dignity'.[2] His invective against dictatorship and its follies assumes added concentration in his denouncement of Saddam Hussein's invasion of Kuwait in August 1990. In an essay titled 'Hard Lessons', dated 27 September 1990, he writes, with Saddam Hussein as the immediate example in his mind, but by extension of any dictator: 'Disaster generally lies in any autocratic leader who imposes himself by force and who controls the media to the point where he appears to himself and to his nation as a superman, speaking from revelation, acting on inspiration, and coming to his senses only when he is in the depths of the abyss.' He follows this with a set of painful, rhetorical questions: 'When will the Arab countries recover from this deadly scourge? When will they be ready

1 For Democracy Ever and Always, 31 August 1989.

2 Our Hopes for the New Year, 4 January 1990.

to live in the present times? When will they believe in freedom and respect for human rights?'

In December 1991 in Algeria, after winning the first round of elections, the Islamic Salvation Front (FIS) was poised to win outright in the second round against the ruling party, the National Liberation Front (FLN). At that point the military intervened, cancelled the elections, banned FIS and arrested a great many of its members. The result was a guerrilla war between armed Islamists and government forces that was to last for the next ten years. A stout believer in democracy and the binding force of the ballot box, and totally unaware of the brutal war that was to ensue, Mahfouz was horrified at the cancellation of the second round of the elections and describes the act as a 'convulsive setback' that struck 'the newborn democracy in the cradle' and allowed despotism again 'to loom with its horns and its monstrous gaze'. He rails at despots who think they know what is best for their people and would use democracy only when they thought it could grant their rule legitimacy and scupper it if it did not. He finishes by saying that any new despot ruling Algeria 'may find many justifications for his policies, but he will never be able to claim that he rules in the name of the people'.[3]

All this concern with democracy and denouncement of autocracy East and West has its deep roots in Mahfouz's own experience as an Egyptian. One sin he never forgave the 1952 revolution and Nasser's regime for was the abolition of democratic life and the establishment of dictatorial rule from which Egypt never recovered up to Mahfouz's death more than 50 years later and indeed since. Autocracy was the revolution's cardinal sin which neutralised all its other achievements and eventually led to disaster in 1967, when Egypt was defeated in war and Sinai was occupied by Israel, not to mention parts of Syria and Jordan's west bank. Mahfouz believed that this national humiliation and its far-reaching consequences from which the region never recovered had been in the making for many years and had its root in the totalitarian state founded by Nasser.

---

3 Algeria's Experience, 16 January 1992.

Mahfouz's disillusionment with the revolution and Nasser is expressed time and again in his fiction during Nasser's lifetime, especially in a series of novels published in the 1960s. After the death of Nasser, he became more open and direct in his criticism of the period in a manner that would not have been tolerated by the regime earlier. This attitude started under Sadat, who was happy to see his predecessor discredited, and continued until Mahfouz's death. In the essays collected in volumes ii, iii, and iv of this series of books, covering the period 1974–1994, there are numerous essays where the author's negative views of Nasser and his era are repeated time and again. On every anniversary of the revolution (23 July), year in year out, he recalls its history and goes through the mantra of its achievements before dwelling on how all this was laid to waste because of the grave faults of a totalitarian rule.

There is another date which Mahfouz also observed every year without fail: 23 August, only a month after 23 July. But there is a substantial difference between these two dates: 23 July was a national holiday behind whose celebration the whole apparatus of the state stood, while 23 August was a date that only Naguib Mahfouz observed timidly, if untiringly, and a date that but for him would have passed unnoticed, as indeed it did until Mahfouz decided to make a stand for it and to bestow symbolic meaning on it. August 23 was the date Saad Zaghloul, leader of the 1919 revolution against the British occupation and founder of the Wafd party, died in 1927. By coincidence it was also the date of the death in 1965 of Mustafa al-Nahhas, Zaghloul's political disciple and successor as leader of the Wafd and champion of the Egyptian national cause during the 1930s and 1940s, and five-times elected prime minister of Egypt, until Nasser banned political parties in 1953 and placed al-Nahhas under house arrest until his death.

These two iconic leaders of 20th-century Egypt, both of whom were marginalised in Nasser's history books and propaganda machine until nearly forgotten by new generations, were Mahfouz's heroes. He sees them as 'the two symbols of the 1919 Revolution' and the 1919 revolution as 'the eternal symbol of the return of the spirit to the age-old Egyptian people'. Unlike the 1952 revolution which originated in a military coup led by Nasser, the 1919 revolution was a popular one: 'it was born in the street in a wonderfully spontaneous spirit and exploded among the populace, driven by an all-engulfing popular consciousness.' Mahfouz considers it a revolution which tapped the creative energy of the people and led to a flourish in all national activities: political, economic, literary, artistic, etc. He takes particular pride in the unity of purpose and solidarity it brought among the two major religious communities of Egypt, the Muslims and the Christians.

In an essay titled 'Saad Zaghloul and the Return of the Spirit' dated 24 August 1989, Mahfouz extols the 1919 revolution for establishing democratic rule in which individual freedom and human rights were respected. All these remarkable achievements of the popular 1919 revolution, the praises of which Mahfouz sang on every occasion, represent the very opposite of the 1952 revolution, whose shortcomings he never tired of denouncing and condemning. It was a military coup in origin. It came from above and imposed its reforms by force. It abolished democratic life and nurtured a cult of the sole inspired leader who knew what is best for his people who were turned into passive observers rather than agents in the affairs of their nation. It also allowed the sectarian unity forged by the 1919 revolution to disintegrate, such that the Christian minority of the country felt insecure in its own homeland.

Writing in the 1990s when a bloody conflict was afoot between armed extremist Islamist groups and the state, Mahfouz was conscious throughout the raging battle that the ban on the creation of religiously based political parties was a contributory factor. He writes that as the result of this ban 'the arena has been left open to extremist groups on the streets and campuses'. Hence, he calls for the political arena to be opened for all and to let the people choose, and reminds readers that 'our people have never once made a bad choice in their not-so-short democratic history', a reference to the constant support for the Wafd in the pre-1952 period.[4] These words and the stance behind them foreshadow what he was to write three years later, quoted above,

4 Towards a Better World, 16 February 1989.

about the cancellation of the Algerian elections, when the initial results looked certain to bring the FIS to power. It is to be remembered that this willingness to accept the result of the ballot box, whether in Egypt or Algeria, was being emphatically and repeatedly voiced by an author whose fiction consistently expressed an antipathy to fundamentalist thought and the politicisation of Islam; a progressive, liberal thinker with pronounced leftist leanings. Yet such was his commitment to democracy and belief in the will of the people that he was prepared to live with an Islamic government if it came to power by the ballot box.

Ever the voice of reason and the advocate of a balanced, multi-sided view of issues, he writes a courageous article in 1994, at a time when terrorism was being treated by the state as a security matter to be suppressed with brutal force and nothing else, describing terrorism as a socio-political phenomenon, and a by-product of the ills and injustices of society. He bluntly proffers the view that terrorism is as much practised by the state/society as by the terrorists. He bases this argument on a simple definition of terrorism as 'the use of illicit force in order to achieve a certain aim […] Everything that is achieved by force, not by law, or through legitimate means, is a form of terrorism. And force means not only bullets and bombs – there is also the force of influence, nepotism, party affiliation, family, faction, and religion'. For him these kinds of terrorism are no different from 'the terrorism that we hunt down morning and evening'. Given that this list is universally acknowledged to be at the heart of corruption in the Egyptian state/society, his invitation to readers to judge for themselves whether theirs is 'a society of law and legitimacy, or […] one of terrorism' is poignantly rhetorical. The terrorism of an unjust society is the cause of the terrorism of the bullet; that is the case he was making at a time when the state's attitude was to counter bullets with even more bullets.[5]

Reading the articles of this volume is not an exercise in cheerfulness. In fact, it can be very depressing. At times Mahfouz sounds like a voice shouting in the wilderness, like a prophet or visionary who warns against dangers that no one else can see and no one believes in. Week

5 Terrorism and Its Kin, 14 July 1994.

Naguib Mahfouz (1911–2006) is often named as the greatest Arab writer of the twentieth century. Born in the old Islamic Quarter of Cairo in 1911, he began writing aged seventeen before entering university to study philosophy in 1930. He is the author of over thirty novels. In 1988, he was awarded the Nobel Prize for Literature.

Rasheed El-Enany is the Dean of the School of Social Sciences and Humanities and Professor of Arabic and Comparative Literature at the Doha Institute for Graduate Studies. He is also Professor Emeritus of Modern Arabic Literature, University of Exeter, where he became Director of the Institute of Arab and Islamic Studies. He has authored several books on Mahfouz, including *Naguib Mahfouz: His Life and Times*.

R. Neil Hewison is the author of *Fayoum Pottery: Ceramic Arts and Crafts in an Egyptian Oasis* and *The Fayoum: History and Guide*. He has translated a number of other works by Yusuf Idris, Yusuf Abu Rayya, and Gamal al-Ghitani.

after week for four years he portrays a dismal scene of his country and the whole region. Ironically, amidst all this doom and gloom, the only ray of hope shines from inside him, from his indomitable spirit, from the optimist deep-rooted within him despite his tragic sense and acute awareness of the human condition. He once argued that if we only look at the present moment, there is every reason for pessimism, but if we look at the moment in historical perspective and mark the progress humanity has made to reach the present, we can only be optimistic and have faith in the future. This mindset comes through in the essays of this book. For despite the bleakness of the subject-matter, he never writes in a despairing tone, but always suggests solutions and always appeals to the spirit of persistence and positivity in his reader. The title of an essay written on 30 November 1989 says it all: 'Leave Hopelessness Behind and Get on with It.' And so does the title of another essay written four years later: 'Do Not Lose Hope.' In this essay, dated 2 April 1994, after enumerating the endless woes of humanity locally, regionally and internationally – from wars and famines, to minority persecution and weapons of mass destruction, and from drought and environmental pollution to the expanding Ozone hole – he switches keys to remind us that at the same time 'humanity has reached a peak of civilisation never before dreamed of', and goes on to count the achievements in science, health, space, human rights, the arts and so on. He concludes on this high note: 'Do not lose hope. Evil is not there to push you to despair, it is there to urge you to sharpen your thinking and your will, and to prepare for the perpetual revolution.'

By the time Mahfouz had written the last essays of this collection, he had already published what was to be his last novel, *Qashtamar* or *The Coffee House*, in 1988, while his last collection of short stories was to be published two years later in 1996, though it is almost certain the stories were written before 1994; most of his works were normally complete in his desk drawer, as he put it, a couple of years before publication. It can therefore be assumed that throughout the 1990s and until his death in 2006, the main gateways to his thinking about all things Egyptian were the short weekly essays in *Al-Ahram*. For the sixty years or so before that, he expressed the same views in great works of fiction that made the local reflect and articulate the universal human condition. After the assassination attempt, his imaginative writings were few and far between, taking mainly the form of very brief, surrealist and highly poetic accounts of his dreams, which he dictated to an assistant. Those dreams, known in their Arabic version as *The Dreams of Convalescence* and published in book format in 2006 (translated into English as *The Dreams* and *Dreams of Departure*), together with the earlier *Echoes of an Autobiography* which was written in similar fashion in 1994 but not based on dreams, represent Mahfouz's distillation of his lifetime wisdom in a lyrical mystical style, whose beauty sometimes lies in its very abstruseness. In other words, it is at the other end of the spectrum from these essays.

In an essay in this collection titled 'The Reader and the Writer', dated 14 April 1994, Mahfouz muses upon the definition of a writer and the relationship between writers and readers. In the end he writes: 'Some writers please the elite, some please ordinary people, and some please both, but in all cases, it is the audience that certifies the writer's existence and defines his worth.' Where do we place Naguib Mahfouz in his own suggested categories? I believe his genius lay in being one of those authors who pleased both the elite and the ordinary people.

May 2020
Rasheed El-Enany
Professor Emeritus of Modern Arabic Literature
University of Exeter

Translator's Note

Over the years in my career as an editor, I had the pleasure of working on a number of English translations of Naguib Mahfouz's novels and short stories, as well as fiction by many other Arab writers. Working with a variety of translators on a variety of texts, I soon learned that translators are constantly making choices, and that – as the pioneer translator of Arabic fiction Denys Johnson-Davies always insisted – translation is an art, not a science. A few years ago, for a translation slam hosted by the British Council in Cairo, I asked two translators to translate the same few pages of a modern Egyptian novel. One version came in at 739 words, the other at 842, and there was only one sentence that was identical in both versions, a sentence of a single word: 'What?' It was an instructive illustration of how different the results can be when two translators tackle the same text, and a reminder that there is no such thing as a 'literal translation'. I mention this only as a caveat to the reader of any translation, including this one.

In working on this collection of Naguib Mahfouz's non-fiction writings I found I had to leave behind the question 'What does this word mean?' to ask instead 'What did Mahfouz mean by this word?'. For example, the word *'ilm*, which can be variously reflected in English as 'learning', 'knowledge' or 'science', comes up quite frequently in these passages. It is usually (but not always) clear from the context whether Mahfouz is referring to what we would call science or to what we would call knowledge or learning. Similarly, *riqaba* could be 'censorship', 'oversight' or 'scrutiny'; *ibda'* could be 'innovation' or 'creativity' – there are many such choices to make. I have always hoped to be guided in these cases by context.

Meanwhile, Mahfouz sometimes seems to use the 'we' form of the verb to talk about himself, though the boundary between that and the more inclusive sense of 'we Egyptians' or 'we Arabs' is not always distinct. For this reason, I have translated 'I' or 'we' just as he wrote them, without attempting to clarify the referent of the 'we'.

There are many stylistic choices to make too, such as which of several possible words sounds better in the English sentence, or whether a sentence works better when constructed this way or that. In the course of my work, I often felt like a pale ghost, scribbling in the path of the great man, attempting to express his ideas in an alien medium.

It should be noted that typographical errors are not rare in the published Arabic texts. This is partly at least because to the end of his life Naguib Mahfouz always wrote by hand, pen on paper. His handwriting (until the knife attack that affected his control of the pen) was neat, but misreadings could nonetheless occur when a compositor then transcribed the handwritten manuscript for print in the *Al-Ahram* newspaper. The archived columns were then transcribed again when they were collected many years later for publication in book form, potentially allowing further room for error. Whenever I was confident in identifying such errors I have translated according to the apparently intended meaning, but of course it is possible that not every error was obvious enough to catch my attention.

Naguib Mahfouz was not only a great writer, he was an inspiring human being, and the breadth of his interests, his compassion, his modesty, his optimism and his ability to guide you to a different understanding of things all come through clearly in these writings. In working on this translation I have learned not only much more than I knew already about the magical intricacies of the Arabic language, but also something of the workings of Naguib Mahfouz's mind; so my first debt of gratitude is to that wonderful man himself, for all the years he dedicated to his craft in creating week after week these eloquent and thought-provoking reflections. And I am grateful to my friends at Gingko for inviting me to share with them in making this work available to a wider, English-reading audience.

I am grateful too to all the people – the hundreds, perhaps thousands of ordinary and extraordinary people – who have, mostly unwittingly and always informally, taught me Arabic over the years: my teachers have been and continue to be the people of Egypt. One in particular, Omar Ahmed Abdel Ghani of Fayoum, helped me mount the difficult steps of Arabic in the early days: with no English, undeterred by the language gap that existed between us, and determined to drive the conversation forward, he always found imaginative and animated ways to make me understand what he was saying, and to help the new vocabulary and structures settle in my mind. To the memory of Omar, whose friendship we now dearly miss, this translation is dedicated.

I am indebted to another dearly missed friend, Denys Johnson-Davies, for first inspiring and encouraging me, many years ago, to try my hand at translation; and to Hartmut Fähndrich, the leading translator of Arabic literature into German, not only for his encouragement and for many stimulating discussions about the challenges, rewards and mechanics of translation from Arabic into our two different target languages, but also for introducing me to an online resource that I found particularly useful in my work on this translation.

My very grateful thanks are due to:

– Mustafa Ibrahim and Ayman Azabawi, two vital friends, who have both given me tremendous support and encouragement along the way, as well as linguistic help with the translation when I needed it.

– My brother Alan Hewison for his help in finding the right English terminology for sections where the author discusses the Egyptian economy – economics being one of Alan's fields, and certainly not one of mine!

– My sister and brother-in-law Jean and Mike Scott and their dog Honey, who generously hosted me in their welcoming New Zealand home for four months while I escaped the Egyptian summer heat and worked on this translation in their spare room. Thank you for the frosty mornings, the daily dog walks, the empty beaches, the bush treks, the white kiwi and the Waipawa M&D production of *Mamma Mia!*, among all else.

– Mohamed Salmawy, who for many years was a close friend and collaborator of Naguib Mahfouz, for his keen support and insightful help in identifying some of the events and people referred to in these topical historical texts – he wears his erudition and cultural knowledge lightly and elegantly.

Finally, it is more than true to say that I could not have completed this translation without the constant support, enthusiastic interest and great linguistic and cultural skills of my dear friend and spiritual sister Habiba Ahmed. Over the course of fourteen months, wherever either of us was at the time (Cairo, Fayoum, Birmingham, New Zealand), whether sitting together or connected online across the world, she never tired of listening, carefully following the Arabic text as I read aloud my English translation of each piece. As we worked, both of us appreciating the discovery of Naguib Mahfouz's thoughts and approaches to the world, she answered my linguistic queries, cleared any stubborn stumbling-blocks, and stopped and corrected me if I had apparently misunderstood a word, a phrase or an idea. Habiba claims to have learned from and enjoyed the process as much as I did, but I am nevertheless greatly in her debt. It goes without saying – though it must anyway be said – that while this translation is undoubtedly vastly improved by Habiba's invaluable input, any remaining failings are of course my own.

R. Neil Hewison

Towards a Society Not Based on Violence

There are violent events that deserve grief and anger. And there are cruel outrages that we have not experienced since the days of colonialism and despotism. If we are still enjoying a general air of stability and peace of mind, that is thanks only to the determination of our security forces, and to the temperate and forgiving nature of our people. We need stability to endure and to become deeply rooted through a climate of purity, universal justice, abundant blessings and high principles, so that we are able not only to overcome violence, but to build a worthy renaissance together. That is what is important – that is the goal.

We must invest all our energies to make this comprehensive development in our society happen, piece by piece. Our attitude to life must be serious, and capable of dedication, sacrifice, selflessness and self-restraint; we must firmly put aside all forms of foolishness and dissipation.

We must chase down corruption without limit, without equivocation, without leniency and without any slackening of pace, in order to restore trust in ourselves, in our country and in life.

We must give full care and attention to political reform. Let us start right away by striking down the laws restricting the formation of political parties, as a first urgent step towards eliminating the grounds for the unjustified exclusion of some sections of the population from the political process.

We must respond without hesitation – and in good faith – to the demands of the judiciary to support a stainless justice system and to uphold the true rule of law over both ruler and ruled, innocent and accused, and take a decisive step towards an enlightened age.

We must double our efforts to spread the true spirit of religion in our rising generation through education, and in the general populace through the media, so that it becomes fixed in the depths of their souls as a formidable force for piety, noble conduct, work, learning, tolerance and respect for human rights.

Then we can rightfully confront those who have let themselves be seduced into showing contempt for the law – and root them out and eradicate them.

19 January 1989

A Long-Term Treasure

What the Arab character has revealed of steadfastness, strength, determination, patience and faith during the Iran–Iraq War and the Palestinian Revolution is dazzling, and excites admiration and respect. The people of Iraq entered deep into a long and fierce war that lasted a little more than eight years,[1] fighting with brave determination, making martyrs of detachment after detachment. They faced rockets and bombs; cities were emptied of their inhabitants; other cities lived at the mercy of death night and day. Heads were bowed under the emergency conditions of war and its pressure on citizens to endure restrictions, privations and sacrifices. Truly, a steadfastness deserving of all pride and praise, a great treasure to be stored away for a shining future!

The Palestinian Revolution has now lasted for a year and has greeted a new one.[2] It neither falters nor pauses nor retreats, and it pays no heed to brutality, suffering or blind hatred. We are familiar with revolutions whose lives are counted in months, and whose effective struggle can continue only if their natural surroundings provide them with a stronghold, such as mountains or forests. But the Palestinian Revolution has no such stronghold to protect it, only its faith in its sacred right, its superior courage and its extraordinary, outstanding heroism. Truly, a steadfastness deserving of all pride and praise, a great treasure to be stored away for a shining future!

We do not love wars, unless they are in self-defence, and we do not call for revolutions unless they aspire to liberation, freedom and dignity. But we must welcome the fact that these events in the world of our deep-rooted Arab people reveal elements of strength that must be transformed with the rising wave into building and reconstruction,

---

1 The Iran–Iraq War actually lasted just under eight years, from 22 September 1980 to 20 August 1988.

2 The 'Palestinian Revolution' Mahfouz refers to here is more commonly known in the West as the First Intifada. It began on 8 December 1987 and lasted until 13 September 1993.

creativity and culture, in the shade of righteous peace. Has the time now come for our long night to transform into a shining dawn?

26 January 1989

Work Is a Sacred Trust

We are accountable for work at all times, as a sacred trust that we carry in this world in order to improve it. And at this period in our lives in particular, work becomes an obligation, which we cannot for a moment let out of our sight.

It may not be enough to live by work. Rather, we should love it, since there is nothing like love for energy and impetus. Indeed, not just love work: if we are lucky we will love work more than the fruits that we anticipate from it, even if by just one degree. Certainly, the fruits are the legitimate right of every worker, but what greater hardships a person will face if he loves the fruits more than the work itself. Then work becomes nothing but a means – one that in times of frustration or weariness a person may exchange for other means, soon sliding into dissipation or falling into ruin.

It may have been the love of work more than its fruits that sustained your humble servant through long years of frustration, uninterrupted by any gleam of hope: in work I found a purpose that wanted no other purpose, and despite occasional bitterness, life did not lack joy, curiosity or zeal. This is where patience acquires a new meaning. Patience does not mean unbound or unconditional contentment with things as they are; it means devoting oneself to work, and work alone, with absolute faith in it and in the sublime values of life. This is positive patience, not negative; flexible, not rigid; self-reliant, not reliant on others; taking no account of luck or superstition. And it is a democratic patience too (if that is the right way of putting it), as it looks around itself with a scrutinising eye, criticises and raises objections without rancour, tells the good they have done good and the bad they have done bad, rejects duplicity, scorns illicit means, disdains trivialities and endures hardship. But it refuses defeat and ruin – so do not be surprised if it is destined by God to sweep its path clear of cheap victories, dross and false frippery.

2 February 1989

This Democracy

I am in favour of recognising our democracy for what it is in reality, just as I am in favour of insisting on more of it, in order to reach the perfection we aspire to. At the same time, I am not in favour of denying its existence, disparaging it or making fun of it.

We enjoy a respectable democratic life. We have sovereignty of the law to a considerable degree, and we have a house of representatives in which the opposition performs its duty and has its voice heard. We also have a remarkably free press, and we have political parties that are active in disseminating their message, even if that activity has not been devoid of constraints. All this has had its effects, certainly in countering the prevailing negativism, exposing weaknesses and rooting out corruption.

It is no secret that there are exceptional laws left over from the past and that we are living under the shadow of a state of emergency. The reasons for this are accepted by many, and the laws have not been applied outside their stated remit. Of course we call for the complete independence of the judiciary and the earliest possible revision of the constitution, but we cannot deny our democracy or denigrate it, nor talk of it without due esteem and respect. And do not forget that we live in an age of democracy born in the lessons learned by the state from painful, unforgettable experience, and in its understanding of the pressing need for popular participation and for the revival of the positive energy we had lost. It is the offspring of reason and politics and so, with persistence and perseverance, it develops and grows through persuasion, dialogue and good example.

And I would like to remind the opposition, with whom I have a great deal of sympathy and on whom I build great hopes, that they did not bring about democracy – on the contrary, they came into being thanks to the establishment of democracy. So on the one hand we must not stop calling for the rights of the people, and on the other hand we must honestly and sincerely acknowledge the reality and its merits.

9 February 1989

Towards a Better World

It is not easy to assess the scale of the political currents that run through our society. This is because there are currents that are still not allowed to create parties, while others have succeeded in forming parties but under such constraints that their activities in the street or on the college campuses are restricted. The result is that the arena has been left open to extremist groups on the streets and the campuses, as long as they act in the name of religion, not politics. They may thus appear to be larger than they really are, to be more influential and to have a louder voice. They frequently clash with the authorities; violence erupts, and blood flows. Warts appear on the face of democracy and stability. Then the moderate men of religion set out to quieten the extremists with honest talk and sincere lessons. It is as if the field is empty of all but the government and the religious moderates and extremists.

Where are the parties? Where are their principles? And what is their role in this rising struggle? Where is the popular majority, and what is its role? There can be no objection to whatever the people choose and want, so long as there are equal opportunities and a call to commitment and positive participation. Those of the parties that are able, will prevail; the weak will become a thing of the past, and truth will become as manifest as the light of the sun. Even the government is struggling alone, as if it was merely an administrative body and not a government based on a parliamentary majority. Perhaps it is responsible for its own isolation by holding too firmly onto the bonds that tie down democracy. At the same time, the clarification of rights urgently requires full democracy, as a final means in the struggle, and as an honest inquiry into the will of the people.

We must face reality, whatever it may be, but it is enough to remember that our people have never once made a bad choice in their not so short democratic history. It is time for those whose views coincide to unite, for those of like mind to come together, and for all to know that this is a crucial battle, and that we will overcome every obstacle in our path to the world of progress and success.

16 February 1989

Reason in Everyday Life

One of our common mental ailments is that we think too much with our emotions, without realising it. And even more seriously, this phenomenon is spreading among the educated and even among the intellectuals. To elucidate:

We rush to judge based on groundless premises reached without reflection or examination, consideration or scrutiny, and without any evidence at all. Then we use reason to support these emotional assumptions, reactions and whims, to create illusory truths out of nothing. We go on to draw conclusions, and imagine conspiracies and spectres. In the end we live in a spurious world built of our own delusions, which has no relation to the truth, and we are its primary victims.

How many formulas there are in our discourse for expressing affirmation and certainty. A speaker will begin with 'There can be no doubt' or 'For sure' or 'Everybody agrees that … ', and then proceed to build his oration brick upon brick, without consideration for the foundation on which it stands – which may be nothing more than rumour, or common opinion generated by argument, or wishful thinking or presumption. The cure for this malady can succeed only if we begin with early education built on the stimulation of thought, instead of rote learning. But without doubt the media also have their role to play. Just as they treat our endemic and other ailments both directly and through radio and TV dramas, they should apply themselves to our mental maladies, by calling on the populace to respect reason and objectivity, and to beware of subjective reactions and personal emotions.

This may be their starting point for gently and patiently disseminating the spirit of a knowledge-based methodology, and accustoming the people to using reason in their everyday life. If the heart has its place, so also does reason, and the only result of mixing the two is chaos.

23 February 1989

A Squall from the World of Darkness

What happened in the People's Assembly[1] is akin to a climatic event, when a depression blows in from somewhere to change the weather from its annual average, and the temperature suddenly drops to near freezing-point, or rises until it competes with hell. The democratic climate of the assembly was disturbed by a current of low pressure, bearing the tensions of subjugation and authoritarianism, which disordered its equilibrium and disfigured its face with warts and ulcers.

What happened was not caused by democracy, and does not point to any lack of capacity for freedom on democracy's part. Nor was it the fault of inclusive debate. It was a sudden squall that struck the moderate, stable system due to the pressures of life, the suffering of the people and the poison of corruption; and it brought to our lives a faithless defection to the ignorance of tyranny and despotism, and of contempt for human rights.

The era of darkness loomed over us with its cudgel. Violence became sovereign; the rule of law was nowhere to be seen. Women wailed, children screamed, grief took root in the dignity of men; and rage struck the chamber of ideas, reason and legislation. Mouths bellowed bombshells, hands rushed to punches and slaps, and the transitory rule of authoritarianism triumphed, for an hour or two.

What happened, happened. In any case, it was not so very unusual – how many parliaments have seen fights involving fisticuffs and chairs? But everybody must restore their tranquility and reassess their situation, and each in their own way repent for their apostasy.

If we take account of the problems that challenge us, and of the resolutions we need, we will find potency in our international success, from which we will derive strength and hope; and instead of squandering our energies in screaming we will mobilise them in the service of the people and the homeland.

2 March 1989

---

1 In February 1989 a number of Wafdist members of parliament criticised the heavy-handed policy of the then-minister of the interior, Zaki Badr. The confrontation developed into a physical fight.

Towards Integration and Civilisation

One of our great national accomplishments is the economic agreement between Egypt, Jordan, Iraq and North Yemen. Once its goals have been realised, history will add it to the scroll of achievements we can be proud of, such as the liberation of Sinai and the return to democracy. I hope it will be the first step on the road to Arab economic integration, or a firm foundation for a modern Arab developmental awakening. As we know, the precepts of the Arab League encompass principles for its growth and advancement, but politics has taken over centre-stage, and disagreements have broken out, leading to ruptures and divisions. Any hint of cultural interests has occasioned derision and scorn, and in this rancorous turmoil we have forgotten that in the contest of the age, our prime adversary is underdevelopment.

The commencement of economic cooperation between the four states demonstrates clearly that any delay while waiting for full integration is no longer tolerable. A partial beginning is better than a wait of unknown duration, and its success will be a clear and open call to the indecisive or the inattentive. It also indicates that we have woken up, if a little late, to the importance of a solid economic base and to the value of civilisation in an era when human advancement is measured by the worth we place on a civilised life and the gift of, and participation in, human development in general.

It is an era of cultural alliances and blocs, in place of the political and military alliances that characterised relations between states in both the recent and more distant past. These are blocs that require more than just strength alone; they require ascendancy in the world and in productivity, openness in culture and respect for human rights. It is true that all Arab states practise regional development to different degrees of success, but cooperation opens up for them new horizons for business and new solutions for problems, and supports them with renewed energy on both the spiritual and the material level. I hope to see with every rising of the sun a coming civilisational light.

9 March 1989

Cultural Unity

Whatever the divisions and differences of the Arabs, there is an ever-present unity among them, which is their culture. Relations between the Arab countries may be prone to weakening, temporary suspension, or boycott, but culture is never completely absent. It remains an urgent spiritual need that creates a state above states, a friendship among enmities, an innocent and unblemished forum where the people can laugh at the caprices of their governments. In this way it has preserved various levels of continuity and interaction, even in periods of colonial rule, political rifts, or foolish rivalries; and thanks to modern media its power has dominated and broken barriers. But the time has come when we should not leave its effectiveness to cultural trips, fairs, festivals and bootlegging. There must be preparation, organisation and conversion of the piles of proposals in the archives of the Arab League into realities of thought and behaviour.

We are at the gates of an educational revolution which will carry us from one age to another. Our minds and our customs are preparing for a new future full of difficulties and adventures, so we must exchange experiences and opinions in order to discover new foundations for the revival of minds and souls. And we must agree on a long-term policy of cultural exchange, as well as fruitful cooperation in the field of radio and television broadcasting. Equally importantly, we must convene a conference of ministers of culture and finance to remove the impediments that hinder the free flow of books into the Arab market, and to protect intellectual property from forgers and pirates.

It may even be time to establish a distribution company on a regional level, to allow books and tapes to reach every place where they may be read, heard or watched. To this I might add a suggestion to set up a regional agency for translation from and into Arabic, equipped with all modern means to create our own renaissance – one that will lift us to the same level as all other fellow-travellers in this fast-moving world.

For years we have been calling for cultural unity, as well as economic unity. Together they are the unshakable foundation for the reawakening of this region to assume its anticipated civilisational role.

16 March 1989

On Production

You may have noticed what is published now and then about the productivity resulting from our human efforts. The figures certainly are very distressing, especially when compared to other countries. And since we have all come to believe that production is the best way to escape the grip of suffering, and the serious challenges that are hovering over and closing in on us, they are more distressing still. More than once we have resolved to convene a conference on productivity, but the days pass, and the conferences pile up, yet the desired convention does not materialise. The truth is, I do not accept the published rate of productivity as a measure of the ardour of the workers in our nation. It is inconsistent with reality and history, and with what we know of our people's perseverance and endurance.

We may find the explanation when we remember that the low-income citizen puts only part of his energy into his main occupation, saving the rest for his secondary work in order to just scrape by. The total effort he expends to earn a living is no less in degree or vigour than that of others, but it is split between two jobs.

The state turns a blind eye to the behaviour of its workers because it cannot afford to pay fair and adequate salaries that would leave them free to concentrate on their principal occupation. But it can oblige them to carry out its work properly, in exchange for overlooking the extra work undertaken out of undeniable necessity.

Serious scrutiny and follow-up is needed, as well as the establishment of a system of well-founded incentives. The state must also make a good example of itself in integrity, discipline and austerity.

As for the long term, those who plan the renovation of the education system might set their sights on what will make a citizen an earnest individual, loyal to his country and reverent of learning, work and earlier values. This is also the duty of the media and the pulpit. In religion and history we will find support for our calls and the realisation of our aims, and only circumstances will impede us – and bad circumstances are a cause for the redoubling of our efforts and determination.

23 March 1989

Fame

Do you love fame? First you have to understand what fame is. True renown is for a person to be known by those who comprehend and appreciate his work – in other words it means success in one's work and winning the esteem of experts in one's field. The only way to avoid renown is to renounce progress and success. And as is clear to see, it is relative and cannot be absolute. The extent of a scholar's renown is limited to the scholars and students working in the same or related areas of specialisation, while the fame of a comedian extends to millions of people. So we must not be upset over the restricted fame of the scholar compared to the comedian, so long as each of them has reached the peak of his profession. Nor is the general public to be blamed for being familiar with one and not the other: each faction loves the one it knows and is interested in what he does.

There is no way to accuse the masses in this case of ignorance or ingratitude, for affection here is a sign of allegiance to whomever you love, or whomever you have the capacity to love. Fame does not in any case always correlate with worth. Science continues to sit at the peak of human endeavour, even if its practitioners win the least part of general fame. Besides, justice finds its own path to realisation – limited renown may last for generations through the strength of its originality and its continuous effect on knowledge and life, while another type of fame may be gone within a lifetime.

I say all this in relation to what has been written about the honouring of some extraordinarily popular athletes. Whatever was showered upon them by the public was born out of the people's love, liberty and loyalty, without reducing in the slightest the value of science and scientists.

30 March 1989

War and Peace

Land will always be the hope of humankind; our dream, and the stirrer of our passion and our fervour.

Its independence will remain a goal of life, an emblem of dignity, a symbol of sovereignty. This is why we celebrate the liberation of Sinai every year – indeed, this year we celebrate twice: once for Taba, once for the whole peninsula.[1] The commemoration invokes memory: we recall the glorious October War,[2] which liberated the soul of the Arabs from the humiliation of defeat and the grief of ruin; they retrieved confidence from the depths of frustration and once again cleaved to their great history, their heads held high.

It was one of those rare wars that the human conscience can sanction and that piety can bless, as it was a war of liberation and justice. Indeed it has been demonstrated that its sole aim in the end was a comprehensive, just peace, which was the right of this key tract of land in which long ago the worship of the One God was proclaimed, and the call was made for freedom, justice and human brotherhood.

Blessed is the free land in the shade of peace, blessed too is the first step on the road to the liberation of all stolen land, so that peace and cooperation may spread instead of usurpation and subjugation.

Peace be on the souls of the soldiers whose blood coloured the land of Sinai from 1948 to 1973. I salute the great leaders of our struggle: 'Umar Makram, Ahmed 'Urabi, Mustafa Kamil, Muhammad Farid, Saad Zaghloul, Mustafa al-Nahhas, Muhammad Naguib, Gamal 'Abd al-Nasser, Anwar al-Sadat.

And I salute and congratulate President Hosni Mubarak, leader in war and peace.

Let us derive from these memories and these great names a spirit

---

1 The return of Sinai (except Taba) to Egypt was completed on 25 April 1982; Taba was finally returned on 19 March 1989.

2 On 6 October 1973, Egyptian troops crossed the Suez Canal and broke through the defensive lines of the Israeli forces occupying Sinai.

with which to confront the challenges of today and tomorrow. And God is the supporter of the patient.

6 April 1989

A Call to Self-Defence

If we weigh our problems on the one hand against the efforts we exert to resolve them on the other, we find that the side of the scales bearing the problems is still the heavier. Before the unknown takes us by surprise, while engrossed in our daily lives, we must think about a comprehensive defensive front in order to decide on a course of action, and the sign pointing the way is a clear one. We – as individuals, as parties, as organisations, as agencies – do not fall short in considering our present state and our tomorrows: just look at the number of articles, studies, books and recommendations we produce. But all of that is going on in a tower isolated from reality and implementation, as if it were no more than an effort to salve our conscience or simply to pass the time, while stagnation remains around us – or at best, a slow hint of movement that is not commensurate with the enormity of the problems or the impending disasters.

As a nation we must come together to clarify our position in the face of the challenges of our age. Our parties – both registered and unregistered – must unite, along with whoever in the national councils, the trade and labour unions and the universities has the right experience. They must come together to look into the problems and come up with solutions. They may reach consensus on one or more matters, or a majority opinion on others, and they may disagree on the rest. But through coming together, we will be guided to decisions by way of greatest agreement, and we will not hesitate to put them into action. These decisions will apply to the majority, and will encourage the government to issue their decrees. And even on points of disagreement, what is hidden from the casual glance will be made clear to us. We must move forward, so as not to appear to the eye of history as a people drowning in stupefied negligence, waiting for something to come from nothing. For how can a people remain indifferent when their lives are tossed on the waves of problems such as debt, population growth, unemployment, low productivity and corruption, and the challenge of reconciling Islamism, national unity and modernity?

12 April 1989

A Revolution in Education

It is not to be doubted that the education minister is thinking about the problem of education from a revolutionary starting point. And it is not to be doubted that this revolution, if it is destined to succeed, will play a fundamental part in shaping a new future for the Arab world. Nor is it to be doubted that an enlightened revolution in the arena of education will not be restricted to education alone, but will spontaneously spread to kindle a revolution in the fields of production, politics, society, health, culture, sport, family, allegiance, personal relations and a general vision of humanity and existence.

Whoever leads a revolution in education is doing nothing less than modernising the foundations on which to erect a new world of true faith, one that demands authentic worship and the improvement of this world, as well as respect for human rights, the sanctity of learning and labour and the opening of our arms to receive everything that is great and beautiful in creation and in culture.

And whoever leads a revolution in education is doing nothing less than working to reawaken our minds from their sleep and save them from mechanistic deafness, so that they race ahead into the world of originality, creativity and democracy. He is working diligently to create lovers and disciples of culture, faithful supporters of the nation and national unity, outstanding giants for humanity, glorious champions in sports, fighting colossi for the challenges of life and selfless heroes for sacrifice and solidarity. In a word, he is working to create people who love God and are loved by Him – who are working for this world, to become worthy of meeting Him in the next. So let us pray for the success of the revolutionary minister. A prayer for him in his revolution is a prayer for Egypt and for humanity.

20 April 1989

The Sporting Spirit

It is no exaggeration at all to define sport as one of the fine arts. It is a healthy regime for the human body, and by extension for the mind and the soul. It is a means of increasing a person's dexterity and agility, and it reveals the constitution of one's personal, social and moral character.

But unlike the arts it is a universal obligation, and everybody must devote a portion of their time to it whenever possible, as a service to their internal systems, as a way of taking care of their health and as pure enjoyment for their spirit. It earns a wide following in all the countries of the world, where people love it dearly, and enthusiastically shower their sporting heroes with admiration and affection, and show an attachment to them that in its essence is a devotion to skill, talent and beauty. It is by no means fair to scoff at an interest in sport, while having regrettably little interest in other activities. The blame here should not fall on sport itself, but on shortcomings in education and the negative atmosphere that alienates many from an honest devotion to culture, politics and scientific knowledge.

But as much as we may like sport, we are lacking in the sporting spirit. And what is the sporting spirit? It is to love sport without fanaticism, rage, malice or rancour. Sport itself is your aim, and you gain your satisfaction from your proficiency in it or your enjoyment from following it, regardless of winning or losing.

It may be that both winner and loser are deserving of admiration, and displeasure is aroused only by the slovenly, the lazy, the half-hearted or the breaker of rules. In the old days we used to say to anyone facing defeat or loss: 'Accept your fortune with a sporting spirit.' By which we meant the maintaining of a good-natured disposition in time of loss, just as in triumph.

This is the spirit in which we should follow sporting fixtures both here and abroad, on the local and the international stage, in order to be true lovers of sport rather than speculators on victory. And perhaps we need this spirit not only in sport but in other fields too.

27 April 1989

Between Defence and Reform

We have the resolve to deal firmly with drug offences and rape, and we are relentless in promulgating just and deterrent laws to protect human dignity and national security. There is no doubt that all the corrupt deviations that are crippling our national progress deserve that same resolve. The smuggling of wealth, bank fraud, currency speculation, artificial inflation of prices, mistreatment of the people, influence peddling, class favouritism – all these create an inhumane situation, and are extremely detrimental to millions of people. They hamper our progress forward. They overtake us and our children with frustration and negativism. They drive some to extremism while tempting others to wrongdoing. But we must beware of deluding ourselves that punishment is where our pains and efforts finish, or is the end of the line. Punishment is of no use as a fundamental line of defence, and as a means of reform it ranks lowest. It is nothing but the easy way out when more beneficial methods arrive too late, or when we neglect to employ them.

The true remedy is to be found in an intricate and integrated network of achievements: in the economy, in politics, in culture, in morals – what we properly call comprehensive development. This is the national project for those who are searching for a national project; that is, it is a project that puts overcoming underdevelopment and launching ourselves into modernity at the top of its agenda. Every time we take a step forward towards achievement, we are also automatically making advances in the service of country, youth, intellect and decency, changing the perspective of the life ahead of us and raising our position in it. It allows the blood to flow in our veins and hope in our hearts.

Decisive punishments are certainly necessary, but our youth are in need of someone to save them from the crises that grind them down, to guide them to the straight path even as they plunge into the shadows of the darkest night. We welcome decisive punishments: may there be in them an opportunity to set our crooked affairs straight and cleanse ourselves of villainy.

4 May 1989

Facing Up to Problems

The general conference of the National Democratic Party will be held in early July, and we have read in the newspapers that it will focus this year on the discussion of a single topic: unemployment – the scale of it and how to deal with it. In principle, we welcome this, and we wish the conference good fortune and success. However, we see our problems as interwoven and interlocked, no single one of them separable from the rest. Stability, democracy, debt, productivity, government transparency, drugs, waste, population growth – all these are units in one structure, and unemployment may be nothing more than the bitter fruit of a flaw in one of them. So we had hoped that the conference would be concerned with all the problems together, and that its attention on them would act as a comprehensive review of the first five-year plan and the beginning of the second.

The issue under discussion is a serious one, and on it hangs the future of the country's youth, the backbone of the present and the hope of the days to come, so concentrating on this one problem is an obligation that cannot be put off, and cannot be lumped together with others. But our problems are nothing new; indeed, they are the pivot of every plan and every budget, and the study of them has not ceased since we began devoting our attention to our domestic concerns. Hence their discussion will not begin from zero, but will take the form of exhaustive examination and self-criticism, and suggestions that arise for modifications and amendments.

I hope the opposition parties prepare similar conferences to examine, research and suggest solutions. Because at this point in time, Egypt needs every mind to be occupied with our problems and every heart to beat with our concerns. There is no excuse for hesitation, self-interest or apathy.

11 May 1989

Science and the Cave

Al-Ahram newspaper has brought us the announcement of a scientific revolution in the field of energy, with the success of an experiment in nuclear fusion for the production of cheap power that is radiation-free and will have no effect on the ozone layer. This breakthrough comes at a time when many scientists are coming together to tackle the imminent dangers that face our planet, and publishing important recommendations on counter-measures and prevention. Talking of dangers, there are those who continue to express their distrust of science and technology, and to warn of perilous consequences. The bad side cannot be denied – industrial effluent, atomic waste, nuclear bombs, chemical weapons – even though most of these are to be blamed on the misuse of science and its discoveries, rather than on science itself. And we may also note here the technologies that will allow the modern media unauthorised access to our homes, and surveillance that will convulse our firmly grounded traditions and culture.

Be all that as it may, it is not possible to restrict human curiosity for knowledge or to limit exploration to a certain point or within the range of a given mandate. However, this will not mean capitulation to a tenebrous fate, for what is not in doubt is that science corrects itself by its own devices and rids its output of any defects. Moreover, in the age of science we demand the luxury of scientific vision and self-confidence, just as we demand a sound education, both intellectual and moral. We demand that our minds be educated in independent and critical thinking, relying on elevated principles, so that we can achieve a civilisation that moves towards unity and inclusion, for which censorship, withdrawal, or hiding in a cave will not work. The lifebelt is the possession of an independent, critical mind and a disposition founded on high principles: these are the means to a dignified life on this planet in this age.

18 May 1989

The Anxieties of Youth

Whenever a young Egyptian approaches you, you immediately feel the glowing fire burning in their chest. They are always angry, disaffected and dismissive. If they are employed, their campaign is directed against their work regime and its futility, the failure of their salary to meet the needs of daily life, and their failure in the property and marriage markets. If they are unemployed, the complaints are even more calamitous and bitter: what was the point of studying and earning qualifications? And if they aspire to emigrate, why are they faced with such arbitrary conditions and unreasonable demands to fulfil?

At every step personal connections are indispensable, and at every move a bribe is inevitable. There is no end to the complaints, no end to the disaffection. There are so many sad and painful examples and tales. It is as though we are living in a jungle, where the strong annihilate the weak, rather than in a country where affiliation and inclusion alleviate the distress of the weak so that they can stand up to the challenges of life. Of course I know that we are passing through a critical period full of difficulties and hardships, and that we will cross the bridge of anxious times only in the long term. The state, while not asked for miracles, is asked for what is possible, and this can bear no negligence, delay, or indecision.

We must determine the number of unemployed, follow them, support them in finding work here or abroad, and guide them towards the necessary training for it.

We must make a firm and clear connection between education and productivity, and we must prepare the younger generation for work in accordance with its requirements, from the first stage of education to the last, placing public interest above all else and without giving in to complacency or short-term avoidance of pressures.

And the state must treat its citizens fairly and erase 'connections' and 'favouritism' from the dictionary of its dealings, because the perception of real fairness relieves the tormented in this world of many of their torments, and overcomes their feeling of belonging to the wide community of the disenfranchised, who watch the community of the capable monopolise all the good things in the world.

Two great revolutions[1] were staged for our sakes, to realise freedom and justice, so let the adherence to freedom and justice be a fundamental principle of our lives.

25 May 1989

1 Mahfouz is referring here to the revolution of 1919 against the yoke of the British Occupation, and the revolution of 1952, which succeeded in removing the corrupt regime of King Farouk.

Preaching in the Modern Age

The message of the pulpit is that we have been given religion in order to work for the sake of both this world and the next: to worship God in the right way, and to deal with people and the bounds of life in a way that is pleasing to Him. The first of those duties is simple, while the second is arduous and difficult. The first is easy to define and its outline is clear. The second is arduous and difficult because it does not allow for idleness or negligence. The world keeps on turning through time without cease, and every day – perhaps every hour – reveals something new in knowledge and work, and in whatever changes this may bring about in our dealings, behaviour and relationships with others, whether within a single land or across the face of the planet. This requires of the preacher constant awareness, consciousness of the time he lives in, and continuous cognizance of what is happening in the wider world, of what the present moment may unleash, and of what the immediate future may bring to bear.

This must be taken into consideration when setting the curricula of study for preachers, especially in what relates to civilisation and the spirit and requirements of the age, along with the course of human life from the agricultural revolution to the industrial, and the gradual transition to the age of information. Thanks to modern means of communication, we are approaching a kind of global unification, whose rushing waves will not be stopped by any decree, confiscation, censorship or other means of evasion. The question posed for the pulpit and the preachers is: how do we live as Muslims today and tomorrow in this hegemonic world from which there is no escape?

This is where the importance of efforts to respond and engage come in, so that Muslims can share in the innovative life without embarrassment or feeling out of place, or desperate attempts to retreat to the cave of the past. We either make this effort or we go extinct. For this reason, preachers should be affiliated to a higher committee of specialist theologians (perhaps one of the most significant committees of our time), trusted to outline the bounds of the life of a Muslim in the modern age. It is good to remember the saying that Islam is fit for every time and every place. The time has come for us to prove this in deed, in mind and in faith.

1 June 1989

Builders and Destroyers

We have friends and foes in our life: the former build, while the latter destroy. The destroyers may be victorious for a time, but the builders will win in the end. It may be useful to set down and record just who the builders and the destroyers are.

Among the builders:

1. The president, who tirelessly urges action and warns of anarchy, tours business sites at home and roves east and west abroad, pursuing the path of blessings and peace.
2. A serious, diligent minority, working silently, executing the plan with integrity and experience, battling the problems of today, looking towards tomorrow and heralding a better future.
3. An honest, patriotic opposition that does not hold back its opinion or fear speaking the truth to its critics, and is patient in the face of many adversities and difficult circumstances.
4. A faithful group of policymakers and experts on the national councils, who are constantly thinking and issuing recommendations, and attentively following up on each of them, great or small.

Among the destroyers:

1. The negligent, the lax and the apathetic.
2. The plunderers of aid and the smugglers of wealth.
3. The tax evaders.
4. The dealers in death through the smuggling and distribution of drugs.
5. Those who exploit the suffering of the people and make a profit on their daily bread.
6. The deceivers who employ the finest words for the basest intentions.
7. Those who play with human rights and their worth and hopes.

The builders deserve the nation's appreciation. The destroyers deserve to die.

8 June 1989

The Meaning of Stability

Egypt's stability is a shelter of hope for us all, and a guarantee of peace. This holds true for every nation or society, for there can be neither development nor progress without stability. But what is meant by stability? It is a reasonable degree of confidence and hope that enfolds separate individuals as well as a broader community-based society of individuals and organisations, to allow an appropriate climate for fruitful work under the auspices of satisfactory human cooperation.

This is a definition some way from the ideal, but it represents the minimum that is necessary for work to begin, which is attained by the following:

1. That the state enjoys authority and confidence – and this must be a respectable authority, and the degree of confidence must be like that of a father in his firmness and his compassion. This will only be possible, or partially possible, if the state is a model of probity, justice, vigilance, veracity and strength.
2. That the elected assembly performs its important duty of representing the people, dealing with their problems, championing their wishes and promulgating laws that safeguard their progress and prosperity to match their dreams, aspirations and values.
3. That the judiciary is totally independent, so that its honour is elevated and its pillars are strengthened, and its judgements are applied swiftly and without wavering, dawdling or wrangling, thus extending the protection of the law, its sovereignty, sanctity and integrity, and affirming equality before its scales. Thus no individual is ruined, no matter how insignificant his state, and no person evades justice, no matter how high his position.
4. That all political currents operate in the light and above ground, and that covert activities created by oppression and despotism disappear.
5. That all human rights are respected, so that no discrimination penetrates our ranks based on belief, colour or race.

6. That rising generations find patronage based on justice, equal opportunities, and the availability of a range of activities according to the various provisions and needs of society.

This is the meaning of stability at its minimum. Perhaps this will lead us later – through work, innovation and progress – to stability in its most ideal sense.

22 June 1989

A House of Wisdom

The Arab League should reconsider its functions in the light of the present times. I don't mean by this that it should change its traditional mission, or add amendments to its charter, but that it should apply itself zealously to breaking through our challenges, solving our problems, eradicating our differences and consolidating our cooperation, brotherhood and peace. And it should redouble its activities in regard to the present state of our civilisation and its future:

1. It should align its member states in what amounts to a complete revolution in education and a reinvention of the Arab mindset, in order to face the future in a suitably humane and worthy manner.
2. It should propose a general cultural plan that will acquaint each person with his own identity and with the character of the time he lives in, returning the breath of life to his consciousness – this in collaboration with educational and media institutions.
3. It should propose the necessary legislations to protect intellectual property rights, to create a common Arab book market and to eliminate forgery and the theft of ideas.
4. It should examine the plan for Arab economic integration, aiming at self-sufficiency, food security and employment for the new generations.
5. It should work to establish a massive scientific research agency, ensuring that its financial, organisational and human resource needs are met.

This is a call to urgent and immediate action, to make the Arab League a centre for the dissemination of learning, culture and well-being, and a house of wisdom to which every Arab who yearns for life and light can belong.

6 July 1989

A Quiet Word between Brothers

No system of government possesses magic powers to solve problems and bring about justice, progress and prosperity. It all comes down in the end to the people who run the government, and to competence, integrity and enlightenment. This does not mean that all systems are equal in the capabilities they can bring to a project or in the choices they have. Democracy will always come out on top in providing freedom, dignity, scrutiny and respect for human rights, and the individual and the populace may benefit from participating in the work and cooperating in shouldering the responsibility. There is no reason to consider the military regime in Sudan as a defeat for democracy,[1] since most military regimes are subject to failure, and most totalitarian regimes lead their country to ruin and barbarity.

It had been hoped that Sudanese democratic rule would succeed, as a good example to the Arab world of democracy in practice and a distinguished demonstration of how it can overthrow oppression and tyranny. But things turned sour, in spite of the favourable and healthy climate in place for it to work. Corruption, weakness, blind factionalism and tribalism triumphed, and affairs sank to the lowest level domestically and internationally. All we can do now is to wish the new rulers good fortune and success, in the hope that another period in the precious life of Sudan does not go to waste. And we hope they will avoid the pitfalls of dictatorship, and that they really do see themselves as a rescue team, aiming at a decisive remedy for every rampant ill and handing over in the end to the people, who have the sole and legitimate right to determine their own rule.

12 July 1989

---

1 Omar al-Bashir led a military coup in Sudan on 30 June 1989. His rule lasted until 2019.

Towards a Better Scientific Life

We are not outside the age of science, but we have not yet entered it as we should. It ought to engage our attention and interest wherever it may be applied, as the axis of our modern life. The matter cannot be postponed or neglected, for this *is* the age of science: only through science can we attain a true awakening with which to solve our problems, further our interests and conquer our underdevelopment. How often we have said: our civilisation must stand on faith and science. The religious awakening confirms the strides taken in the realm of faith, through the educational revolution and the heated debate in our society, but science needs to enjoy the same enthusiasm and attention. Praise God, we have many colleges of science and plenty of specialised scientific personnel, we have a ministry of scientific research, and researchers charged with studying many of our problems and finding solutions to them. In spite of all this, as I said, we are not outside the age of science, but we have not yet entered it as we should. For that to happen, I would like to see the following come to pass:

1. That we teach the scientific curriculum in a simplified and gradual manner from the beginning of preparatory school to the end of secondary school.
2. That we raise the science colleges to the highest levels in terms of teaching staff, equipment and curricula.
3. That we make firm plans for scientific research based on teams working together, concentrating at this time on whatever relates to production.
4. That the necessary technologies be made available, as well as financial support – and how good it would be if we could work together with other Arab countries on this.
5. That we confer on the researchers whatever encouragement and honours may be apt, and give them an appropriate standard of living, so that they can continue to be free to carry out their important work. They are our guiding lights on the path of progress and modernity.

22 July 1989

Work Is Life

How can we provide a job for every citizen able to work? Firstly, by preparing citizens for all kinds of work and activities. This is a goal that should be taken into consideration from the earliest stages of education, and it must be planned for thoroughly, carefully and securely, and on the basis of the interests of society from first to last. Because after the period of basic education, there begins the judicious appointment of students in service of the country's overall plan and realistic needs, according to individual aptitudes. This should be done in such a way that the higher specialisations are filled only by the most competent and able, who are selected in an open manner, above the slightest suspicion. And the number of students in any college or institute should not exceed the maximum to ensure a sound and complete higher education that can be expected to reveal innovators and leaders.

Secondly, through the continuous creation of new jobs. We possess encouraging indicators in this area, such as stability, peace and good relations with the countries of the world, especially the Arab states. Moreover, we are in the process of promulgating a new investment law that we hope will clear the way of obstacles, simplify necessary concessions and rid investment of the shades of deathly bureaucracy that haunt it. This will encourage local and foreign capital in employment and production, and bring careful attention to the public sector, so that it may fulfil its anticipated national role.

Thirdly, by preparing the surplus work force for systematic emigration. This will come about as required only if the Ministry of Labour carries out two important tasks: an investigation of the needs of foreign countries in terms of workers; and the training of the reserve labour force to fill the gap left by the employment of qualified workers.

Fourthly, by spreading cultural consciousness in the schools and the media. Culture is essential for every individual and is everyone's right. What matters here is that it has always had an effective and spontaneous link with family planning, since before overpopulation became a national problem.

29 July 1989

The Aims and the Reality of the July Revolution

On examination, the July Revolution of 1952 can be crystallised along two lines: the line of intentions and goals, and the line of practical application and reality. We certainly remember the aims and goals of the revolution, just as we have lived with its practical applications and realities. And in one phase of its history we have found ourselves in dire straits, which has caused some to label it one of the calamities of our time and to wish it had never happened. This is a hasty and mistaken view. What pricks the soul is that the revolution's wonderful beginning could have led to an even more wonderful end – but when dealing with history there is nothing to be gained from 'what if'. What happened, happened; and the curtain has in any case not yet been lowered. This is nothing more than a phase loaded with suffering, the bitter fruit of bitter mistakes. But by learning the cruel lesson for which we are all effectively responsible, we will be able to face the challenges, to overcome the false steps and to rejuvenate body and spirit. Today we have undoubtedly learned that:

1. Social justice is the soul of any society deserving of life.
2. Democracy is the sound foundation of any sound government.
3. National unity is the basis of our revival.
4. There is no substitute for facing modernity on a foundation of science and culture.
5. There must be a religious awakening free of superstition and inflexibility, whose essence should be prized as the source of refined values and human brotherhood.
6. Arab brotherhood is indispensable, as it represents a brotherhood of civilisation, culture and economy, starting with advancement and ending with generosity.

Those who properly comprehend the disaster that has befallen them can with time account it a formative element of their good fortune.

30 July 1989

To Have a Civilised Life

Why are we not at the same level as the Japanese, even though we began our revival years before they did?

This is a question posed by the perplexed from time to time. But all they need to do is to read our modern history – whether in detail or at a glance, it makes no difference – and they will find that instead of concentrating primarily on our own shabby house, we aspired to exert influence in external affairs while unaware of the changes of modern times around us. Thus we received two mortal blows that put an end to both aspirations and reform.[1] Then there is also autocracy, which places us at the mercy of whim, whether that whim comes from the ignorance of a perverse and stupid ruler or the folly of an enlightened and reformist one, or from the frivolous caprice of a jesting fate.

And they will find foreign invasion, which shut down state-building and economic momentum.

They will find too the fossilisation of the religious leadership, at whose hands religion has been turned from a universal spiritual revolution into superstition and mental and moral defeatism.

They will find instances of the disintegration of national unity and the fragmentation of our single family.

They will find corrupt administration, in whose putrid vastness the rule of law, the spirit of justice, the values of moral excellence and human rights dissolve, as society becomes a rich grazing land for profiteers, thieves and miscreants.

And when they look up from their reading of history, the signs to the right road will appear to them, the road that we have missed so many times, and these are:

1. That our aspirations be limited to a civilised way of life and civilised sharing.

---

1 By 'two mortal blows' Mahfouz is probably referring to the defeats of the Palestine War (1948) and the June War (1967); the 'perverse and stupid ruler' would be King Farouk in 1948, and the 'enlightened and reformist one' President Nasser in 1967.

2. That we cling to political and social democracy without hesitation or mitigation.
3. That we continue our spiritual and religious awakening.
4. That we preserve our independence and national unity.
5. That we resist the beast of corruption with all the strength we possess.

3 August 1989

The Prize for Innovation

News has come of the establishment of an international Egyptian prize for innovation. For us to have an international prize is a beautiful dream that chimes well with our national pride, as well as matching the aims of our minister of culture and his tireless path to resurgence and progress. But the international prize is a serious venture; it will necessitate great amounts of money, executive bodies and many experts of the highest calibre for a multi-faceted, broad-ranging and thorough investigation, which such high aims can barely support. It is not appropriate to push ourselves forward in a field if the effort, implementation and fruit do not bring honour to the name of Egypt, its place in history and its ongoing struggle. It may be that if some of the burden associated with this project and some of the effort promised to it were to be directed to the support of *local* innovation, this would do a great deal of good and remove a great difficulty.

Serious culture is in urgent need of serious support. New innovative talents are cleaving their path through rocky ground and sending out their melodies in a desert spoiled by crises, unemployment and bigotry, in addition to competition from our spellbinding modern media.

Real innovation requires continuous hard work, a broad and comprehensive culture and a well of patience, and its recompense in the end is negligible. In this climate, the innovator (if he hold commitment in esteem and stand above temptations) is expected to be content with asceticism, whereas serious encouragement is needed if we are to fly beyond our suffocating crises. We must be as liberal as possible in discovering new talents, recognising the eminent and honouring the great. In my estimation, the value of the 'Encouragement' prize should be no less than 10 thousand Egyptian pounds; the 'Distinction' prize no less than 30 thousand; and the 'Appreciation' prize no less than 100 thousand. We call on those responsible for culture to stand by the serious innovators, in order to face up together to a gloomy time with all its disgrace and temptations.

10 August 1989

No Escape from the Inescapable

We have been through times that have warned of danger that is approaching us, or that we are hastening towards. There is no need to be reminded of these times, for they stand out in our consciences and ferment in our sentiments. The people are still suffering the bitterest torments, fighting on more than one front, chasing out the spectres of perdition represented by rising prices, drugs, violence and disrespect for the law.

All this confirms that it is time for the patient to put an end to his irresolution and begin to take conclusive decisions, because life – above and beyond everything – is a sacred trust that must be afforded its proper place and be treated with seriousness and honesty, no matter what sacrifices may be required. But the solution cannot be limited to making decisions: it must come in the form of an overall policy that spreads its wings over everybody, based on confidence, respect, strength, impartiality and sincere intentions.

The administration must reinvent itself, purge its negative aspects and grace itself with justice and integrity, for it is calling the people to action, patience, fortitude in the face of adversity, loyalty and sacrifice. It must be an example of performance, of respect for human rights, honour and the sanctity of law. It must make the simple citizen understand that it is of the people and for the people, and that it provides him with freedom, security and justice, and that together these form an indivisible single entity, working towards the single aim of prosperity and progress.

If we were accustomed to following the policy of step by step, then we must lengthen our strides. If we were accustomed to depending on others, then we must depend on ourselves and arouse our minds, our hearts and our wills.

We have endured many crises in our history, and these crises have passed by and vanished, and life has rushed on, crowned in victory.

17 August 1989

Saad Zaghloul and the Return of the Spirit

Saad Zaghloul and Mustafa al-Nahhas are the two symbols of the 1919 Revolution, and the 1919 Revolution is the eternal symbol of the return of the spirit to the deep-rooted Egyptian people. The people's revolution rose up to end the British Protectorate and begin the walk to independence, but in the vastness of its long struggle there crystallised some fundamental characteristics no less important or glorious than independence itself.

First: it was born in the street in a wonderfully spontaneous spirit and exploded among the populace, driven by an all-engulfing popular consciousness. The Egyptian people have never known such effective assurance – or initiative, or self-confidence – as they did in this revolution's creative space. They turned with all their strength towards public life, commitment and immersion in the political struggle. In the revolution's embrace they created an economic revival, a women's awakening and a burst of creativity in the fields of science, literature, theatre, music, painting and sport. Stars shone in all these fields, representing the pioneering cream in politics, economics, writing, science, art and intellectual endeavour.

Second: it made a reality of national unity among the masses. The Egyptian people moved forward like a tightly constructed edifice to confront the challenges of foreign colonialism and home-grown despotism, and to defy all messengers of doom and disruption, nobly and proudly paying them no mind.

Third: it followed its tireless path to create a democratic system built upon the shoulders of the people for the sake of the people, safeguarding in it human freedom and rights, and plunging on its behalf into continuous battles with the king on the one hand and the British on the other, never losing sight of its aim until the last moment of conceivable action.

It came as a revolution to complete the journey, and here we are today enjoying independence and democracy and standing up for peace and prosperity. So let the 1919 Revolution be our reference whenever we wish for perfection in our democracy, for security and safety in our national unity, or for conviction, commitment and struggle in the spirit of our people.

24 August 1989

For Democracy, Ever and Always

When we follow the achievements of science on earth and in space we are dazzled and overcome with admiration and wonder; and we have perhaps forgotten that the long road of science began with the discovery of sound scientific procedure and concentrated on the study of simple principles. It is also thus with democracy, as we know it from the developed nations, where the marks of freedom, the respect for human rights, the strength of institutions and the supremacy of public opinion dazzle us, refresh us and fill us with cheer in front of an ideal and noble life. But we usually forget that this life is the final fruit of a long, violent and blood-stained struggle, and that it passed through periods when relationships and social compacts broke down, and consciences were bought for the lowest prices. So there is nothing more unfair than to cast doubt on democracy with the excuse that we are unfit for it through poverty, ignorance or corruption.

Democracy is a way of life that cannot be matched or even approached by any other. This is not to say that it is a magic wand that can perform miracles, solve problems or ward off corruption. Problems and corruption can exist in democratic countries, and will always exist in autocratic ones, and they become excessive when they are secure from scrutiny and beyond hope of change. At least in the vicinity of democracy there is no veil over failings or faults – the forces of good wrestle the forces of evil, and there is hope for correction in the opposition parties and in public opinion at elections.

It is a good thing for democracy to be given its chance, to be subject to reward and punishment, and to plunge into the floodwaters of experience both sweet and bitter, in order for its true character to stand out and its latent strengths to be released. Doesn't autocracy impose itself for decades, in spite of its corruption and its failures? So why would anybody begrudge democracy a few years?

The fight is between good and evil, and good will never be defeated no matter how long the fight goes on.

31 August 1989

The Workers

The sit-in by workers at the iron and steel factory calls for reflection. And on reflection, certain truths suggest themselves to us that we hope will not escape the attention of reasoning people.

1. If the survival and continuation of rule is based on the representation of the majority, then the workers stand together at the forefront of that majority. It was they who returned the 1952 Revolution to the centre of authority when events had moved it away, and they were the ones who profited from its revolutionary laws and institutions, just as the Revolution also profited from them. So these two parties have been closely bound together from the start, and this bond needs to continue even more strongly to face the present and build the future.
2. We are passing through a difficult time and crossing a bridge full of hardships, and our only salvation is in work and productivity. This is the duty of every citizen everywhere, but especially so of the workers. They hold this position because they are the first to be thanked when things go well, and they are responsible for any slackness or inattention in times of failure; any negligence or mistake on their part cannot be excused.
3. Industrial action, even though it is an accepted democratic right, should be avoided in circumstances like those we are passing through, and should be considered – at least for now – a grave offence. We must explore all avenues except that which threatens us, and most of all the workers themselves, with ruin.
4. Injustice is also, like industrial action, a grave offence, and likewise threatens ruin. So we must all deal with our problems far from stupidity, arrogance and red tape, far from force and bullets. Every worker must know his legitimate path, and the authorities must do their national duty, as must the unions and party committees. The family must come together again, reach a mutual understanding through dialogue and consultation,

and exchange mutual respect under the shade of the rule of law and the sanctity of justice.

The ship is overloaded and cannot withstand unexpected storms.

7 September 1989

Crime in the Media

Every society has its share of crimes and ills. They may be fewer when a society achieves more spiritual and material equilibrium and bears the stamp of civilisation and mental health, or they may be more when a society is out of balance and is assailed by ignorance, poverty and underdevelopment, so that dissolution, hopelessness and apathy flow through its veins. Thus the fight against crime is really just one aspect of the broader fight against underdevelopment, and a declaration of civilisational war on ignorance, low living standards, oppression, the mockery of human rights and contempt for the sanctity of law and values. What should the ideal position of the media be in relation to such crimes and ills, of which no group or class is free?

They cannot ignore crime for the sake of security and good reputation without betraying one of their most fundamental missions, which is to supply people with information on what is happening at home and around the world, and to get to the essence of crime and urge its opposition and eradication.

And they cannot present crime in a spirit of excitement, suspense or horror, which would lead to an exaggerated image, accompanied necessarily by the spread of panic and despair, possibly even tempting the weak or the mentally ill to become involved in crime themselves.

The only way is to report the news seriously and objectively, and to go to the experts for comment: the security officers, the psychologists and the sociologists. It is up to the journalists to keep in mind the real goal of their mission in this tragic aspect of life, which is to inform, educate and set straight, and to defend the life of society and its values, as far away as possible from entertainment and commerce.

14 September 1989

Illegitimate Legitimacy

It is the right of any regime to defend itself, and this is also one of its most sacred duties: to defend lawfulness and stability, security and safety, and the rights of the people to all these, as well as to the realisation of their dreams of development and progress, both spiritual and material. But the regime must defend itself in a manner in keeping with the principles of its legitimacy, and in line with its values and high ideals. For as much as it demands vigilance and resolve, it must operate under the umbrella of the law and with a respect for human rights, and must not deviate from those by one hair's breadth. For in reality it is defending democracy, law and human rights, and it must not violate any one of those lofty values or be negligent in how it treats them. Otherwise it is no longer a fight between legitimacy and those outside it, but a fight between two factions that are equally outside the law and legality.

We support the regime in its legitimate defence, we invoke a blessing on the struggle of its members and their battle, and we appreciate highly the sacrifices that have been made and the blood that has been shed. But it pains us that this ongoing battle is blemished in its dealings by a departure from its fundamental principles and sacred values, which damages its otherwise good reputation – one that we hope will be emulated in the East and earn its deserved appreciation in the West. Those in charge should know that the achievement of democracy is the only achievement whose merit is immediately recognised and its benefits felt at once.

They operate in many fields related to reform and reconstruction, and every field requires a long time for its fruits to ripen and for the toiling citizen to attain them – except for democracy, freedom and the respect for human rights, which people are able to enjoy and practise as soon as they are established and acknowledged. So the utmost care must be taken of these accomplishments, and we must hold them sacred no matter how tough the struggle or raging battles.

Who points out your mistake is a friend; who lets it pass is an enemy in friend's clothing.

24 September 1989

Art and History

The problem raised by the connection between art and history should never have come up. Art is a creative force that stands alone. History is a science that has its methodology and its fundamentals. We look to art for the purpose of spiritual and sensual enjoyment and insight, and we turn to history for knowledge of the facts of the past and illumination of the present. Those who would make art a path to the revelation of historical truths malign both art and history, and themselves as well.

But sometimes an artist aims through his work to bring a period of history to life or to subject it to scrutiny, thereby entering the field of history and the historians, and perhaps exposing himself to criticism far from the essence of his art. But even in this case we must not forget that the subjectivism of the artist is more important to him than the objectivism of the historian, and that his goal is artistic vision, not scholarly historical examination. We must admit also that artistic vision is what in large part enriches the intellectual and objective dimension.

This kind of discussion can go on in a serious cultural context or among serious intellectuals. But what happens when art is transferred to a popular mass medium such as television, in particular when we remember the illiterate millions who follow it so attentively and passionately and who at the same time make no distinction between what is history and what is art?

Here we find ourselves in a dilemma, and presentation may turn unwittingly into a deception of the audience, falsifying history for them, and greatly damaging their cultural awareness.

We will only emerge from this dilemma through one of two ways:

1. Either we choose to show only those works that agree with accepted history,
2. Or we show our history only through documentary films, short or long, provided that historians write the scholarly text and review the visual content. No doubt this will be both beneficial and entertaining.

28 September 1989

The Sixth of October

It is the anniversary of revival and peace.[1] It was a victory, but a victory not so much over the enemy as over despair, depression, futility and nihilism. In it the Arab spirit was revived, radiant and open, as history knew it in the first times. From a starting point of wise planning it moved on to calm execution, to confront obstacles and seek peace. This great historic leap depended on two foundations that in any true leap forward our people cannot do without: faith and learning. Our faith in God moved us beyond the most stubborn hurdles, both material and psychological, and brought blessings on the march of our soldiers who were facing death in the theatres of war, as well as on their precise organisation, superb training, and complete understanding of the latest, most intricate and skill-sensitive weaponry. And thus in a historic moment we found a leadership that combined wisdom, bravery and patriotism with soldiers graced with faith, courage and self-sacrifice. They snatched Egypt up from the quagmire of shame, defeat and despondency, and set her down in the abode of pride and dignity, opening for her the doors to peace, stability and civilisation.

This was right and proper, as it paved a road for the nation towards a complete resurgence, spiritual and material. And how the faithful delighted and rejoiced, for they believed that the night of sorrows would unveil a bright rising morning sun. But the exploitative profiteers showed themselves to be more deadly and cruel to this country than its worst enemies. They lurked like crows, then swooped down through the windows of the Open-Door Policy, jeering at the martyrs' sacrifices and the mothers' bereavements, making dirty money and sneaking it abroad, and spreading corruption throughout the land,

1 On 6 October 1973, Egyptian forces crossed the Suez Canal and broke through the Bar-Lev Line into Israeli-occupied Sinai. This breakthrough was seen as a great victory and morale-booster after a series of defeats, most notably in the Six Day War of 1967, referred to in the final paragraph as '5 of June.' After the October victory, President Sadat introduced the Open-Door Policy, designed to encourage investment in Egypt and revive the economy.

drowning the country in debt, drugs, disintegration, extremism and violence.

Remember 6 October and say: We will erase the villains as we erased 5 June, and we will cleanse the land of the poison of selfishness and greed. We count on sticking to the two foundations that victory was based on – that any victory is based on – which are: faith and learning.

5 October 1989

On the Intellectual Path

Let October be the month of victorious commemorations. As we celebrated 6 October in the field of war and peace, today we celebrate another victory in a field that is considered the most important in our age for civilisational advancement, and that is science. We celebrate the announcement in *Al-Ahram*'s science pages of the choice of the Egyptian emigré scientist Lotfy Basta to join the community of the twenty-five most prominent leaders in politics, media and the economy, one of just four scientists in the whole of America to be selected. He is counted among the consultants to the US president, for his work as a professor and as Chair of Cardiovascular Diseases at the University of Oklahoma.

In France, the Eleventh Congress of the European Society of Cardiology confirmed the acceptance of two important studies by two Egyptian scientists at Cairo University's Faculty of Medicine: Dr Yehia Saad and Dr Mohsen Ibrahim.

In West Germany, at its Fourteenth Congress, the European Academy of Allergy and Clinical Immunology extended invitations to the Egyptian scientist Samir Khidr and to Dr Mounir al-Mahairy to carry out their specialist research.

In Britain the Egyptian scientist Dr Abu Bakr Farrag has been carrying out research among sufferers of bone disease that has excited the greatest interest in this specialist field.

These are scientific victories, and not the first of their kind. They are steps towards an age of light, innovation and discovery, of which we hope to continually hear more news from Cairo and other Arab capitals, as has begun to come from abroad under wreaths of glory and excellence.

Scientific research knows no boundaries and brooks no bonds, striving always towards a universal humanity, but the straitened circumstances of the Third World enjoin us to concentrate on the problems of construction and production. There is nothing wrong with focusing our studies on tackling the obstacles that stand in the way of our resurgence, or with our research lending all its power to comprehensive development. We should have been in first place in the training of researchers in agriculture, irrigation, desert reclamation and our indigenous diseases, but we now consider that scientific research has come to be at the forefront of our intellectual concerns and our civilisational goals, and has become the object of attention and care.

12 October 1989

Art and Freedom

The objective of art – it seems – is the presentation of human experience through the viewpoint of the artist in an aesthetic form. However, this presentation will not meet with any kind of success if the artist has not been furnished with freedom of execution and expression. For freedom is the life-force of art, which can have no true life without it. Not all societies are prepared to provide the life and freedom that art aspires to. They respect freedom in art only as much as they respect freedom generally, and they grant art only the freedom that they customarily grant and are able to practise. If art crosses the boundaries it is thwarted, whether by law or by public opinion, and it becomes entangled in an unending struggle with society.

This is why art thrives and bears fruit in free, democratic environments, while it withers, fades, and becomes sterile in the shadow of subjugation and repression. We may sometimes find exceptions to the rule, but that does not alter the rule. Nonetheless, an artist is free always if he so wishes and determines, even if he lives under a brutal, repressive regime, just as he is a slave if he so wishes, even if he lives under a free and emancipatory regime. For you may find in a democratic system those who sell their freedom to authority or commerce, as you may find in a totalitarian system those who practise their freedom bravely and pay a high price.

The artist is free if he wishes, a slave if he wishes. He has no excuse, no matter how much his circumstances turn to the worse, and we must recognise that he is both free and responsible. Freedom does not relieve one of responsibility. The artist must weigh his freedom on the scales of the general good, of the present and the future, then make his decision and bear the consequences. Freedom is not a game, not an adventure, not a business. It is a serious activity that aims at truth, eminence and eternal human values.

The artist strives for the sake of goodness and ideals. Who chooses security, it is granted; who loves profit, it is possible; and who insists on truth, it is given and it is precious. Life was never and will never be a pastime or an amusement.

19 October 1989

Your Health

I am pleased by the initiative of officials in replying to the criticism that has arisen of matters in their areas of responsibility. This is an extension of the discourse that goes on in the People's Assembly between the members of parliament and the ministers, but this time it is taking place directly between the people and the officials. There is nothing more troubling to the soul than for a serious story published in the press to be met by silence from the state and indifference from the people, for this reveals a general condition of capitulation to mistakes and a despair of reform, and warns of total societal death.

One of the good instances was the story of the tainted children's milk, which could potentially have had tragic effects. Less than a day passed before the story in its published form was denied, and while at the same time admitting that mistakes were made, the responsible body acted quickly to contain the situation before any harm could be done. This was good, and even better was the fact that no milk was distributed to the people before it was confirmed fit for consumption: it was subjected to inspection on a regular basis to protect the public health.

But I could not understand the meaning of the story that appeared about the banning of the production of the 'Mineral' brand of bottled water, based on the results of tests. I could not understand this because this brand has long been available in the market and was selling well and widely. It and similar drink products earned the confidence of the people based on their trust in the Ministry of Health, and the responsibility it carries in that field. This is what we expect, and we could not expect anything else, otherwise the health of the people would be exploited for greed, avidity and illicit profit. So how is it that tests uncovered the truth about this water only in the late summer of 1989?

The health of our population is a sacred trust, garlanding the neck of the Ministry of Health, which we hope will always have the population's best interests at heart.

26 October 1989

The People's Assembly

At the beginning of this month, the People's Assembly resumes its regular sessions, returning after a break in which it took something of a rest at the end of a year filled with activity, and crowned with the promulgation of laws concerning inheritance, drugs and investment. I am one of those who miss it when it is away, and who always love to hear the voice of the people raised high in all its many tones, both in support and in opposition. It returns as the idea has firmly taken root in the conscience of all those who follow world affairs that nations are no longer satisfied with an alternative to democracy as a system for their political life (which is as true of capitalist as of socialist nations), and that the whole world is moving towards a new life of unity, the formation of blocs and newly minted economic groupings, and is embarking boldly on a period of global transformation. This requires of all its peoples – especially those of the Third World – strength of purpose, flexibility, untiring alertness and an aspiration towards tomorrow, with whatever it may harbour of social upheaval, natural disasters or the battle against ego and vice.

In this kind of atmosphere we always like to hear the voice of the people, and to watch them as they face challenges old and new, and appreciate them expressing their positions on our wishes, our pains and our dreams. And our fixed hope is that we will always find a constant broadening of the embrace of the majority for our representatives, and an increasing adherence to objectivity and seriousness in the opposition, with a level of argument that is honourable and patriotic.

We all hope that the new year will unveil a solid mooring for ideal democratic customs, true sanctity of the rule of law, complete respect for human rights and the dignity of the citizen, and progress appropriate to the age in purifying our democracy of the imperfections that stand in its way and of the shackles inherited from the time of totalitarian rule. We are looking forward keenly to the issuance of new laws to rescue our economy, to a change in the way our affairs are managed and to the cleansing of corruption and negativism from our life.

The People's Assembly is back, and we welcome it as a sanctuary for every citizen, as a home for every reform, and as a sunrise for every enlightened hope.

2 November 1989

Nobel 1989

Señor Camilo José Cela has won this year's Nobel Prize for literature. According to the Spanish news agency, he was born in the town of Iria Flavia on 11 May 1916 to a Spanish father and an English mother. He has spent most of his life as a soldier, a bullfighter, an artist and a movie actor. In his youth he enrolled in a medical college, and studied philosophy and law, but did not complete his studies because of the outbreak of the Spanish Civil War. From an early age he was interested in literary studies, launching himself into experiments in poetry, fiction and theatre. His first novel was *Pascual Duarte's Family*, which is considered one of Spain's most influential novels and has been translated into twenty languages. He is distinguished by his wide-ranging speaking engagements at European and American universities, and he has also taught at many institutes of higher learning. He is a member of a number of scholarly and literary societies.

We should stress here the Spanish interest in Arabic literature, and note that a number of leading works have been translated over the last quarter century. Spanish activity in this field increased after Egypt won the Nobel Prize last year.[1]

The least that can be expected of us in return is that our media and literary centres should pay attention to the winning writer and arrange introductory meetings with him. Specialists should undertake studies of his work, and indeed his works should be translated into Arabic, as they have already been translated into twenty other languages up to now. These ideas are addressed first and foremost to Dr Samir Sarhan, to add to his continuing services to the Arab book world a new service, combining art and good faith.[2]

This is the kind of attention we should pay to all Nobel prize winners, as well as winners of important regional literary prizes in

1 Mahfouz is being coy here: he, not Egypt, won the Nobel Prize for literature in 1988.

2 At the time of writing, Samir Sarhan was the chairman of the General Egyptian Book Organisation (GEBO).

France, Britain and the United States. If we had already done this, by today we would have had a library of the greatest literary works to enlighten and entertain our youth and to inspire writers in their work and reveal the clarity of their authenticity. And may our request not be disappointed at the doors of those in charge of our culture.

9 November 1989

Leave Hopelessness Behind and Get On with It

I have come to recognise two varieties of the hopeless. The first has no confidence at all in our ability to overcome our current problems, such as debt, the population explosion, corruption, low productivity, unemployment, the economic crisis and moral dissolution. The second does not consider the solution to these problems to be remote, but despairs completely of catching up with the developed nations, which have been transported by technology to the farthest horizons, while we are still stumbling at the beginning of the road as the distance between us and them increases exponentially, so that continuing in the race and quitting it are equally difficult.

The first kind is ignorant of history (both the history of nations and the history of his own country), high-strung, slow-witted and always inclined towards collapse and defeat. There is no doubt that we have the resources, the abilities and the workforce, and we lack nothing but more organisation, perseverance, follow-through, oversight, determination and reliable social and scientific leadership. We will conquer the various hardships of the present and move ahead on our road to distant goals.

The second kind imagines that the great resurgence will only come to pass if we sit on the summit, in science and technology, with the leading nations. But the world has more than one acceptable level for nations, and more than one means to life, wisdom and happiness. Is it not enough to make our countries independent, exchanging benefits and peace with other nations? To make our citizens good examples of learning, culture, faith and work? To make our governments humane regimes that bring security and respect to the people under their shelter? And for the Arab world to believe in truth, goodness and beauty, and not to hold back on all possible effort for the sake of science?

It is a project that can be realised, that can pave the way for us to a decent life, and that can give our presence its worthy due in this world, even if we do not scale its summit or advance its march into space. There is no place for hopelessness, in either the short or the long term.

30 November 1989

Storm in the Arab Teacup

What is going on in the land of the Arabs? First we hear from some of the workers returning from brotherly Arab countries of the mistreatment and malicious attitudes they sometimes face. Then we are shocked by unexpected violence, as happened in Algeria and Egypt during football matches. And finally we are alarmed by the arrival of Egyptian bodies from Iraq in their tens and hundreds.

The observer reflects, recalling the renewed hope in cooperation, integration and brotherhood, and a tremor takes hold of him: are we dreaming waking dreams that are based outside reality?

Are we building castles of sand on the edge of a tottering precipice?

In truth, in my opinion, we must not downplay what has happened, just as it would not be right to exaggerate it. We must not downplay wrongs, whether they stem from negligence at home or excesses abroad, not only to preserve our dignity and protect the lives of our children, but also to defend higher Arab interests.

And it is not right to exaggerate, overstepping the bounds, shaking the cornerstones of our public policy, or departing from our fixed goals.

It is good and wise to establish relations with our Arab brothers on a platform of reality, far from poetic ideals – reality with all its contradictions, shortcomings and negative aspects, which are part of human nature. When higher interests or the will for life necessitate the awareness of turning towards integration, cooperation and brotherhood, we must all – as Arabs – look towards that desired life, without expecting that this will change human nature and rid us at one stroke of our propensity for egoism, distrust, rivalry and everything else that comes from working in close proximity.

Things similar to those that have happened to Egyptians abroad sometimes happen here in Egypt, between individuals, groups or affiliations, without hurting the unity of the nation or its general path to the future: indeed, they may happen in a family between brothers and sisters.

We must come together to rectify the aberrations that have occurred, but this must occur in a framework of integration, cooperation and brotherhood.

7 December 1989

A Complaint to the Discerning

We commented recently on the announcement about 'Mineral' bottled water,[1] wondering: how was this water left for people to drink for years without account, before this announcement was made warning the public against drinking it? We expected to receive an explanation or an investigation, but the wave of indifference once again flooded in. Then our astonishment was compounded when we heard that the company producing the water was as perplexed about the matter as we were, and that it was eager for a fair investigation to replace doubt with certainty, and to reassure the public about their health and about the integrity of their country's administration.

Then I received a letter from the company describing its growth and success at home and abroad, and how it had faced an unjust war from rival companies and interference by the administration; it was taken to court more than once and was found innocent. The company was then surprised in the summer of this year to have its factory's electrical supply cut off, sustaining heavy losses and leading to some 250 families being left destitute, not to mention the effect on the reputation of the country in the summer tourist season.

In publishing these words, we can neither confirm nor refute the veracity of the contents of the letter: the knowledge of that will be revealed only by a speedy and fair investigation with the sole aim of truth and justice. This is what the company is calling for, and it has addressed its complaint everywhere that complaints may be expected to be heard. In the end, we live in a state governed by a constitution and laws, and by civilised traditions going back thousands of years, not in a jungle inhabited by brigands and beasts.

What concerns us more than the company and the water is the reputation of the country and the suffering of the miserable people of the land. We are also concerned about the confidence that is needed to encourage investment and open doors for our dispirited youth. Somewhere there must exist a trace of conscience as yet uncorrupted by this gloomy time.

14 December 1989

---

1 See 'Your Health', 26 October 1989.

The Scheduling of Problems

The president addressed the People's Assembly, setting out problems and pointing to solutions. All that remains is to wait with patience and hope for the work to begin.

Some solutions require deep thought, careful planning and successful execution, such as putting a programme in place to narrow the gap between exports and imports, manufacturing the tools of production locally, fully comprehending modern technologies, developing economic performance or solving the debt problem. All of which need time, and while I cannot imagine that we have not already made a start on these in one direction or another, it is now the moment for us to redouble our endeavours and strengthen our determination.

There are other issues that can be tackled head-on, without delay, and that we should not need reminding of, like doing what is right before such is demanded, effecting a faster rate of achievement and productivity, pursuing proficiency and innovation, establishing a principle of rewards and penalties, encouraging special bonuses and involving the citizens in decision-making.

This last point relates to the role of the People's Assembly, and includes continuous communication with the popular bases, vigilant review of the implementation of decisions, setting up fact-finding committees on important issues and the cooperation of all political parties on the national goals.

What is new in foreign relations – in addition to earlier Arab and African initiatives – is the rapprochement between Egypt and Libya, and our support for the decisions of the National Dialogue Conference in Sudan, which was characterised by flexibility, broad horizons and a readiness to embrace all kinds of differences of opinion.

In truth, everything calls for unmitigated action. The worries are many and the burdens are heavy, quite apart from the problems for which we know no quick solutions, such as unemployment and population growth, and the resulting drugs, crime and moral dissolution.

We must fight, fight, fight; and not give up fighting until victory comes easily to us.

21 December 1989

Towards a Global World

On previous occasions – as we remember our history – it has become apparent to us that our external politics have been an essential cause of the difficulties in our domestic revival and the whittling down of the great effort exerted on internal reconstruction. This happened in the time of Muhammad 'Ali Pasha,[1] and again in the early years of the 1952 Revolution. Our concern here arises not from a radical rejection of any foreign policy, but from our conviction that the country may pass through periods that call for a concentration on putting our own house in order and reinforcing it, and the necessity of placing this before any other priority. This is not to say that we should not have any foreign policy at all, but that in our policy in this field we should bear in mind two important considerations:

First: a firm grasp of the dimensions of international politics, especially the politics of the most influential and strongest nations.

Second: that our policies should match our strength and our capabilities, so that we do what is right without exposing our country to danger or our development to setback.

For this reason we now welcome the international engagement of our government in Arab, African, and global affairs. We hope that this will count among our most successful, appreciated and reputable achievements, and that in time it will place us in a significant position as a nation on the path to wealth and peace, as well as to the defence of those deprived of their rights, the victims of racism and the martyrs of exploitation, all of whom have given their persecutors no provocation at all.

It is a policy based on a comprehensive understanding of the world and its transformations and a true knowledge of our own worth, without undervaluing or overestimating it, as it aspires forever to the highest human ideals, and furthermore – unlike earlier policies – it reinforces the foundations of resurgence and reconstruction, opening

1 Muhammad 'Ali Pasha ruled Egypt from 1805 to 1848 and introduced many important reforms.

the doors of fruitful cooperation and mutual interests. It also renews the search for international solutions to domestic problems. No official can be allowed to postpone our domestic issues, let alone ignore or neglect them, but we are plunging into a new era in which the boundaries between the internal and the external are disappearing.

23 December 1989

Gifts to Celebrate

Sport enjoys enduring merit in the training of body and soul, but in our modern history it has a special place, as it is inscribed among our most glorious national exploits. What joy our football team gave our people in November, for the first but I hope not the last time.[1] This is a glowing link in the string of shining pearls that adorns the neck of our country. In weightlifting we have won three international championships in successive years at the hands of Sayyid Nusayr, Mukhtar Husayn, and Khidr al-Tuni, as well as crossing the English Channel for the first time, with Ishaq Helmi. Likewise, football stars have shone, excited the attention of the international press, and moved hearts, among them for example the legendary player Husayn Higazi, as well as Mar'i, al-Husni, al-Suwalim, and Mahmoud Mukhtar.

In those days we were a small nation, folded under the wing of the British lion. The army of occupation was the collar around our nation's throat, and sitting on its chest was a despotic king who collaborated with the occupiers. Its defenceless populace fought arrogant forces in a continuous one-sided battle. Things did not look good. Then a blessing appeared from the heavens in the form of these sporting victories, which breathed a spirit of courage and hope into us and showed us our green flag fluttering with the victorious in the arenas of the world, amid a roar of acclamation and zeal, soaring with us over the haughty heads who had looked down on us and dismissed us as a contemptible adversary, numbered among the defeated.

Yes, in those days we knew triumph on the world stage once we knew it from our sporting heroes. We were even happier that they were all sons of the people, who forced the oppressors to cede to them their rightful position both at home and abroad.

Sporting heroes are the leaders of global triumph. They reached it before its arena was lit up by the front rank of science, whose noble

1 On 17 November 1989 Egypt beat Algeria, to qualify to play in the 1990 World Cup.

examples in turn include Khalil 'Abd al-Khaleq, 'Ali Ibrahim, and Naguib Mahfouz Pasha.[2]

We say welcome to sport and to its athletes. May the gifts you bring continue and grow, as they dispel our sorrows and open the doors of hope.

28 December 1989

2 Mahfouz is not referring to himself here, but to the well-known obstetrician who attended his difficult birth and after whom he was named.

Our Hopes for the New Year

Here we are, bidding farewell to one year and welcoming another. And on this demarcation line between two years it is pleasant to look back and remember, in consideration and reflection. Unfortunately, we are not one of those who record events as they happen, so we rely on statistics and studies, but we are left with a spontaneous impression, with whatever meaning it carries. And there is no doubt that the year just gone was a distinguished and exciting one.

On the international level the year saw rapprochement and understanding between the leading powers, giving a good prospect of peace on a level hitherto unprecedented. It also saw a tempestuous revolution for freedom set off by the peoples of the bloc that laid the foundation of totalitarian rule and sanctified it – indeed, this outburst in a startling manner at the hand of the ruling leadership at the head of the bloc and its central authority, convinced us in the end that there could be no justice without freedom and dignity. Moreover, they are directing the bloc towards reconstruction on modern, contemporary foundations that cannot be ignored. The year also witnessed triumphs for human rights, represented in the continuation of the Intifada, in the independence of Namibia, and in African Americans taking up important positions of leadership in the United States. There has been progress in the conquest of space, scientific focus on the protection of the environment and change in the way debt is viewed, and the obligation to come up with a just solution to this issue that will suit both the rich and the poor.

On the local level, Arab attention towards cooperation and integration stands out, as does Egyptian foreign policy in the Arab, African, and international realms, and the wise policy that Arab opinion has settled on in solving the Palestinian issue – not to mention our special interest in a revolution in education, culture and agriculture, and a review of our economic life.

Yes, our fund of negative points is still ample: what happened in Lebanon is a return to the dark ages, as is the military coup in Sudan, which swims against the tide of universal freedom.

Our hope for the new year is that the positive steps of the past year will be completed, with confirmation of peace and human rights, recognition of the rights of the Palestinians, progress in scientific research and protection of the environment. In our own country we also wish that the year will see the complete triumph of democracy, human rights and the rule of law, as we hope too for real advances in the economic field and in addressing all our problems.

May God make it a happy year and a clear beginning.

4 January 1990

Terrorism and Cleansing the Country of Corruption

We must confront terrorism with all lawful means, not with one means only. We must confront terrorism with redoubled determination so that the attack that targeted the head of the country's security is not repeated.[1] There can be no leniency for those who allow themselves to be seduced into unsheathing weapons to murder innocent people, overturn stability and abuse the efforts exerted to save the ship from sinking. And there can be no debate about society's right to defend itself with the requisite firmness and force, and with full consideration of the legitimacy and honour of the battle, and its conduct under the shade of the law and respect for human rights.

We must not neglect this urgent, lasting and genuine defence. For it is not only defence, it is society's human duty to itself, to its children and to civilisation.

We must cleanse the country of corruption in order to restore balance to our lives, and confidence and hope to our souls. We must demolish the pretence of those who condemn society to deterioration, decline and licentiousness, so that it can become a true and proper society deserving of defence and sacrifice.

We must push forward with all resolve and determination on the road to reform. Time is calling us to action, seriousness and devotion, while everything that is happening in the world around us screams in our face: wake up from your sleep, before the flood sweeps you away! Terrorism is nothing but the bitter fruit of hardship, corruption and adverse conditions.

We must continue on our democratic path, respect the law and human rights, and establish a sound climate for a sound life. I say this in the knowledge that a democratic country is not free from corruption, terrorism or extremism. But with freedom and popular positivity

---

1 Egypt's minister of interior at the time, Zaki Badr, narrowly escaped an assassination attempt on 16 December 1989.

the hope of overcoming the hurdles is greater than it is in the slough of totalitarianism, tyranny and oppression.

Once we seriously address accomplishing this, we will mobilise the strength, meaning and support for our battle with terrorism and establish just cause for our security forces, one that is worthy of sacrifice and devotion; so that they set off on their noble mission as heroes, rather than as functionaries charged with defending one variety of wrongdoers against another.

11 January 1990

Examples of the Age

November of last year witnessed an important occurrence in the history of the United States, or one could even say in the history of humanity. It saw African Americans becoming mayors in New York and three other cities, and winning the governorship of the state of Virginia. The governor of Virginia won after beating off the white former attorney general of this state, which had been one of the strongholds of racism in the past and a supporter of slavery and bondage in the last century, at the time of the Civil War. And the mayor of New York won the support of a third of white voters, in addition to the black votes, in the largest city in America.

This is a victory for African Americans, a victory for the United States, a victory for humanity and a victory for civilisation. In it we find some solace and much encouragement in the face of what is happening in South Africa, what is happening in Lebanon between sects and families, and what happens night and day in the Occupied Territories between intolerance on the one hand and the desire for emancipation on the other. Indeed, it comforts us and gives us hope in regard to what is happening to free people everywhere, and in regard to the crimes committed in prisons and internment camps that take us back to savage and bloody eras of human history.

This century has witnessed the Wilson principles,[1] colonial revolutions, the independence of peoples, the great revolution for social justice and the declaration of human rights. Everybody in the world with a responsibility for human life should be aware of the era he lives in and look closely at where its path is headed, in order to conform with it and not to swim stubbornly and foolishly against its current. We are not ignorant of the suffocating crises that seize our souls, nor do we give in to rose-tinted dreams, but we must derive direction, strength, hope, determination and resolve from the spirit of our age. And we must anticipate tomorrow, citing every good victory. It truly

1 Woodrow Wilson's principles, the 'Fourteen Points', were published at the end of the First World War.

is an unending battle, and its outcome is for the steadfast and the patient.

25 January 1990

The Government's Path

We have no dearer wish than that the government carry out what it has promised, that it succeed in implementing its overall plan and that it move the country forward in decisive steps towards salvation. I have not forgotten its statement in front of the People's Assembly, which truly lifted the soul above its worries for a while, infusing it with ease and hope. At the same time the government released a statement about the achievements of 1988, a statement full of positive action on a variety of vital activities in both production and services. But this all seemed like the extraordinary measures taken to save a ship that is still battling the waves in the middle of the ocean and has not yet reached safe harbour. The imminent danger to those on board may distract them from giving fair credit for the effort exerted, and from directing appropriate praise and encouragement to those exerting it.

But what is to be done, when the current administration has inherited a mound of ruins that has compelled it to carry the burden dumped by others, and to labour and borrow in order to provide the people with the services they take for granted – services that are barely noticed when they are there, but which when absent or intermittent cause panic and set off painful memories? Based on this difficult situation we sympathise with you, and wish you success. And based on that sympathy, we remind you that populations who have enjoyed far more of the good things of life than we are wishing for our people have risen up against their conditions and agitated forcefully for a new order, indicating that 'man does not live by bread alone' (and even bread is not free of problems), and that freedom and human rights are venerable demands for which no substitute is acceptable.

Thus we ask that universal reform keep pace with political reform, or even better, precede it. How urgently we need not only an effective solution to the people's problems, but also leadership for them in the battle against underdevelopment, corruption and wrongdoing. Purify democracy of its defects, remove the restrictions on those seeking to enter politics and submit to the rule of law completely and sincerely – then perhaps the spirit will return to the people and inspire them to productivity, labour and creativity. Among the crush of parties (both current and yet to be formed), you represent the moderate centre – but you must bring all others of the centre together in your sphere. Then you will need only to be bold and to rid your towering tree of its dry yellow leaves.

1 February 1990

A Disease Called Dictatorship

Listen and beware:

A Soviet economic expert has announced that there are thirty thousand millionaires in the Soviet Union, who made their fortunes trading in the black market, and that thirty million people are caught up in the nets of the black market, which trades in commodities and services that are not generally available.

The truth is that we have never adopted a fanatical attitude towards the Communist regime, though we rejected its philosophy, which it imposes by force. Philosophy is something for open and limitless discussion, not something to be turned into compulsory thought. We also rejected its dictatorial system, for its cruel effect on individuals and on their dignity and creative powers, and for the disastrous consequences it usually leads to in politics and general behaviour and treatment.

At the same time, we admired its attention towards social justice, as we appreciated its achievements in the fields of production and services and its demolition of the circles of exploitation and profiteers. We thought it a nation in which humanity had reached a high degree of happiness and which always promised more.

Yes, we learned much about the inexcusable cruelty that went on, and the unavoidable corruption on a limited scale, but it never occurred to us that it was a country of crooked millionaires, and that uncontrollable corruption was rife in it.

How did this new humanitarian experiment turn to tragedy? It is dictatorship that has done this, dictatorship more than the economic system itself. Dictatorship is the first foe of humanity, the enemy of freedom and dignity. It has injected its venom in Russia, as it did in Nazi Germany and Fascist Italy. The Third World is the victim of the one party and the single ruler, and the consequences follow one after the other – the wars, the decline in production, the negativism of the citizens, the black market – and it ends with the transformation of the proponents of revolution and justice into cutthroat brigands and millionaires.

I am not saying that democracy is a paradise free of gloom, but I believe it reins in evil, monitors corruption, hunts down the corrupt, respects human rights and calls the populace to leadership and action.

Curses on dictatorship and dictators! They have tainted history with blood and shame, and there is not one fool among them who has not left behind him a nation stripped and torn apart, its hopes destroyed.

8 February 1990

An Essential Plan

On 7 January, the *Al-Ahram* newspaper published a report submitted to the People's Assembly on the government's plan for the current phase. In it the government confirmed that the necessary measures were being taken to develop, increase and improve production in various sectors to attain self-sufficiency in essential commodities and to allocate an amount for export in order to reduce the import–export gap. These measures depend on:

1. Effective oversight of the work of state employees and their productivity.
2. Objective foundations for incentives linked to the performance of each worker.
3. Concentration on technical education and a limit to university admissions.
4. Independence of the public sector, and the introduction of regulations to preserve invested capital.
5. Provision of guarantees and the independence of controlling bodies in decision-making.

These are ideas that are spot on and bode well. They give rise in our souls to a pure, cool breeze for a suffocating people. With all our love for our country and hope for its salvation from its suffering, we truly yearn for these ideas to be converted into actions, firmly and without delay. And we yearn to feel the reality of this in executive decrees or, more importantly, in the desired results that will come when they are implemented. That is, in increased production, in self-sufficiency, in export growth, in regulated administration and in the end of misery for the downtrodden of the land. We salute this thinking and long for its serious implementation, and we dream of harvesting the fruits and easing the burden on the people.

To be frank with Prime Minister Atef Ebeid, I am a little uneasy, because this fine talk has made me happy several times in the past, and perhaps under several different administrations. And furthermore, these are steps that should have been the basis for clear action since their foundations were first laid in the 1960s. So it is barely credible that we begin the process as agreed, then think about a firm plan to put it into action thirty years later ... but what is to be done?

Let us hope that this time it truly is for real, and that Atef Ebeid's words are not like those of his predecessors. Egypt, the East, the West, the world *and* the hole in the ozone layer all demand commitment and action. And may God not deny us the recompense from this best of works.

15 February 1990

Diagnosis and Treatment

There were fine promises in the government's statement to the People's Assembly, and an announcement of valuable accomplishments made. We mentioned this last week, and we made clear the positive effect this information had on the long-suffering people, plagued by worries about current events. But it seems the government is not revealing all its secrets, concealing those that would upset us or multiply our anxieties. This may be considered polite in dealing with our feelings, but it is of no use in the face of the overwhelming reality. For the reality must be known in any case, so that we know the truth on the one hand in order to respond to the treatment if necessary on the other.

In an article in the financial edition of *Al-Ahram,* Dr Khaled Fuad Sherif talks about 1989, telling us that the performance indicators give no comfort: Central Bank statistics confirm that exports fell from $3,274 million in 1987/88 to $2,545.9 million in 1988/89, while at the same time imports increased from $9,841 million in 1987/88 to $10,078.9 million in 1988/89, meaning that the balance of trade deficit rose from $6,567m to reach $7,533 million. Similarly, the current account deficit in the balance of payments (excluding remittances) rose from $4,626 million in 1987/88 to $5,696 million in 1988/89. Dr Sherif wonders, and we wonder with him: how long can Egypt continue spending more than it receives in hard currency?

Certainly, this survey of the economic situation over a twelve-month period should not pass without accounting, investigation and review, nor without an explanation to the populace, who carry the debts and bear the repayments generation after generation. What state would we be in if loans and aid were suspended? Clearly, we must increase production to the highest level and reduce government expenditures to the lowest level, and we must rectify performance and watch the administration closely. And clearly, we are in urgent need of creative ideas and firm actions. And clearly too, time is running out at the speed of lightning, and it has no mercy on the remiss or the timid.

22 February 1990

A Call to Those Who Care about the Political Centre

Global transformations and our domestic circumstances urge us to redouble our vigilance, action and clear-eyed reading of the future, and this in turn urges us to pull together all our energies and abilities. The formation of one complete political bloc may be impossible, because of the gap between the different currents: the centre has a particular vision, rallying under its banner the National Democratic Party (NDP), the Wafd,[1] and the Liberals; the left has another vision, to which the Tagammu and the Nasserists belong; and the Islamic current has a third vision, bringing together the disparity of the Muslim Brothers and other groups. The formation of a homogeneous bloc of all the above may not be feasible, but it should be possible for the centrists to merge into a single party that would lead to the creation of a broad popular base, and solid national unity.

The differences between the centrist parties amount to no more than side issues and executory procedures. They do not differ on principles, since they agree in general with regard to foreign policy, the form of government and economic vision, quite apart from their agreement through faith in God and religion on how to legislate and what course to take. If there are differences beyond this, they will be of the kind that can be found between one wing of a single party and another. So perhaps the urgent step to be anticipated is the broadening of the NDP to include the Wafd, the Liberals and all the independent intellectuals, as well as the liberals who from way back have been affiliated with socialist democracy.

This will bear fruit only in the context of total political reform; one that allows for party diversity as a prelude to holding fair elections that will yield true representation for the people and propel them to participate effectively in the building of their future. The country awaits the

1 Sometimes known as the New Wafd, a revival of the earlier Wafd Party of the royal era.

leader to effect the unification that is possible, to put an end to artificial disarray and to move beyond historical differences and personal remnants. These cannot be allowed to impede the destiny of a nation embarking on one of the most delicate, critical and intense stages of its history. It is essential that we have a parliament that represents the real world and its trends (as any parliament that does not honestly reflect reality is merely symbolic, even if it is innocent of all procedural or legal suspicions). Our hope for this to come about is reinforced by a commitment to democracy on the part of those in charge; one that goes beyond words to genuine action in this most critical situation, a situation that is also the most conducive to regression for those who embrace the reasons for regression.

So let us take the decisive step forward. God looks after those who act.

7 March 1990

A National Project

It is astonishing that thinkers are coming together to search for a national project to unite around. A national project is one that invites people to acknowledge it, proclaim it, and demand that it be fully embraced. It comes into being of its own accord in the course of history, bursting out through political, social or national circumstances as a definitive necessity, then needing only a signal from an individual or a group to become life's aim for a whole nation for a period of time. This was how the national spirit came to life in the era of the British occupation, heralded by the old National Party.[1] This was how the independence movement came about following the Armistice and the announcement of the Wilson principles, its banner carried by the Wafd Party.[2] This was how democratic rule was established after the signing of the 1936 treaty, fought for by Mustafa al-Nahhas.[3] This was how social justice was introduced, adopted by the men of the 1952 Revolution. There was no choice among alternatives: each period had its project, and each project had its champions.

It seems that today there is no national project in its full sense. But two projects are in play, known to all:

The comprehensive development project (on which all domestic institutions and organisations are working together) aims for an Arab, African and global foreign policy, based on wise and balanced foundations, and is attempting to enrol in modernity while holding onto religion, values and national unity. It is a project that all who believe

---

1 The British occupied Egypt in 1882, declaring a Protectorate in 1914; the last British troops did not leave until 1956. The National Party (no relation to the later National Democratic Party, in power at the time Mahfouz was writing) was founded in 1895 and dissolved in 1952.

2 Woodrow Wilson's principles, the 'Fourteen Points', were published at the end of the First World War. The Wafd was Egypt's most popular party from its founding in 1919 to its dissolution in 1952.

3 The Anglo-Egyptian Treaty of 1936 required Britain to withdraw its troops, except from the Suez Canal. Mustafa al-Nahhas (1879–1965) was prime minister of Egypt five times between 1928 and 1952.

in these goals can rally round. It may not attain the level of diffusion and zeal it deserves, due to the failure of its proponents to establish the appropriate popular base and to their wavering, which has prevented them from adopting full democracy, as well as to administrative corruption, which arouses resentment and negativism.

The other is the fundamentalist project, which has a solid base but is mired in the past, behind the times and the spirit of the times, provocative and inflexible, given to violence, alienating Muslims more than anyone. To this group, even the tolerant, enlightened Islamic opinion-leaders are suspect, and have not been safe from their hands and their tongues. If this project cleansed itself of its damaging aspects and returned to the true spirit of Islam, and if its adherents followed the enlightened groups in reconciliation, it could be an adviser, a reminder, a counsellor to the first project.

As for those who are searching for a national project, they should sign up to one of the two above, and rid themselves of their negative attitude, which deprives the nation of their knowledge and experience.

8 March 1990

Description de l'Égypte[1]

Let us take a brief look at our situation, as a kind of preliminary closing of accounts to this period that sees us at such a low point. Let us ignore the history, not because it is not important but because everything that can be said about it has already been said. So, how do we see our face in the mirror of time?

1. A foreign policy characterised by vitality, sagacity, far-sightedness and sound planning.
2. A resurgence that gives cause for hope (to varying degrees) in construction, agriculture, transport, electricity, education, irrigation, security, culture and scientific research, besides the achievements made in the military and the infrastructure. Here we must not be unmindful of what is happening around us, nor neglect matters of maintenance and renovation.
3. A democratic system of government tarnished by the remnants of a previous totalitarian regime. Mixed together in it are freedom and emergency laws, and liberty with shackles.
4. An economic system feeling its way carefully and slowly towards reform. It has not yet proved its capability in the face of inflation and general hardship.
5. A sinking administration suffering from a lack of efficiency, faded integrity, and a failure to establish justice and respect the law.
6. Then there are the problems of youth with unemployment (both apparent and disguised) and dead ends in basic human requirements.
7. Drugs are still a problem, and their savage onslaughts still continue.
8. Last but not least, the deadly viruses that sneak their way into morality and human relations.

---

1 Mahfouz playfully uses here the title of the encyclopaedic publication of Napoleon's *savants* after their exploration of Egypt during the French occupation of 1798–1801.

I present this closing of accounts only as a reminder. It contains much that is not pleasing, but it is not a cause for despair or apathy. The great nations have gone through the same, or worse, and have come out of the dark shadows only through work, science and faith.

15 March 1990

National Unity

It is like a nightmare lived by a tormented sleeper: people believe a strange rumour, one of them rushes forward, and they burn and destroy. Then the lie behind the rumour is exposed, but the damage remains, testimony to the depth of the tragedy and the grieving of a nation.[1]

How did some people come to imagine what did not exist? Why were people in such a hurry to believe? Why did others willingly join in the destruction?

I have witnessed an age that we might call the age of national unity. It was a living reality, a genuine sentiment, a firmly rooted foundation. It had its political opponents, who never ceased attacking it with insinuation as well as directly, and with the fabrication of lies, but it deflected any aggression on its edifice without the least need for the intervention of security forces or religious leaders, and we considered it a deep natural instinct, like love for country and family, in no need of motivation or cultivation.

What on earth is happening today on Egypt's precious land? Rumours are believed, suspicion is rife, assaults take place and sorrow spreads its wings over heavy hearts.

How did this downfall occur?

Perhaps we have been infected by harmful germs from abroad. Perhaps it is the pains of successive wars and the wrathful economic crisis. Perhaps it is the remnants of the totalitarian regime slowing down the progress of democracy. Perhaps it is the heedless repetition of misused expressions about crusades that undermine national feeling and drive a wedge between the children of this single nation. National unity is the basis of our life, the starting point for any more complete unity.

Today reformers call for dialogue, arbitration and resolve, but the

---

1 Mahfouz is apparently referring here to instances of sectarian violence that occasionally erupt between Egypt's normally neighbourly Muslim and Christian communities.

matter requires greater action – action that will apprise every party, every trade union, every authority of the patriotic role it will play in it. They come together for the sake of political and constitutional reform, which is a good thing, but national unity will be no less important than these noble aims, if not more so.

You must all make your voice clearly heard, then reach out to the popular base with good examples and good words.

22 March 1990

On Culture

In our cultural life there are positives worthy of note and praise, as well as negatives that demand our continuous effort and honest work. At the head of the positives is the diffusion of general culture, thanks to radio and television, which penetrate the depths of the countryside, not just the cities, and reach the educated, the half-educated and the illiterate. This is a political, social and artistic culture, in keeping with a nature of general awareness and a religious, patriotic, humane and fun-loving environment; and if it were not for the miracle of modern technology it would not enjoy such wide dissemination, even over centuries of time.

Another positive aspect is how responsive readers are to books on religion and politics, including valuable books distinguished by their depth, their comprehensiveness and the nobility of their aims.

But it seems that free culture is passing through a period of uncertain steps and regression. By free culture I mean that which one accepts not for academic gain or to gratify a religious or political agenda, but out of a love of learning or a quest for fine artistic pleasure, as represented in thought and literature. Its lovers in relation to the size of the population are a tiny minority, a select few lost in an enormous ocean. Certainly the spread of modern technology has had a major effect here, but this has been compounded by the lack of cultural education in schools, the economic crisis and the currents of extremism.

It is true that the Ministry of Culture is doing great work and is always thinking of new projects. Likewise, radio and television offer tangible and varied services for serious culture, as does the press in its dedicated cultural pages and the exposure it gives to the views of writers and thinkers. But it is also true to say that the disease is latent in the population itself, for the reasons we have noted, and that its cure lies in an increase in services in defence of free culture and its role in building character. So I permit myself to make the following suggestions:

First, that the radio redouble its attention to culture, and strengthen and promote the Second Programme.[1]

1 The Second Programme, now known as the Cultural Programme, began

Second, that television devote a weekly programme to books, to look at the new publications of the week and discuss one of them, examining its depth, its useful lessons and the information it provides to all generations about their country or modern times. And how nice it would be if the discussion took the form of 'a book for the readers', with a panel of specialists to hold a dialogue with the competitors, and a prize of selected books for the winner.

Third, that each major newspaper produce a literature and arts supplement (without needing to raise their prices), focusing on:

1. Critical presentation and evaluation of the works of the rising generation.
2. Translation of some of the world classics, to be published in serial form.

I have no doubt that true reform of culture is linked to reform in general, or to the success of comprehensive development, which will restore people's equilibrium and direct their latent desires towards culture and values, but we must do the best we can in this time of trouble and uncertainty.

29 March 1990

---

broadcasting on 5 May 1957.

In Defence of Serious Culture

People are the first foundation of any renaissance. Civilisations did not begin with organisations and institutions; before this, human groups confronted their destinies and interacted with their environments, strengthening their muscles in their struggles, sharpening their senses, extending their mental faculties. Thus they devised their organisations and institutions in order to coordinate their activities and support and protect them with principles, laws and traditions.

There are numerous institutions and frameworks in Egypt – and I'm talking here about culture – that offer splendid services in a variety of areas and fields. I have no need to remind you of what the Ministry of Culture provides in the way of books, theatre, music, fine arts and cinema, or of what the radio and television provide for the millions. But we are all of us slipping into a recession in serious thought and art. I have already said that the disease is latent in the people themselves,[1] for global and local reasons beyond their control. The state is battling the slide with its successive five-year plans, but we must focus on education and give it all the care and attention it deserves.

Our educational establishments, from nursery school on up, are laboratories for the incubation of the citizens of the future, in politics, thought and art. Their role in this is paramount and irreplaceable. Indeed it must be extended to mesh with the activities of other institutions if we want to guarantee the spiritual health of the sons and daughters of our nation. Institutions are nothing without people, but good people can create the institutions needed. If we possessed a cultural base in keeping with the size of our population, all the problems that overburden us in our search for appropriate solutions would be solved. A cultured population, by its very presence, would resolve the crisis of writing, publishing and literary criticism, as theatres and stages would be built for its sake, exhibitions opened, magazines and literature and arts supplements published. Literary and cultural programmes would multiply and be more varied, and public and private

1 See preceding essay.

capital would compete to serve the population and comply with its wishes.

So let our first concern be the creation of a cultured class. Our not so distant past saw a serious cultural renaissance, and in the recent past our schools have not been short of examples of education in culture and refined taste, but today we are aspiring to something greater and more universal.

5 April 1990

The Arab World Facing the Times

In its long history the Arab world has met fierce challenges: epidemics, famines, savage invasions, colonialism on all its lands, and geographical discoveries that tore out the roots of its economy.[1] But despite the heavy loss of life and damage to civilisation, it has stood up to the challenges and clung to its existence. And here it is today, undergoing a great awakening and making progress between distress on one side and hope on the other, while the global changes in nature and politics form new challenges in its path. It must think and plan carefully to find its place in the new order, and the best ways of dealing with it. Yes, the Arab world has not solved its internal problems as it should, nor has it settled some of the disputes between its individual countries. There are nonetheless unmistakable signs that show it is moving towards harmony and realism in following what is happening around it, energetically tackling political and social reform and determinedly taking on its proper role in the human family.

The Arabs today are coming together through cooperative blocs and issuing directives that will be effective in development, reconstruction and civilised progress. The matter is no longer limited to speeches and the promotion of slogans; Arab scientists are researching and planning, and managers are eagerly going ahead with implementation. This bodes well for unity in economy, culture and security. There can be no real life for this deep-rooted people without such unity in these areas.

Today, investment capital in the Arab region is being watched carefully from a comprehensive viewpoint and a national standpoint, with the aim of defending its civilisational and humanitarian position and planting foundations for a thorough resurgence built on faith and science. These hopes have extended to the wider Islamic community, as wise voices have rung out in its meetings, calling for cooperation and economic integration, which promise broader benefits and greater

---

1 Mahfouz is probably referring here to the European discovery of the sea route round Africa, which drastically reduced Arab control of trade along the medieval Silk Road.

progress. Our higher duty is to continue on this path without hesitation or weakness, to redouble our efforts and our actions and to be liberal with what we have, in hand, word and heart. We must provide the coming generations with enlightened faith, creative science, genuine culture and radiant civilisation. We must be loyal to our past in order to build a future that is better than the past, notwithstanding what has been handed down of glory and great repute.

12 April 1990

The Lifeline

There may be no overwhelming disagreement among Egyptians about faith in religion, but there certainly is disagreement about the relationship between religion and daily life. There are those who see religion as an intimate bond between individuals and their God, and a strength from which a spirit flows that strives to make God's world a safe refuge for humanity, and in whose corners truth, justice, freedom, knowledge, beauty and love can take form. They derive inspiration from the sharia and they promote diligence and openness to the world and its civilisations and culture, while taking good care of our national unity, human rights and authenticity. And then there are those who go too far in their religion, shutting their eyes to the times they live in, going beyond the bounds of tolerance, tending towards violence and scorning others, both as people and in their ideas, civilisations and cultures.

The differences between the two groups will only be settled in an atmosphere of freedom, dialogue and respect for human rights. To this end, I call for the application of freedom in the formation of political parties, for openly declared activity and for legitimate competition, with detailed programmes, so that everyone knows where they stand. And I likewise call on all in the first group to join a single national front, under any name, old or new. I call on the National Democratic Party, Wafd, Labour, Liberals, Nasserists, and Tagammu to come together in this open front. There is no real difference between the National Democratic Party and the Wafd, the Liberals, and Labour. And there are now probably no differences with the Nasserists and Tagammu, after the global changes that have led to a new form of the international Left, from which there is now nothing to fear.

Every day we come across a new warning that reminds us to look closely once more at our historical differences and painful memories in order to save Egypt and its unity and promote it to assume its fitting status in this age.

O God, may we be among those who are grateful for guidance, not those who fall into temptation only to regret it.

19 April 1990

A Call to Self-Interest

How do we address the indifferent majority of our population? At first sight they arouse disgust, but after a little contemplation they stir hidden reservoirs of sadness and sorrow. In any case, since we love them just as we love our dear country, how are we to reach them and rouse them to awakening and change?

We have no shining hope in them, or in any quick solutions or dazzling miracles for them, and we know very well how they have suffered from poor education, anxiety about the future, unjust treatment and bewilderment at the deluge of theatrical performances that contradict our miserable history. Because of this, rhetoric, poetry and references to bygone glories count for little, so there is nothing left but to appeal to their self-interest.

It can be said that self-interest is an active natural instinct that no living being is free from. Loyalty may be present or not, duty may be pursued or not, but self-interest is always and ever evident, and it is in no need of being invoked – so why do we call on the indifferent majority to embrace it?

We urge them to self-interest because I have come to believe that indifference has begun to have a fatal effect on that old instinct. If someone proceeds recklessly on the path of dangerous drugs, it is obvious that his self-interest has become enfeebled; if someone's lust drives him to the gallows, it is obvious that his self-interest has been blinded; if someone invests his wealth abroad or otherwise damages his country's economy, it is obvious that his self-interest has erred or been deceived – we no longer take account of tomorrow, of our children, or of the consequences of revolutions and upheavals. You can adduce as many such testimonies as you like, but they all go to show that self-interest is no longer what it used to be – an exaggerated love of the self – and that it has mutated into a different instinct, one that conceals hatred and the annihilation of its host and his family.

Thus I call on everybody to return to self-interest in its traditional, old and well-known form, the self-interest that really does love the self, and with that love makes us act with more intelligence and wisdom.

So let us start with the call to this mindful self-interest, even so that the fruit of it then transports us to a new thinking person's quest and allows us to converse in that noble language: the language of religion, nation and humanity.

2 May 1990

Sectarianism, Real and Transient

It is rare for a society to be distinguished by complete homogeneity in all aspects of race or religion, but the differences do not always lead to discord and chronic problems. Sectarianism leads to a real problem and civil strife only if peace is unfeasible and agreement is impossible, and social relations give warning of its disastrous consequences – as is the case between whites and blacks in South Africa and between Hindus and Muslims in India.

Egypt is free of sectarianism in this sense, and has never known it in any period of its history: the different races and religions have lived together here in peace. The country's differences in this matter are no more than the differences between members of one family. The Egyptian village is the best witness to this, in the way it takes under its wings people of varying origins and different religions; the city alley is the same. But it is true to say that social relations have sometimes involved tensions that have grown or receded according to circumstances and conditions, and they can perhaps all be traced back to social, political or economic problems that spoil things when they are bad and fix things when they are good.

Let us look more closely at the reasons, to better understand our situation, so that we are better equipped to rectify it:

Tension may originate with the state itself, if it practises discrimination between its citizens in employment or services. Religious bigotry is not behind it, as demonstrated by the fact that discrimination is also practised among Muslims to the advantage of the elite. So the fault may actually be in poor administration, corruption and exploitation. This can be fixed through integrity, honesty and justice, to bring stability and peace of mind to Muslims and Copts alike.

Tension may arise from autocracy, when an individual or a small group appropriates power and denies the populace any participation in it. In truth, this exclusion falls on all, but members of the minority may feel that it is aimed at them. The only cure for this is democracy and respect for human rights.

Tension may be caused by an adverse economic situation, and a fear of poverty, when people, their families and their neighbours are in straitened circumstances.

And tension may be ignited by the threat from extremist currents, who espouse hostility and tend towards violence. The ranks of these extremists grow beyond their natural size by attracting those who are embittered with life as a result of administrative, political or economic obliquity.

The sectarian tension that troubles us today has no relation to real sectarianism; it is a temporary disturbance resulting from general conditions, and a warning that impels us to redouble the effort to bring about a leap in reform. It is a problem of civilisation, not religious dispute.

3 May 1990

Looking Again

We have already expressed our opinion about religious deviation and the dire consequences it has on our resurgence, on thought and on the unity of the nation. We linked its growth to the climate of politics, the economy and the performance of the government, and saw how comprehensive reform is the appropriate way to achieve the return of equilibrium to society and the restoration of a sense of integrity, tolerance and national pride. But this does not prevent us from treating the topic on its purely ideational level, as doctrine and propaganda, in order to seal any cracks we may find.

I say: Islam is a complete, humanitarian religion that radiates eternal principles such as freedom, social justice, human rights, tolerance, and a deep-seated love of learning and work, besides its character of moderation, its avoidance of excess, and its effective message of an abode of peace. Meanwhile, the deviant currents are known for excess, bigotry and narrow horizons, and they do not hesitate to use violence and promote malice and hatred.

How did these currents become strong enough to muddy the clarity of such a clear religion? Was there nothing better suited than religion to stand up against politics, the economy and government, to act as armour against corruption, dissolution and aberration?

What is astonishing is that the true religion has the institution of Al-Azhar and its establishments of learning, along with thousands of professors and preachers, the leaders among whom are counted as possessing the cream of intellect and conscience. It also has all the means of education and communication – schools, mosques, radio, television – while the deviant currents have nothing but secret propaganda and limited immediate means. Should this not prompt us to look again at the religious curriculum and its teaching? What should the role of the religious school be? And the mosque?

What is the role of radio and television?

The crucial factor is not a question of how much, but of how – and of the kind of men involved. And the question on the table today and tomorrow is: what form should religious education take? And what form should the call to religion take in the age of information, direct broadcasting and unlimited, universal culture?

We have many enlightened men of religion, and many enlightened thinkers, and those who work for religion are in fact working for both religion and the world we live in.

10 May 1990

The Summit of Hopes

No Arab country is free of internal crisis, whether political or economic. But just as the solution is internal, it can only be achieved by seeking help from abroad. This is because we live at a time when the internal and the external are mixed together, especially among countries whose roots and branches have interconnections going way back, and what concerns one Arab country concerns them all. At this historic moment, which is flooded with disruption and alarm bells, the Arab summit appears like a ray of hope and a beacon for the future.[1]

We hope, first of all, that the summit will clear the air of emotion and light the lamp of reason, which is the best guide in a tempest.

We hope it will reconcile the outstanding differences between some of the sibling nations, so that all the countries can end up as one community in direction, thought and policy.

We hope it will confirm its desire for just and comprehensive peace, a peace that takes in Palestine, Golan, and the Iran–Iraq conflict, setting out its recommendations and the right path to their accomplishment.

We hope it will adopt a resolution to rid the Middle East of all kinds of weapons of mass destruction, in support of the push for peace and to avert from the region the threat of ruin with an end known only to God; and that it will demand that the world shoulder its responsibility in this matter with sufficient strength and clarity.

We hope it will also announce that the only alternative to ridding the Middle East of weapons of mass destruction is the natural race to acquire them for self-defence, for as much as we aspire to comprehensive peace, we refuse to live at the mercy of others.

We hope the summit believes – as surely it must – that our solidarity in these times is essential to life and survival, that the times will not allow us to overlook the outcomes that lie in wait for us, and that any complacency in this will herald an end beyond description or solace.

We ask God for guidance and success.

24 May 1990

---

1 The Arab League Summit Conference, held from 28 to 30 May 1990 in Baghdad.

A Call to Hope

I believed in the public sector before there was such a thing in Egypt, and when it was launched I was steeped in the light of hope for the future of my country and its people, because I had been brought up in the embrace of two great fundamental principles: freedom and social justice. I considered the public sector to be both the symbol of social justice and its supporting pillar, and I adored its declared motto: copious production, fair distribution.

I was employed in the public sector, and I had the leisure to breathe its atmosphere and contemplate it at length. I will not hide the fact that concern dogged me from the first, not in rejection of it as a system, but in disquiet at the methods of those who worked in it, and in objection to the way they treated it and to their bureaucratic dealings with the public. I felt that if it had the kind of workers that the socialist countries had, it would produce the yields that they did, and it would take this country bounding forward as they had theirs. Thus things remained until the socialist world turned on itself and looked firmly towards a reconstruction of its vision, system of government and economy, and I became convinced that the public sector was no more free of malady than those who worked in it.

If the public sector and the private sector today each have their partisans, I have suffered from both. Nothing is left to me of my old history but my faith in freedom and social justice. The economic sector that I unreservedly and unconditionally lean towards is the successful one – and the successful one is the productive one, which allows room for business and produces good commodities, with a surplus that can be exported to attain balance and pay off accumulated debts. And freedom and social justice will remain the responsibility of a watchful populace and a judicious government.

Let us have one objective: success. It is the lifeline in the worries of the hour, it is action, it is hope, it is the escape from negativism, apathy, discord and criminality; it is the eternal call until the arrival of the dawn.

2 June 1990

Our True Wealth

Population growth is a destiny we have to live with, an inescapable reality. I do not mean that we should neglect the family-planning programme, indeed we should exert all possible effort on its behalf. Our endeavours will not disappoint us as a nation. But the torrent will keep on flowing until it reaches its limit: complaints alone are of no use, and despair goes against life and is not a quality that gets things done. So we need to ask ourselves the question: how is it possible to invest this human wealth for the good of our country and humanity? For the multitude to be converted into wealth it must be governed by a calm and conscious policy, working towards both the short and the long term. And the curse can then be turned into a blessing deserving of praise and thanks.

The first thing that comes to mind is that we should leave nobody, male or female, without proper education, training or preparation for life, so that we convert them from simply a passive living being into the potential for productive or creative work, wherever they may be. Everybody must be prepared to cover all needs, at home or abroad in Arab or other friendly countries. There is a constant need for security personnel, for workers in agriculture and industry, and for higher specialisations in science and technology. Our extensive deserts could be transformed through science and hard work, and there are promising indications of the possibility of making fresh water from salt water and of the broad capacities of new methods of irrigation. And we are not short of cities that need to be demolished and rebuilt, or just restored and renovated, quite apart from the new cities that need to be constructed.

The Ministry of Workforce needs to broaden its operations and must be prepared to fulfil its vital guiding duties for the future. It needs to work together with our embassies abroad to understand the needs of countries near and far and the conditions for successful employment in them, and to draw up a plan to prepare the workforce anywhere they might be needed.

We will soon discover that our prime wealth is our human wealth, and our most important goal is the investment of that wealth.

7 June 1990

A New Era

The decision of the Constitutional Court is not just related to a particular electoral method; it is a historic condemnation of political duplicity, an unambiguous and definitive call to respect the constitution, and a firm anchorage for the buttress of stability, the sovereignty of the law and the prestige of the state. It has created a rare opportunity for the clear-sighted to review our political life, to cleanse it of its negativism and its defects, and to build a new foundation for democracy and legitimacy; an effective adherence to reality and a confrontation of economic and social problems with the requisite courage and genuine will.

We must beware of agreeing to an amendment to the electoral law that would take us back to a rigid regime that does little and talks much, surrounded by an indifferent silent majority and a gang of robbers who make a mockery of the law.

Now the opportunity is there for the president to let the presidency stand separate, relinquishing his party position in order to put his powers at the service of whoever wins the trust of the people, and to become the third symbol[1] of the popular will and the protector of the constitution.

Now is an appropriate opportunity to repeal the emergency laws[2] and to respect human rights when it comes to the law of parties, free from anybody's directives.

We must now sanctify electoral freedom and afford it a range of essential guarantees so that we can hear the voice of the people, long denied its expression.

I am not saying that this will present us with a magic key to solve problems or step over obstacles, but it will provide the best atmosphere for action and for delivering popular confidence, scrutiny and participation.

---

1 After the People's Assembly and the Shura (Consultative) Assembly.

2 These underpinned the state of emergency that had been in effect since the assassination of President Sadat in 1981.

We must change, we must shake off our fear and idleness, and we must face adversity neither with force nor as slaves, but with the courage of men.

14 June 1990

A Call to the Crooked

Rightly or wrongly – or perhaps both together – distrust has become an almost inescapable plague. No person, grand or base, and no project, even if it is an act of piety, is safe from suspicion and idle talk. And one cannot deflect or change this by saying it is exaggerated, or fabricated, or the result of a conspiracy, for we are plunging into the depths of a gloomy era in which morals have been reduced to the lowest level, and where people are surrounded by crises, worries and troubles. There is no way we can perform our duty in the struggle for life without an authentic moral foundation that includes even the minimum of national feeling and human conscience. So what is the path to deliverance?

Deliverance requires the thorough reform of all institutions of society, as well as a deep and discriminating education, and sound tools. But we have to wait a long time for these – and the longer we wait, the more the chances of salvation slip away. So there is no alternative but to save what we can with what we have to hand, until the reformers catch us up with the advances we seek. On that basis, I direct my call to the crooked of all kinds and on all levels, and say to them: crookedness does not come between a person and his love for his country, especially if his disillusion has come about as a result of adverse, overpowering circumstances. I remind them that English pirates performed the greatest services to England, one of them earning titles from Queen Elizabeth I.

I remind them too that the day the eternal leader Saad Zaghloul returned from exile, Egypt's burglars and pickpockets made a pact to abstain from committing any crime that day, and indeed the day passed peacefully, despite the houses being empty of residents and the streets being overcrowded with humanity. This shows that love of country can bring the crooked and the straight together.

I am not asking that you mend your behaviour, or that you cease your crooked ways: be as you wish to be, and as the times wish for you, but do not forget your sad country, do your full and complete duty, devote yourselves to work with purpose and proficiency, respect those of the people who deal with you, and reinvigorate the fields, the factories, the offices, the hospitals and the streets.

Whatever happens, one good deed deserves ten, and you will find a place in the embrace of your nation, which will remember what you have done and will forgive you all your bad deeds, for what are you but good people swept away by the current of calamities, crises and the instruments of misfortune? And may you one day return to your good origins, your benign behaviour and your illustrious excellence.

28 June 1990

Driving Out the Spectres

We are following the initiative of our president, Hosni Mubarak, on weapons of mass destruction with the great interest it deserves. It is a simultaneously national, Arab and humanitarian initiative, so it is gaining support, and all that remains is for it to lead to a result of similar importance in ridding a vital region of the world of the spectres of fear and tension, and preparing for it a better atmosphere of mutual understanding and reconciliation.

What threatens the world as a whole must be confronted by the world as a whole. It is an international obligation, and every nation must perform its duty as far as it is able, without hesitation or prevarication. The world must adopt a united and cooperative position in the face of pollution, drugs and weapons of mass destruction that goes beyond the damage these cause to one country or one environment. And in order that decisions in this matter are not subject to political whims, they must be deliberated in the United Nations and unanimous resolutions must be issued, whose implementation nations must adhere to, whether through universal boycott or through material penalties. Moreover this must happen with integrity and transparency, to remove any suspicion of bias or capricious tendency.

We do not want a repetition of what happened when doubts about weapons of mass destruction first arose, met one time by a preventive blow, another time by exemption and leniency. The world must take a united stand against any country that pursues a programme of such weapons. The matter should be clear and deterrent, and carried out in a humanitarian and just framework – if not, it will become a new face of colonialism and subjugation, far removed from any serious attempt to confront the universal evils that threaten human civilisation and existence.

If the issue is not dealt with decisively, the world will find itself hurtling in shame towards global destruction. All the same, it is unthinkable that a nation should neglect to defend itself or live at the mercy of others.

5 July 1990

Elections

We hope that research will result in a legitimate and well-constructed electoral law, and that this will come as part of comprehensive political reform, that will bring with it a sound environment for freedom and action. Perhaps it is pertinent at this point to return to my stated and long-held view, which I have expressed more than once, on elections by popular list. I have always seen these as extremely simple and practical. Votes are cast at the various polling stations for the competing parties, then the votes won by each party are counted up, and seats in the People's Assembly are unconditionally assigned according to the proportions. Each party then chooses its representatives to take those seats, either by internal elections or by any other agreed means.

This electoral process achieves the following:

First: no vote is wasted, and the assembly represents all voters fairly and precisely.

Second: it teaches the people to vote according to principles, rather than by personalities, families or tribes, so the assembly represents the general public interest.

Third: through the electorate voting for the parties, and through the parties selecting their representatives, we guarantee the best people for the job.

Fourth: this electoral method respects minorities and strengthens their standing. We live in an age that demands a palpable degree of political awareness that may not always be as well developed as we might hope. But let us remember that freedom involves ceaseless effort, education and lessons, and it does not matter if it meets a few obstacles in the hard upward climb.

12 July 1990

Developing the Achievements of the 1952 Revolution

A true celebration of a historic event such as the 1952 Revolution should tend towards a re-examination, with an aim to revitalise it, as made necessary by the unceasing march of time. We have spoken enough about its positive aspects, with the realisation of social justice and the advancement of society in a range of amenities: all this has been said often and repeatedly, and we have been happy when it has gone well and unhappy when it has not. And we have spoken enough about its negative aspects, from which we have derived lessons and warnings for all to see. What we now need to focus on is how to develop its visions and directions in a world that is moving steadily towards political democracy, economic freedom and cultural unity, under the shade of universal human values.

Certainly the revolution established the indispensable human value of social justice, but this came at the price of individual liberty and political human rights. So today we must lay the foundation for our way forwards on the two values together: both social justice and political, economic and intellectual liberty. This is something that people used to say was impossible, that we had to choose one way or the other, and we were accused of distortion, idealism and fantasy. But it has been affirmed now by the reconstructive revolution in the Eastern bloc, and indeed in the entire Third World.

The new situation requires enduring dynamism, the elimination of fanaticism and an escape from the grip of slogans. And it requires a bold and honest re-evaluation of everything, in bringing about unconditional and unfettered justice and liberty, and in the pursuit of perfection for the sake of creating a better society for the benefit of all, without discrimination between one social class and another or between ruler and ruled.

For the good of everybody we must look again at our political and economic life, at our services and at the positions of leadership that should be held by magistrates and scientific researchers. And we must understand that clinging to the achievements of the revolution as they were first formed is to condemn them to death for being out of date, and that to develop them in order to catch the train of the times is to revive them and to avoid squandering the toil, blood and torment that were expended on their behalf.

19 July 1990

The Electoral System

It is good that it has been decided to run the elections for the Consultative Assembly on the individual candidate system; this is a progressive step that should be followed in any election. But that does not prevent me from declaring that I am a supporter of proportional representation, and that I was the first to call for this system in the time of the late leader Anwar Sadat, though I must note that the general list did not occur to me at that time, nor the statutory minimum. The idea I had was to consider the whole country as a single constituency, in which the voter would cast his vote for a given party and the party would then choose their representatives according to the votes they had won. There are advantages to this system, which I can summarise as follows:

1. It excludes independents. I cannot conceive of an independent citizen, when there are so many viewpoints and ideologies available, but if a person decides anyway, for some reason, to maintain his independence, he should move away from practical political life and leave it to those who are able to bear its consequences openly, far from any reservation or expediency.
2. No citizen's vote is wasted or lost, no matter how small the trend he belongs to, and any assembly that reflects the reality of the population becomes its strongest and fullest expression.
3. It trains the citizen in national democracy in the short and the long term, and arouses in him tendencies of allegiance to the principle before the person, with the knowledge that the person will not disappear from the picture altogether, since it is he who promotes his party in one constituency or another.
4. It guarantees the selection of the best elements by each party, as it is like an election in two stages: the first on principles, decided by the people; the second on competence and commitment, which the party carries out by the method of its choice.

And perhaps the most important thing about this system is that it may propel more than two parties to the assembly. Nor does it enable a single party to form an overwhelming majority. But we must accept the assembly in any form, since the people are its source and its fashioner, and the people know best what is good for them and what suits their needs.

19 July 1990

A Return to Loyalty

Loyalty applies to friendship, love, and the awakening of feelings of responsibility, while it is manifested most strongly in work. It may be expressed in the written or spoken word, and the heart may blaze with it out of sincere love, to say the least. One of the best models of loyalty is that which binds together the members of a family, though in this case it may arise from something like a natural impulse, without the need for any effort or inculcation. Loyalty to society, on the other hand, is a disposition that is acquired and nurtured, formed as a result of people coming together in a particular environment built on proximity and cooperation, and subject to personal, social and civilisational influences; circumstances that may raise it to the peak of potency, or that may oppose it and weaken its force, and even plunge it into the abyss of extinction.

In times of resurgence – or of strength – loyalty grows, even at the cost of familial affiliation. And in times of disintegration or regression, common loyalty weakens, leaving nothing but loyalty to family, or if the collapse becomes more intense, only loyalty to the self. And the question that faces us at this stage in our life is: how can we strengthen our common loyalty, so that it becomes a mainstay in facing challenges and building a sound new society? There can be no true advancement without true loyalty; indeed, the degree of advancement is directly proportionate to the degree of loyalty. It is humanity that is the foundation, that ensures the success of all other factors, for humanity is more important than money, or technology, or planning – without loyal people, money may be plundered, technology may break down and planning become only ink on paper. But what are the factors that have a strengthening or weakening effect on loyalty? They are:

1. Political organisation. The system in which the state does everything, which is not based on practical popular participation, invites the citizen to abandon the burden of constancy and tempts him to be concerned only with his own affairs, as long as the system aligns with the attainment of his aims and the

realisation of his goals. But if he is unsuccessful or is overcome by failure, his self-concern may extend to indifference, crude negativism or resentment of the state, and he may become lost between that and dark despair, and become involved in crime and drugs.

2. The general climate of society, and the governing attitude in its treatment of the individual. It exhausts him in his quest for his daily needs such as food, clothing, education, health, hygiene and transportation. It does not uphold his rights as a person in the street or in government departments, so that he feels he is living in a hostile society that begrudges him love and respect, and he responds with dislike for dislike, contempt for contempt.
3. The disregard for values and laws, and the consequential dominion of the unscrupulous and the crooked. The citizen finds himself between a rock and a hard place: to rebel against society, or to fall into the chasm of corruption.

So if we are to create loyalty, we must – while keeping a close eye on education, the media and the preachers – establish the rule of democracy, treat the administration with firmness and scrutiny, and relentlessly chase down corruption and the corrupt.

21 July 1990

Electoral Memories

There are memories associated with elections in our history, and what memories! They are a testament to the national pride, strong loyalty and keen awareness of the Egyptians, and show how people have a natural disposition to be led by the light of these qualities, even if they are steeped in illiteracy. You have heard about the prime minister who ran the first elections in our modern times and was defeated, beaten by an ordinary member of the public. And in another constituency the overwhelmingly Muslim masses chose a Coptic candidate who was not from the area and had no direct connection to anyone local; it was his principles, his party and his overall nationalist approach that recommended him and propelled him forwards.

In our constituency of Abbasiya, two men were standing. One was an everyday pasha who had gained that rank through seniority and promotion, without personal distinction in either knowledge or competency, though he was known for his patriotism, his popularity and his hard work. The other was one of those Egyptian pashas accounted for his learning, experience and politics, though he was known for his loyalty to the king and his haughtiness towards the people. Both were equally sons of Abbasiya. The people chose the man who was loyal to them, and he outstripped the brilliant other one, who even lost his deposit. We can confirm from this that the people know well how to choose the person who will represent them, despite his unsophistication, rather than the person who will represent the king, in spite of his great merits.

There were certainly those who turned against us for preferring the plain man over the scholar, but we must distinguish between elections to an academic position and political elections, which first and foremost are about principles, not personalities. How many battles have the people plunged into at the time of elections, and how much harm and pain and damage have they suffered through their insistence on the respect of their principles! Our national record has preserved the martyrs of democracy as much as it has the martyrs of independence, and there is no doubt that their souls are hovering around us these days to assure themselves that their sacrifice will not have been wasted or disappear to no avail. May God guide our people to choose the most deserving of trust and the most worthy to abide.

26 July 1990

Inspired by Reality

In following events – and especially after the president's speech on the anniversary of the 1952 Revolution – some serious and essential truths have become clear to us.

Today we enjoy friendly and constructive relations with the whole world and full and fruitful cooperation with the Arab countries, promising great hopes for the future. And we are striding firmly towards true democracy, which brings together freedom and social justice, ahead of the revolt of the socialist nations against totalitarian rule and rigid slogans.

We have spent 93 billion Egyptian pounds in the latest phase of the revolution in investments to revitalise the basic structure of great national projects, with a tangible revival in agriculture, industry, power, transport, housing and new cities, and in the beginning of a revolution in education.

Our future goals are crystallising in the light of all this, confirming our role among the nations, our standing in the Arab world, and the development of our society towards a degree of modernity that qualifies it for business, for production, for the exercise of freedom and for the enjoyment of human rights.

This is our national project – for those who seek a national project. This is our allegiance – for those who suffer from apathy. This is our endeavour – for those who give in to laziness or plead excuses.

But is it not strange that after all the effort and the money expended we remain victims of suffering and distress, of so much negativity, and of misunderstanding by the World Bank? This may mean that we have fallen into the worst stages of ruin, or that the effort we have exerted is still not sufficient and that our moral standing is still not at the level we are aiming for, but in the end it defines our plan of action and its goals: that we increase our good relations with the world, that we confirm our close Arab connections, that we lengthen our stride towards full democracy and respect for human rights, and that we redouble the workforce and provide it with a good, sound environment.

In a word: that we overcome every obstacle and encourage every initiative, heedless of any slogan except progress and success accompanied by our highest values.

3 August 1990

The Crime and the Mission

In my view there can be no hesitation in condemning the invasion of Kuwait at the hands of a member of the Arab community, and I do not exclude even the people of Iraq from this consensus.[1] For the invasion is an ignorant crime that goes to show that an Islamic culture of some fifteen centuries' duration has not been enough to cleanse some souls of the dregs of tribal arrogance. Moreover it is a blatant contradiction of the spirit of the age and its direction.

But as a result of it, there has begun to be played a strange tune on the strings of despair – a despair in Arabness, unity and cooperation, expressed as confused dreams, clouds of delusion and spectres of the jet-black night. This is another mistake, no less erroneous or disastrous than the criminal invasion itself.

Look at European unity and how it has come about with patience and perseverance, step by step, after centuries of fragmentation, hatred and wars, with millions of casualties and mountains of ruined towns and villages!

Arab unity is a mission inspired by reality. Our needs decree it, our existence demands it, and the realisation of our identity in the modern world enshrines it, as does the solidarity of thought, minds and assets that it entails for the achievement of our goals today and tomorrow.

A reprehensible crime has been committed in spite of us, and other crimes may occur, but we will not let go of our higher aim, and we will not waver in its realisation by all means and by any path, even if the beginning is limited to a core of believers – not as an alliance against anybody but as an open and constant invitation to all who will follow the call sincerely and faithfully.

The road may be long and hard, with many false steps, and its air may be disturbed from time to time by ignorant prejudices or insane tendencies, but we must face any delinquency with solidarity, reason,

---

1 On 2 August 1990, Iraq invaded Kuwait, occupying it for the next seven months until forced to withdraw by a UN-authorised coalition of forces in the Gulf War of January–February 1991.

wisdom and determination. We must correct mistakes, bandage wounds, and support truth and justice. There is no room for retreat, despair, or failure.

16 August 1990

Arab Hopes

In this suffocating nightmare, among the ruins of the heavy financial losses that no Arab nation has escaped, and keeping in mind the calamities that have befallen the peaceful people of Egypt and other countries – in these dark days our minds do not cease from thinking, nor our hearts from grieving, but our imagination can glean a few moments of ease as it floats in a land of hopes. What are these hopes that the imagination hovers around?

1. That the Iraqi president will conquer his own despotic tyranny and return triumphantly to justice – a withdrawal nobler than his retreat before Iran, and one that would save his Arab nation and his national history.
2. That Kuwait will be restored to its legitimate status, regain its sovereignty, its rights and its plundered wealth, dress its wounds, and resume its honourable path.
3. That Iraq will emerge from the crisis sound and unharmed, its people, its infrastructure and its institutions intact, for it is an Arab power, a national pride, and we have the same concern for its safety as we do for our own.
4. That the Palestinian cause will not be damaged, and will once more occupy the centre of attention in the hearts of the Arab peoples, as the primary Arab cause.

It is true that these hopes are like a dream, but if they came true the world would be reassured in its interests and the Arabs could turn to the restitution of their losses, having avoided a fate whose severity no one knows but God.

The dream is not impossible if the ruler of Iraq listens to the voice of reason, if he remembers lessons from the recent and the distant past, and if he thinks it out as should those who are truly responsible for their countries – as well as those who aspire to a place in history, to be recorded in its blank pages.

23 August 1990

The Arab Road

In the midst of the current Arab crisis, President Hosni Mubarak has risen to the pinnacle of civilised wisdom, worthy of this steadfast Egyptian ruler, supported by God with a judicious mind in a sound body. He has given the clearest expression to the voice of Egypt, the civilisation of Egypt and the true spirit of Egypt since the dawn of conscience broke in this blessed land to separate good from evil, and to set down just recompense in this world and the next.

We were pleased by his insistence on the path of peace, sparing the Arab world the woes of war, and we wish him success, as we do all those among the Arabs and other nations who support him. But we will not be happy with peace if – God forbid – it comes at the expense of our values. So our first aim must be the elimination of the effects of aggression and the restoration of Kuwait to its legitimate status and its role in the Arab world, and the return of Iraq to justice, legitimacy, the rule of law and respect for human rights under the Arab League and the United Nations.

It may be right to allow that the crisis has not been all bad, for it has exposed truths among our Arab brothers that needed to be known in order for relations between them to be set straight in a plain and clear manner. It has revealed their philosophies of life, for even if they agree on the long-term ends of liberation and development, they differ on the means. There are those who care about the integrity of both the means and the ends, and there are those who believe that the ends justify the means.

We must unite with the first group to build with them the moral foundation for the Arab world, and we must try by all legitimate means to cleanse the second group of the relics of bygone centuries that we hope are over and never to return.

Meanwhile we may ask ourselves with a sigh: when will we emerge from the darkness of this crisis? When can we continue on our way? When can we devote ourselves entirely to our true goal, which is to take on the role that befits us in this modern age?

30 August 1990

The Passing of the Professor

When I first knew him at the Opera Café discussion group, before the 1952 Revolution, I saw in him a professor who devoted his whole being to learning and culture. He had come to meet the members of the university publishing board, whose sessions were a mix of serious debate and genial conversation revolving around publishing matters, political sorrows and the latest jokes. But our new guest began in a serious and ponderous tone with our duty towards culture, focusing on the earnest work to be done in its publication. Our first discussion with him was about looking into the establishment of a weekly literary and cultural magazine to be a voice for the new generation of critics and writers. Unfortunately though, the publishing board was treading its path with some difficulty and did not have the means to enter into a new project with which none of its members had any familiarity.

Some years later, he joined our Harafish group as a free member, sometimes attending, sometimes not, and the bonds of affection between him and us were cemented.[1] At this second arrival in my circle, his personality had matured as a university professor, a consultant to the ministry of culture, a leading critic, and a thinker distinguished by sincerity, courage and insight, without losing the qualities of gravitas, commitment and sobriety. He participated in serious discussions as though delivering a lecture, he rarely indulged in humour, and he would not play the role of the smiling listener. His true delight was in serious thought and profound comment on political and cultural affairs, in which he was prepared to engage for hours without becoming tired or bored. He seemed to have been created solely to explicate, to lecture and to play with the ideas generated by a present full of ferment and a history rich in contradictions.

He was a luminary of the generation of earnestness, open-mindedness, freedom, loyalty and national unity. His long campaign produced

1 The Harafish was a kind of cultural salon, for which Mahfouz and a number of like-minded intellectual friends met regularly at a café to share views and tales and to hold literary, cultural and philosophical discussions.

a pick of the best and most enlightened followers, a deep and broad critique of contemporary literature and a bold, liberated thinking that you might agree or disagree with, though you could not but revere and respect him. Thus he became one of the greatest symbols of our intellectual life and our noble aspirations for a better tomorrow and a more humanitarian and civilised age.

And now death has taken him when he was at the peak of his maturity and with the most to give, a fruit ripe with excellence, overflowing with virtue, radiating light and grace. He is lost to his family and his compatriots, but he receives the beautiful reward in the realm of the Almighty. Farewell, Louis Awad.

1 September 1990

The War of Human Shields

President Saddam Hussein has decided to turn the foreigners working in Iraq and Kuwait into human shields to protect him from the blows he is expecting. It is pointless to say that this measure is beyond all international laws or humanitarian principles. For what is the use of talking about laws and principles in the case of a man who acts as if he lives in a world where they do not exist?

Even so, how are we to deal with this abnormal situation?

American and Arab forces have gone to Saudi Arabia for defensive not offensive purposes, and there will not be war unless the Iraqi president dares to attack; but if he does, no one will have any choice. And if the hostages cannot be saved, a terrible vengeance will be visited on Iraq, and the first to be swept away by this, unfortunately, will be the innocent victims.

If there is no war, economic sanctions will be enough, even if they are protracted, though it should be noted that – as of writing these lines – the Security Council has not yet determined a blockade, and sanctions may not include food and medicines, for humanitarian reasons. With sanctions in place, the problem may be solved internally as a result of pressure from the Iraqi people, who I cannot imagine consent to the policies of their ruler, and the defensive forces will also have more time to complete their numbers and preparation.

The Iraqi president is behaving like the gangsters of the cinema, who put their victims in the line of police fire with the aim of escaping unscathed. But the police always perform the impossible to achieve their goal without the loss of innocent blood.

6 September 1990

War

The decision of the Security Council to impose a blockade on Iraq is sufficient to achieve what we and the world all want, which is the withdrawal of the Iraqi army from Kuwait and the restoration of Kuwait to its legitimate status. Whether or not the results come as quickly as we hope, they will definitely come in good time. All we have to do is be patient and consolidate the blockade. The time spent waiting will not be wasted, as it affords an opportunity for initiatives and negotiations by those who seek a solution to the problem. What matters to us is that right returns to where it belongs, that principles prevail and that anyone contemplating aggression is aware of this lesson and at the same time understands that they are living in a new world, under whose precepts they must operate.

As for war, it is evil – an evil that begets evils, and no country, whether Arab or non-Arab, will escape its direct or indirect consequences. And its effects will be more deadly on the Third World, whose miseries it will double.

We must not think about war unless it is forced upon us, and it will only be forced upon us if the Iraqi president risks starting a new one. All the troops gathered in the Gulf region are there for the implementation of the Security Council's resolution, or for defence. And whoever was following what happened in the Security Council will have noticed how some countries hesitated for a long time before agreeing to the strengthening of the sanctions resolution, which goes to show that they do not desire or approve of war. Marching to war without necessity is no less inhuman than the criminal invasion itself, or using people as human shields.

To sum up: we care strongly about right, justice and legitimacy, but we do not want war if it is not forced upon us against our will.

10 September 1990

War and Peace

Who are the Arabs?

They are agents of imperialism and international Zionism. It is not I who say this, nor have I ever said it, but it is repeated by Arab tongues or pens in times of disagreement and discord. They may tell you of conspiracies whose traps their leaders fall into, as though they were an easy catch for any cunning hunter.

It is all an unfair and spurious condemnation, unsupported by any proof, certitude, or documentation. It arises and spreads with the force of unbridled agitation and reckless emotion, and the complete absence of thought. The fact is that all Arabs have adopted a single goal. They dream of unity, without entering into the details, and they dream of a comprehensive awakening through which they will step into the modern age as a power capable of fruitful exchange on all levels. They hope that oil revenues will support them in their fight, not as direct subsidy but through investment that will bring returns to all.

So where then does the disagreement come from?

The difference arises in the choice of the appropriate means of attaining this dream. There are those who believe in violence, terrorism and war, and there are those who adhere to legality, legitimacy and rational dialogue and wish to achieve their dreams under the umbrella of Arab treaties and international laws.

And the truth is that we get nothing but tragedies and defeats from the hands of those who believe in violence, while the adherents of discussion and reason have liberated Sinai and paved the way to a comprehensive dialogue through which outstanding cases can be resolved. Today, the two parties confront each other – the one pursuing a peaceful Arab solution, the other determined to reject it, flaunting their power and zeal.

In reality, war throws up such disastrous consequences from which it is preposterous to imagine anyone can escape.

13 September 1990

Hard Lessons

There are harsh experiences in our lives that serve as lessons for those who are willing to learn. So when will we learn? A secure house has been stormed from within by a decision thrown down by one of its sons in a calamitous moment of revelation, without discussion or consultation, all of a sudden dragging the house to the edge of the chasm and destroying in a moment what has taken years of effort and sweat and hope to build up. Disaster generally lies latent in any autocratic leader who imposes himself by force and who controls the media to the point where he appears to himself and to his nation as a superman, speaking of revelation, acting on inspiration, and coming to his senses only when he is in the depths of the abyss.

When will the Arab countries recover from this deadly scourge? When in this age will their house return to life? When will they believe in freedom and respect for human rights?

The Arabs so often give the appearance of a coherent unity blessed with embraces and kisses, while their hearts are at variance and their dreams are divergent, and there are those who wish to kill their brother before their adversary. This is why their differences, whether to do with borders or with history, must be laid out in the light of day. They must work towards settling them permanently, whatever this may cost them in effort or sacrifice, in order to clear the air of the turbidity of loathing and rancour, and so that we do not suddenly confront the world every few years with turmoil and harm. Let us have less embracing and kissing, and more strengthening of our close mutual relations.

There is no doubt that the current crisis has revealed important truths, and has shown each Arab country who is in unconditional agreement with it, who has reservations towards it, and who has such differences with it that there is no hope of a remedy within the short term. We must establish a cooperative council with those countries who share a common purpose and path with us, under the umbrella of the charters of the League of Arab States and the United Nations. Let us take this step without hesitation, not as an alliance against anybody, but as a foundation on which to raise our comprehensive development, our integrated economy, our common market and our cultural unity. This will be an organisation that will draw others to join it not by force or by propaganda, but through sound business, profitable performance and the principles of freedom and tolerance.

27 September 1990

Who Is the Culprit?

It has been asserted – relying on witnesses and evidence – that the United States knew about preparations for the invasion of Kuwait long enough before the fact to have issued an alert and a warning and prevented it happening, and that they allowed events to take their course right up to the invasion itself because they had found a rare opportunity to apply a new policy, an important part of their vision of the new world that is being shaped after the entente, which is to move defensive lines to the Middle East.

The invasion did them a great service, because it threatened an important reserve of energy and breached a security principle that the world in its new direction has come to particularly care about. The Arabs themselves agreed with the rest of the world on that, so they immediately called for the withdrawal of Iraq, and the countries whose security was directly threatened began to ask for help from all their friends. Thus the principles lined up with the interests and the interests lined up with the principles, and the West found it had the chance to put its policy into practice with no trouble, indeed with the complete agreement of the people of the region (and at the invitation of some), and under the auspices of an international resolution aimed at the defence of law, security and legitimacy.

It occurred to some to point the finger and say: 'The world will never change. Its ugly face is always ugly. In the end, this time the enemy comes dressed as a friend.'

But just a minute. Don't blame a state for laying out its future in line with its vision of a new world and a new tomorrow. Blame instead the one who misunderstands and miscalculates and who does not know where his feet will land before he leaps, proceeding with a destructive act that leads him and his people into a trackless impasse. The one at fault is the one to blame. I do not say 'agent' or 'conspirator,' as I deem any leader to be above that. But it is despotism, short-sightedness and pride that lead to such extraordinary acts, unthinkable except through treachery and conspiracy.

Sound governance needs a comprehensive political culture,

abundant knowledge, discerning judgement and overall circumspection, which may be found in an atmosphere of democracy and openness to all viewpoints. But one-man rule – especially when that one man sees himself as inspired – always spills straight into the quagmire of catastrophes. We may find ourselves tomorrow in a delicate situation that will demand the best of our acumen and competence.

25 October 1990

The Security Forces

Egypt's security forces are an institution deserving of confidence and respect. Really and truly deserving of confidence: their arrest of the killers in this short time demonstrates their alertness, efficiency, careful planning, good organisation and courage, along with a readiness to make sacrifices.[1] Every now and then they descend on an illegal group, sharpening their weapons and plotting their deceptions in their den. The security forces safeguard institutions and sites against any malicious intent and they protect the pillars of stability, aiming to keep the country prepared both at home and abroad.

And they are deserving of respect because they accept criticism openly, they believe in dialogue whenever dialogue is necessary, and they are not above admitting their mistakes, should they happen, and making every effort to correct and avoid them.

Yes, one may note their occasional interference in elections, or their heavy-handedness with the populace in some situations in the past, but we must acknowledge who was really responsible for that: the governing regimes of other times. The security forces cannot but perform their duty, as they bear the atrocities of others in front of the people.

To come back to the assassination, it can be said that fighting this kind of crime is the hardest task, and no country is free of it – terrorism is today considered an evil worldwide phenomenon, like pollution. But the efficiency of the security forces is gauged by their overall activity, their well-considered policy and their daily achievements. It may be worth mentioning the great secret assassination group that came into being in the course of the 1919 Revolution, and how it operated for five successive years without anybody detecting a single thread that would lead to it, despite British supervision of the police, and despite the fact that the group was their prime target. A single cell fell in 1924 through internal betrayal, not through the work of the police.

I repeat: the security forces in Egypt are an institution deserving of

1 On 13 October 1990 Rif'at al-Mahgub, the speaker of the Egyptian Parliament, was assassinated in Cairo. The killers were caught soon afterwards.

confidence and respect. And I hope they receive all they need from the national budget so that they can attain their full potential.

I pray for God's mercy on their innocent martyrs, and I salute their men, who work in the service of the people … and of stability.

1 November 1990

The Line between Peace and War

We are among those calling for a peaceful solution to the Gulf Crisis, not only out of a loathing of war and its destructive consequences, nor just for the preservation of the Iraqi people and their role in the Arab world, but also out of caution for what will follow the resolution of the crisis, in terms of the dialogue that will take place with the countries that stood up for the restoration of legitimacy. Because to sit down to discussions after a peaceful solution is better than talking with people that have lost tens of thousands of dead and injured in defence of the legitimacy of the region. Moreover, there are considerations on which civilisation is built, and thought must be given to security arrangements that will put a stop to the storms that blow up from this region every few years.

But if we are among those calling for a peaceful solution, we are at the same time calling for legitimacy, law and fundamental principles, and we will never accept any compromise with aggression or any infringement of the right of Kuwait to exist, of the right of its government to return, or of its lawful right to compensation for the unjust losses that have been inflicted on the Kuwaiti nation.

We want peace on condition that it is an untarnished peace, clear of any flaws. A peace that dignity can be proud of, not ashamed of. A peace for the innocent to rejoice in, not for the criminals to swagger in. Initiatives will not hurt us if they pave and smooth the way, and the Iraqi president may yet have a chance to save face. Indeed it will not hurt us to offer him a commitment to secure his country if he takes the decision to withdraw immediately and without delay. What matters to us is that the Kuwaiti people regain all their plundered rights.

And if persuasion is unsuccessful and all endeavours fail, and if the blockade proves impotent and gets us nowhere, then war, with all its ugliness, is preferred over defeat – the defeat of rights, justice, law, legality and principles.

Humanity is capable of rebuilding after destruction, but we cannot live a life devoid of law and principles.

2 November 1990

A Desirable Step to Peace

The Security Council resolution on the invasion of Kuwait is clear and decisive. It demands the withdrawal of the Iraqi army, the restoration of Kuwait to its legitimate status, and the return of its legitimate government. To achieve this, an embargo has been imposed, increasing in severity to the point of a complete blockade of Iraq.

Resolutions of this type and made in this way are international decisions, expressing the position of the Security Council and the will of all the nations of the world.

The use of force is not covered in the resolutions, and all nations and peoples reject it and are well aware of its disastrous consequences. So following on from this we can say that the outbreak of fighting – if Iraq itself does not initiate it – will be a challenge to the global conscience, like going back on the previous resolutions. There is nothing for the forces massing in the Gulf to do but wait, and the anticipated hour will come sooner or later.

But there are some who fear – rightly – that the gathering of troops in their present numbers could lead to the lighting of the spark of conflict for one reason or another, even without prior planning or measures. So why doesn't the Security Council take a new step, and open a new door to hope without infringing its previous resolutions?

I think much would be achieved if it issued a new resolution in which it committed – as soon as its first resolution is fulfilled – to putting all the issues of the region on the negotiating table, and to following through until all are resolved. These include:

1. The Arab–Israeli issue.
2. Arab–Arab issues.
3. The establishment of a security system for the region, to include the clearance of weapons of mass destruction.

This may bring us nearer to the solution, and eradicate the reasons that cause the Middle East to be the source of periodic disturbances for both itself and the world.

5 November 1990

The Struggle of Good and Evil

At tense moments of history, human willpower takes vigorous leaps, extraordinary events follow rapidly one upon the other, and destinies are decided between good and evil.

Kuwait has been invaded and pillaged, and its people displaced.

The world has come together to demand a return to law and legitimacy.

A minority of the Arabs, dazzled by might, support the aggression, but the majority stand with right, justice and legality.

Many countries are facing heavy losses in their defence of principles and legitimacy.

Our situation in Egypt should not be underestimated: we are being forgiven burdensome debts that we would otherwise only have been free from after a long time and much hardship.

And the oil countries have grasped the lesson and are – quite decisively – finding their way to the path of integrity, to a sensible economic direction, and to real Arab national security based on rights and fidelity.

Talk echoes back and forth both here and in the wider world over the problems that threaten the region with eruption every few years, and firm wills convene to find a solution that can bring about comprehensive peace and complete justice, whether between the Arabs and Israel or among the Arabs themselves.

Talk also echoes around clearing the region of weapons of mass destruction to bring about safety and security.

Thus the events began with the outburst of a malicious spark, but in no time they were contained by rational ideas and good intentions, turning them into a path to a new life that will lead eventually to advantage and growth.

Perhaps this can be summarised on the Arab level in two lines, which is that the events came as a result of:

1. The recklessness of a despotic president.
2. The wisdom of a democratic president.

We may have feared that we would depart this world with our Arab nation still stifled by this nightmare, but divine providence willed that our life be extended to see the nightmare vanish, making way for a radiant awakening.

8 November 1990

Comparing the Two Solutions

As the days and weeks go by, the facts surrounding the Gulf Crisis are becoming clear, and they become clearer still with the statements being delivered by the authorities. I may not be going too far beyond the bounds of reality if I summarise the situation in the following manner:

1. The great majority want a peaceful solution; that is, the implementation of the Security Council resolution, without hostilities. They see the blockade that has been imposed on Iraq as sufficient, along with a little patience. They respect principles and condemn aggression and at the same time have concern for their own interests. But they find war and its calamities abominable, and they want to avoid its disastrous consequences on the world economy and international relations.
2. But some political entities are not convinced of the peaceful solution, even if it leads to the implementation of the Security Council resolution, because they do not want to allow Iraq to attain a strength that will upset the balance of the region. What makes it more difficult is that they also do not agree to the complete eradication of Iraq's power, which would upset the balance in the other direction. So how will they achieve their contradictory aims of both implementing the Security Council resolution and containing the strength of Iraq without eradicating it?

In my view, fighting will not resolve this issue, because once it breaks out, it will only cease with the annihilation of one of the two parties, and the expected result in this case will be the eradication of the Iraqi forces and the spread of destruction in the region.

The peaceful solution will allow for a balance between the forces in the region, while the search for a regional security policy goes on, along with an assessment of the size of a deterrent force sufficient to defend security and stability, especially if this is linked to the resolution of the regional issues that periodically threaten to blow up, such as:

1. The Palestinian problem.
2. The problem of Arab borders.
3. The problem of the possession of weapons of mass destruction.

15 November 1990

A Call to the Greater Cause

When will the Arabs settle down in the age of reason? When will they control their emotions and their excitability? Why do they not put their emotions to good use in their lives as a latent strength, while placing reason in the driving seat in these savage, unforgiving times?

You see them between two extremes: either the cooing of flirtatious lovers or the abuse of feuding foes.

We are not asking anyone to waive their interests, nor are we urging one view over another, but we are now highly convinced of the need for harmony, cooperation and unity of vision and aim. Our hearts have turned towards a single path based on economic, cultural and spiritual integration, and we are truly determined to break into the modern age to understand its components and to contribute to its elements, all the while promoting our lasting spiritual values and preserving our glorious heritage, fulfilling our identity in a manner befitting our authentic character and our past civilisational and humanitarian achievements.

Under this climate, filled with good will, hope and ambition, we must draw up policies of cooperation and mutual defence, and when differences arise we must abide by our limits and precepts. The motivations for concord are more important and more sublime than any superficial differences, and the reasons for rapprochement are more important and more sublime than any conflicts of interest.

If serious disagreement arises, appeal to reason and dialogue; if it persists, turn to the arbitration of your brothers; and if that does not help, an appeal can be made to the League of Arab States. Where there is a will there is a way, especially when we remember the hopes that bring us together and the great goals that urge us forward.

Beware of reckless rage, heedless pride and sightless overreaction. This is a call to the greater cause, the battle against the baser self.

22 November 1990

A Journey into the Future

There is much talk and thought about what life in the Arab region will be like after the Gulf Crisis has been resolved. This of course does not mean that we must wait for change to appear before beginning to think or act, nor does it mean that we should be satisfied to sit and wait for things to happen by fate or by the will of others.

We must sketch and plan for a tomorrow that is full of possibilities. We must consider that this task is *our* task first and foremost, and be prepared for different conditions and possibilities, as well as the demands of the new world that is forming by the hour in this age of concord between West and East, and the dissolution of ideologies in a new, single vision, arising to parade its legitimacy throughout the entire world.

In the context of all this, the visit of President Hosni Mubarak to the Gulf states was a journey into the future, indeed it was a first indication of accord on two important matters:

First, an Arab security arrangement for the defence of the region, and the contribution of its own forces to the balance of international powers.

Second, a positive beginning to the economic integration that is the foundation of any true revival for the achievement of progress and the prosperity of the people.

And I hope that the discussion touched upon the creation of a new vision of systems of governance that can conform with the modern age and correspond with its dreams.

It was not only a journey of exploration to the future; it was closely tied to the accomplishment of what can be achieved immediately. The truth is that not everything that was agreed on was a product of the moment or in reaction to the crisis, but it reflected the inner calls of the Arabs of the last half-century. Perhaps the only thing holding it back was the atmosphere of the Arab world, with its disagreements and crises and mistakes that have always made it leave the most important things until last, and waste much of its energies on matters of no use.

The truth is that the time has come for us to act. We must not put today's work off until tomorrow, and we must not deviate from the unavoidable, certain, straight path, the only path to a dignified life.

26 November 1990

Dreaming for an Hour

With every passing day the harbingers of war loom on the horizon, but the promising signs of a peaceful solution have not yet vanished: it still offers us the hope of warding off the woes of war. The latest we have heard is the initiative of President Mitterrand of France, which perhaps has advantages that cannot be underestimated, as it fulfils the Security Council resolution, even going a little beyond its stipulations, and promises the achievement of a comprehensive and just peace in the Middle East.

Perhaps it is this that has allowed us to sit and dream for an hour in spite of our anxiety at the tense and gloomy situation. So let us dream about what needs to happen in our little world exhausted by war and torn apart by differences.

First: Kuwait must return to independence and sovereignty.

Second: we must move forward with the same determination on the stalled issues of Palestine, Golan and Lebanon.

Third: we must resolve the inter-Arab disputes over borders and minorities, first among them the old disagreements between Iraq and Kuwait.

Fourth: there must be action on economic integration on a fair basis between the rich countries and others. Those that are not rich need to prepare their countries and create a space for confidence, security and investment, while the rich need to finally decide to invest their wealth and reap their profits in the development of the greater Arab nation and leap with it into the modern age.

Fifth: all Arab countries must close the gap that separates them from the modern age in systems of governance, respect for human rights and reliance on science in tackling their problems, all the while supported by their deep-rooted faith and noble principles. And who knows, perhaps this explosion has come only in order to shake us up to confront our ailments, and to bring us to the point of relief from suffering after all our distress!

29 November 1990

Contemplating a Vision

We are looking at a new vision suitable for participation in a new world, and it is my belief that this vision needs movement on two fronts, domestic and international.

On the domestic front, we must concentrate on the following:

First: rounding out the dimensions of our democracy, with all that this entails of tireless work and boundless courage. We need to review the constitution so that it becomes a lamp to light our way, an umbrella to protect human rights, a shield for justice and the judiciary, a force for the people for the sake of the people, a guarantee of national unity and a vessel for humanitarian principles and religious values. It will also cleanse our atmosphere of emergency laws, especially in relation to the courts and the press. And it will be a foundation for the stability we desire, a reassurance for citizen and investor alike.

Second: giving scientific research the faith and care it deserves, and placing scientists where the modern age places them, so that they can take the scientific lead in all activities. We should remember that Germany and Japan – two defeated nations – regained their standing through science, achieving a triumph that they could only have gained otherwise through victory in a third war. Science has the first word in every field, and it is science alone that can ensure equality between the small nation and the giant.

Third: completing the revolution in education, the cradle in which the seeds are grown that are good for the flourishing of democracy and scientific research. It will also build individuals on religious, national and cultural foundations to become loyal citizens who revere work, knowledge and thought.

I have not addressed the challenging problems still current in the overall plan; I am talking about the broad strokes of a new vision.

On the international front, I believe matters are no longer as they were in the past, when nations searched for room to grow or strove for leadership. For while that may still be of consequence, it is more important today for us to know what melody we can play in the international symphony, so that we can participate in harmony rather than in discord – discord that may bring hardships. We have to understand the value of peace with the world in order for there to be opportunities for us to flourish at home.

This is a new world, one that demands of us not strength in the usual sense only, but what is stronger and more lasting: it demands learning and wisdom and tireless labour.

3 December 1990

From the Negative to the Positive

One thing that shows how engaged a citizen is in society is his attention to his electoral card, which is a token of his ability to participate in the selection of who rules on his behalf, and of his commitment to the principles under which he would wish his society to be governed. So how to understand the reluctance to register in the electoral rolls, or the refusal of so many registered voters to perform their electoral duty?

Maybe it is to be explained by a lack of awareness, and perhaps there is supportive justification for this in the extent of illiteracy in the country. But this explanation does not stand, because the educated classes are among the most apathetic. Besides, the working classes are quite excited by our democratic experiment, and many of them have participated in it with laudable sincerity.

Or it could be explained by the suffocating frustration felt by great numbers of our youth. But that very frustration is generally one of the reasons for engaging in politics, and turning to promising principles for a solution to problems.

So let us consider what may create a sound environment for political engagement and positive participation: what is it within the state's power to provide in this matter?

First: the citizen must feel that his vote counts and is not wasted, and that he really can contribute to the selection of his representatives and his government. So the fairness of the elections, and the guarantee of that fairness and its fortification against all suspicion, are the primary stipulations for the seriousness of the undertaking.

Second: there must be unfettered and unrestricted freedom to form parties, so that all points of view are laid out clearly in front of the citizens, and all can follow the direction dictated by their interests and principles.

Third: television must play its national role in the creation of political positivity. It has the ability to bring any subject to the centre of attention and embed it in the consciousness, as it does with its health appeals. It should run a daily programme on party politics, in order to generate a wide interest in parties and their policies, and to make stars of the politicians – not for their own sake, but as a way of drawing attention to their aims and of spreading political awareness.

This way we can build a sound environment in which to function. I have no doubt that our people have the underlying readiness to engage in healthy politics.

6 December 1990

On the Latest Elections

What can be said about the latest elections held in our country?

First: all the participants acknowledged the neutral and impartial security situation, so the state accomplished what it had promised to do. We hope this signals an honest and definitive beginning to our parliamentary life, from which the state can emerge as an example to its leaders and its citizens alike.

Second: the battle was fought between the National Democratic Party (NDP) on the one hand and the Tagammu Party, the new parties, and the independents on the other. Of the other legal parties, the Wafd, Labour, and the Liberals boycotted the election, while the groups that have not yet been given legitimate status did not take part. This means that our political map is now split between the new assembly, the street, and the secret hideouts. This calls for a rethink and a consideration of the opportunities open for all to participate in legitimate political activity, leading to increased cohesion and stability.

Third: not all the independents were entirely independent. Some are NDP, Wafd, Labour, and Liberal defectors, and even if they left their parties over differences of opinion, they cannot abandon their ideals. It is expected that the National Democrats will return to their party, and the others will form an acceptable opposition.

Fourth: the contest was run on the individual list system. Individual listing is not per se incompatible with party politics, for in the past an individual would enter the fray supported by his party, speaking in its name, and sheltering under its ideals, so it was a party/individual system. But in this election, individuals triumphed over parties, and personal promises over political principles. Family affiliations and rivalries played a prominent role, which led to violence and sometimes threatened the neutrality of the election. All this adds up to a step backwards in our democratic history.

Fifth: the scarcity of Coptic and female candidates was painfully obvious, and the truth is that we cannot exonerate the majority party from the responsibility for this. It has revealed a wound that will not heal even after the appointment of the ten discretionary members by the president.

Sixth: it is clear that the voter turnout was much lower than was hoped for. We conceived a solution for this, which we elaborated in a separate article,[1] but let us not go back over that. Anyway, any representative in the new assembly, by performing his duty to the fullest, can fulfil the hopes of those who elected him and persuade the dissenters to emerge from their negativity.

God willing, next time we will enter a contest that is untarnished by any flaw.

13 December 1990

1 See 'From the Negative to the Positive', 6 December 1990.

The Independents

I really distrust the word 'independent' to describe anyone working in the political arena. This may have settled in my soul as a legacy of our political past. Some sheltered behind it, to elevate themselves above the fight, the sacrifices that the fight required, and exposure to the constant dialectical – and often material – attacks. Others had recourse to it out of greed, to secure their interests in front of whoever was in power. And it was feigned out of cunning opportunism by a third group, who put themselves forward for the administrative ministries, which would take office to run free elections – if free elections were ever required by rare circumstance.

Independence from parties, in the sense of not following their orders or proscriptions, is possible, especially if the independent person wishes to maintain a measure of freedom, away from the actual endeavour of practical political life. It is in this sense that independence is essential for intellectuals and historians. But it does not at all mean independence from principles and political views, since it is hard for anyone to find himself among a broad array of parties and not know which party he inclines towards, even by general preference. The only exceptions are those who have rejected the blessing of thought and the feeling of general social obligation.

So the independents who won in the latest elections to the People's Assembly must choose what suits their ideals, within the law. I believe the voters chose them on the basis of their promises, which can be delivered only under the wing of one of the parties – there are currently two standing parties, the National Democrats and the Tagammu. Or they can decide to declare their allegiance to the Wafd, Labour, or the Liberals, without the recognition of the parties themselves. Or they can establish a new party – which is not against human nature, so long as it is born out of honesty and sincerity, for although they have left behind party affiliation, they can do nothing without ideals and some kind of political vision.

This is better than remaining a flavourless and odourless speck, or drifting in time into trading their independence on the stock exchange of party rivalry.

20 December 1990

A President for All Seasons

How can President Saddam Hussein confront the world in this provocative manner? Perhaps this is what tempts some to see a scripted drama, in which he is playing an agreed role, acting with the greatest composure.

But while this conception could be imagined between one state and another, it is difficult to accept it happening between one state and the whole world. Besides, the alleged drama has necessitated the movement of armies, along with preparations the like of which the world has seen only in its greatest wars, and volcanoes of rage have erupted on both sides that outweigh any compact or conspiracy. What is more, retreat without the fulfilment of the international resolution will strike like a lightning bolt the dignity of the great powers and of all nations, as well as the hopes of humanity for the rise of a world new in its intent, its course and its goals.

So the conflict is real, no joke, no drama. Let us ask again, then, about the motivation of this president who is challenging the international will, and let us put aside the assumption of madness and the associated manifestations of despotism. The man debates and spins and hides skilfully behind the issues of the region and its riches. He does not reject peace. He requests talks. He puts the responsibility for the anticipated terrible consequences on his opponents.

What I imagine – and only God knows – is that the man is dealing with the world that he evolved in, in whose ways he was steeped and whose lexicon and its power he learned by heart, and he still does not believe that the world is changing and aspiring to a new life.

The old world was a jungle full of fine slogans, malicious intentions and criminal acts. After the First World War the League of Nations was a federation of the strong for the exploitation of the weak, and after the Second World War the United Nations constantly swung back and forth between good and bad, preserving the veto to protect the strong in delicate situations. Then came the accord between East and West, heralding the birth of the new world.

And it was the luck of the Iraqi president that his customary behaviour would be the first test for this new world in its modern orientation. What we can say is that so far, the world has passed the test, and that it will not accept defeat.

The Iraqi president must know this and must yield to the world's will, and save his Iraqi nation and his greater Arab nation, showing the first good example of respect for legality and conformance with the new world.

1 January 1991

The Birth of a New World

We hoped it would be a new world, but they insisted these were just honeyed words that concealed a tired old conspiracy. They were certain in their misgivings, and we were uncertain in our high hopes, but we followed the promising signs with a clear imagination, waiting for the truth to appear at the testing time. And now events are following one after another to confirm our high hopes and our sound judgement.

The American president is working assiduously and tirelessly towards convening a peace conference, out of a belief in the stability, peace and development that are needed in the region. To this end, he has taken a strong and unprecedented stance against Israel, regardless of electoral interests or the special relationship between that country and his. And he was quick to take a sincere step in support of international peace through his decision to reduce the American nuclear arsenal.

Does this not point to a new world being born, heralding a new spirit, new ideals and a new human outlook?

Certainly, many people are pessimistic about the prospect of one state holding all the power in the world, and this pessimistic view would be worthy of consideration if the world still stood on its traditional axis – a world based on strength and power, a world in which the strong exploit the weakness of the weak for their own interests, a world that spawned slavery and colonialism. But today's strong state holds all the power in a world that has matured at the hands of numerous political, social and cultural revolutions, a world of the United Nations, the Security Council, and human rights. It is a state that will be characterised by leadership, not domination; will bear responsibility, not exploit the weak; will practise fatherhood through time, not oppression.

We must welcome this kind of discerning leadership: it is what is needed to solve international problems, to face natural disasters and perhaps to truly confront pollution, drugs, diseases, backwardness, ignorance, fanaticism and all other human ills.

3 January 1991

Egypt's Battle

One thousand days to liberate the economy. Perhaps it would be more accurate to say that this is the last extension laid down for the liberation of the economy, otherwise what was the point of the previous five-year plans? Or even more accurately, we should consider it an invitation to total liberation: liberation from all the shackles and obstacles in our political life, working conditions, moral vision, cultural programme and thought. Yes, we want complete liberation, we really yearn for it – a liberation from corruption and negativity, from bureaucracy, emergency laws, false idols and empty slogans. A liberation from every adversity, and a firm springboard from which to rebuild and to challenge the times.

There are new circumstances that provide a better climate for endeavour.

Some are the result of global developments that have turned the world – despite unexpected tensions – towards freedom and cooperation.

Others have come about through our wise policies and noble stands, bringing us a not inconsiderable lightening of the burden of our debts and their impact, and placing us in a better position to receive Arab and foreign investments.

But the reduction in pressure must be the impetus for a redoubling of effort, a sharpening of determination for serious action and a shouldering of responsibility, along with complete discipline and enlightened planning.

We must prepare the land for investment, remove impediments and spread safety, security and confidence under the sovereignty of the law.

We must organise the work to be done, providing vigilant oversight and constant review, with rewards for what is done well and penalties for what is done badly.

We must not be lax in chasing down corruption, nor show mercy to the corrupt, for mercy is due more to the nation.

The leap of reform must comprehend both politics and the economy together, as they are two sides of one coin.

We must review our laws, which have become tangled and voluminous, and the judiciary must be given complete independence.

We must choose the best available people for the job on the basis of ability and integrity, for these are the true measures, and nothing else matters.

We must establish a mechanism for the assessment and evaluation of performance.

We must all come together to rebuild the country: this is Egypt's battle for a comprehensive resurgence.

10 January 1991

A Day Unlike Others

I usually write my Thursday column a few days beforehand, having asked myself what I will write about, and having wondered what the day will bring. Will it bring what we feared? Or will that be put off until another time? Will God allow comfort and guidance? If harmless endeavours result in a peaceful outcome that affirms the pillars of legitimacy, then they are most welcome. Let them be the beginning of a new era for a new world and herald rebuilding, development and progress for the Arab region – at the end of a succession of cruel lessons – and a determined leap forward to solve all its outstanding problems, as a preface to the spread of a just peace that will preserve the rights of all who are entitled to them.

And if poor judgement or bad luck eliminates all possibilities but war, let us face it with resolve and patience, let us add new sacrifices to our history of sacrifices, and let our consolation be that we make these sacrifices for the sake of truth and honest endeavour, and in the framework of a global vision that looks to a better tomorrow.

Whatever the outcome – given that it will divert us somewhat from our planned route, which we began in the time of Muhammad 'Ali Pasha and even before it, in the groundwork for resurgence and towards progress and civilisation – we will never allow the sound of the battle to rise above the sound of life. We will not put off until tomorrow what must be done today. And we will not invest all our energies in one goal at the price of our other goals.

It is true that we began our resurgence long ago, and although it was supposed to advance along its path without setbacks and breakdowns, to take us to the level of the developed nations, we lost a great deal as a result of autocratic decisions, personal whims, and global greed that we had not protected ourselves against. We were taking one step forward and two steps back. We exhausted our store of strength in healing our ailments instead of enjoying it to the full in health and well-being.

Welcome to peace if there be peace.

But let it be war if folly leaves no option but war.

And let us welcome the challenge and the hard work in all cases.

Let us play our Arab role as it behooves us, and our global role as it befits us, without neglecting our essential role, which is the service and elevation of our nation.

14 January 1991

The Intellectuals

People sometimes speak about intellectuals – what we call 'the cultured' – as if they were a class apart from all other groups, and wonder what their view is of this or that matter, or their responsibility for this or that occurrence.

The truth is that there is no free-standing class based on 'culture', and there is no college or institute for the graduation of intellectuals. Rather, it can be said that there is not a single person in society who is without culture in the general sense of the word. We assign the adjective 'cultured' to those who attain a high degree of knowledge of intellectual, political, scholarly and artistic currents, so that they possess an awareness of the spirit of the age and the ability to adopt an attitude towards it and develop a vision of it. Intellectuals in this sense are to be found in all parties, organisations and professions, and therefore do not have one view, one attitude, or one vision. They have their differences just as everybody else has their differences, and they agree with the viewpoint of the group they belong to. Thus there are left-wing, right-wing and moderate intellectuals, which means there is no sense in asking about the opinion of 'the intellectuals', as though they were an independent and self-contained class. Writers and authors are no exception to this and are divided among the different groups. Even if one of them officially maintains his independence, he must have a private inclination towards one group, willy-nilly, since complete independence in this situation is practically inconceivable.

As for their stand on principles, the same applies to them as to everybody else. They include the sincere, even if for their sincerity they pay with their blood, with exile, or with neglect and poverty. And they include the duplicitous, who sell themselves for a position or for money, but whatever such a person may claim and whatever masks he may wear, events will reveal him and his history will expose him.

Intellectuals should have an active influence commensurate with their awareness in every field that they operate in, but this will generally only happen in an atmosphere of freedom and democracy. Thus curtailing the role of the intellectuals and isolating them, or corrupting them by buying their consciences, with the exception of the resistant few who regularly stand up to persecution, is a despicable tyranny. We have seen all this in our country, and we have long experienced its consequences, and we are still struggling to be rid of its adverse effects after coming to stand firmly on democratic ground – for which we wish more strength and progress.

17 January 1991

Late-Night Confessions[1]

Under the fluttering banner of hope, the dark clouds of anxiety and apprehension are scudding, but those who depend on the rock of principles have nothing to fear: they know their way and are content with their destiny. The situation gives rise to a strange and tragic image, an image of the world laying siege to a gunpowder store in the hands of an evil man. Notice I am unable to say 'a mad man', since a mad person neither minds nor heeds anything, while this man still heeds his own egoism and is well aware that he has unleashed a hell in all the corners of his good country, while spiriting his wife and children away from its fires, and with no thought for his people, who are suffering night and day and whose pains and sorrows we share.

That man is Saddam Hussein, who is fighting not in hope of victory but in eagerness to spread ruin, destruction and chaos that will affect as many peaceful countries and destroy as many innocent lives as possible. How closely his actions resemble those of the Devil, who performs all the evil he can and more, without the least hope of deliverance. So if he is not forced to issue the order to withdraw and spare his people the fires of hell, the remaining hope is that he can be overcome as soon as possible. He must be overcome quickly in order to confine our losses and pain to the narrowest scope of misfortune and misery.

Let us remember in our tragedy, though, that what we are enduring is the penalty for our weakness, our decline and our abandonment of dignity. There is no need for plots or scenarios of global phantoms.

It is we who create the idols, worship them and enable them to toy with our fates.

There are those among us who are tempted by power, even though it deviate from truth and honour.

There are those among us who welcome invasion if they sense benefit in it for themselves.

---

1 The Gulf War had begun with a coalition aerial bombing campaign on 16 January 1991.

There are those among us who are happy with thievery if they can hope for a share in it.

There are those, and there are those, and there are those … All of which has made us a repository of superstitions, duplicity and mental illnesses.

Let there be an awakening from this earthquake, and an opportunity to see ourselves as we truly are. God does not change what is in a people until they change what is in themselves.

24 January 1991

Interests and Ideals

They say that politics is all about interests and has nothing to do with ideals and morals. The poor reputation of interests comes from two sources:

First, history, which is replete with machinations, intrigues, conspiracies and wars that have wiped out millions of people and subjugated hundreds of nations through the interests of the strong.

Second, daily life, in which people are divided between those who follow their ideals and those who follow their interests and stop at no aberration in fulfilling them.

So the negative image of interests has become firmly established in our minds, along with the significant role they play on the political stage. Today I am attempting to forget what is fixed in our minds and examine the meaning of interests anew. So, how should we understand interests?

The interests of any nation are the assets and means of subsistence on which its life and civilisation are based, like the Nile for Egypt and the other countries of the Nile Valley, or oil for the more recently established countries of the region, and so on. So in this sense, interests are an absolute good, and it is the duty of every country and its authorities to protect them.

But how are interests to be secured?

In this there are many ways and means, according to circumstances and conditions.

If the spirit of power and competition watches over the world, interests are achieved by any means, without regard to ideals or morals, and so there is intrigue, conspiracy, war and colonialism with all its evils.

But if the world learns from its history of cruel lessons, it will lean towards cooperation and legitimacy, and forsake conspiracies and wars, as we see today in Europe's move towards unity and in the rapprochement between East and West. So it is possible to say (and may my hopes not be dashed): interests are an absolute good.

And rational politics are closely linked to ideals and morals, and cannot do without them.

We may not differ with Saddam Hussein and his supporters over the importance of interests, but we disagree over the means. They honour invasion, pillage and plunder, while we hold fast to law, cooperation, legitimacy and peace.

31 January 1991

Know Thyself

Who among the Arabs denounces President Saddam Hussein? And who supports him or sympathises with him?

In trying to answer these questions there is a test for our selves and what they conceal, and a study of our society and the currents that stir it. In ancient times the wise man was addressing everybody when he famously said: 'Know thyself.'

The Iraqi president has been strongly denounced by all who hold to principles and commitments, who believe in Arab security, and who look forward to a tomorrow in which the Arabs join together in unity based on sincerity, cooperation and a shared desire to progress under the shade of peace and in line with international legitimacy.

Supporting him are those who are dazzled by power without paying attention to its ideals. They accept the benefit, however it comes. They have no interest in principles or commitments, nor do they believe that a new world is being formed. The evil past, with its bitter memories and its deceitful practices, still draws them to it.

The two camps have arisen naturally, in tune with their views of life and the degree of their conformity with them. Fortunately, it seems that the camp of the denouncers is winning, if we base our assessment on what is happening in Egypt, what stirs the Egyptian street and the indications of statistics.

But not all those who support Saddam are of the kind that have their special, if perverse, logic. They have been joined by a stream that is devoted to hostility against the West, and so persistently that it has become the main element of their lives and the basis of their world view. There may have been reasons that excused this long ago, but these people have held to it, and while the world has changed, they have refused to change with it. This group supports Saddam not out of love for Saddam, nor out of faith in what he has done, but out of hatred for the West, even when they agree with us on basic interests and principles.

And there is another group of supporters, the opponents of our government for internal political or social reasons: they have taken opposition to the point of supporting whoever the government denounces and denouncing whoever the government supports, in accordance with their emotions and without thinking of adopting a national position in line with reason and the national interest, as others in the opposition have done.

This is an image that reflects our reality to a degree, though it is not our entire reality, as there are small, unstable factions that allow themselves to be swayed by events and hold one opinion in the morning and another in the evening. But I have concentrated here on the stable factions, and although the picture overall is not without its ugly side, it is very far from desperate. I will end as I began, with the famous saying: 'Know thyself.' Perhaps we can improve how we deal with our selves, as well as with others.

7 February 1991

The Hero of the Stalls

An interesting observation not lost on cinema lovers is the affinity and admiration of the audience in the stalls for the villain, if he is particularly daring, crafty and clever in striking and retreating to gain temporary victories over the police before he finally falls into their hands. We have ascribed many excuses to this audience: their young age, their bad upbringing, their helpless tendency to deviate, their antipathy for the law and all that goes with it.

Well, we have 'lived and seen the wonder', as the old song has it. We have lived to hear of the affinity of an Arab audience for an Arab villain who is real, not a cinematic creation, and who is threatening the world with his criminality and rolling the reputation of the Arabs in the dust. And the admiration this time has gone further, and affected men who are considered the elite of society and its most upright sons. These are the ones who today are supporting Saddam and defending his excesses, heedless of the countries, people and principles that are his victims.

I do not deny that the steadfastness of Iraq under the rain of bombs that is pouring down on it deserves recognition and makes us sad. And I do not deny that many times each day I swallow my sadness that all this power has not been stored away for the support of the Arab world, the solution of its problems and the implementation of peace based on justice. But Saddam Hussein has relinquished all this in his recklessness and madness, first in his assault on an Islamic neighbour, Iran, and then in swallowing up an Arab nation, Kuwait. In his misjudgement and sick impulsiveness he has split the Arabs in two, convulsing their community, causing the whole world to condemn and punish him and confirming himself as an agent of destruction, like earthquakes and volcanoes.

He forms an ugly picture, operating outside the framework of the modern world and its hopes and aspirations. He determinedly rejects peaceful solutions, threatens hostages, mistreats prisoners of war, fires his rockets on civilians, flaunts his weapons of mass destruction, pollutes the environment and spreads devastation in his home region without a care for any responsibility or human value.

And because of the adulation from the new audience in the stalls, the ugly picture has now become a symbol of the Arabs and the Muslims, and the mistreatment and contempt they encounter in the outside world is no secret. Efforts are still being exerted to save the criminal, and to justify his crimes at the expense of innocent victims and noble values. Meanwhile there remains no comfort for us amid the grief and tragedy unless the catastrophe ends through the aid of truth, justice and honest human values.

14 February 1991

The Gate of Hope

Iraq's latest communiqué has the tone of a victor dictating his terms, so the attacking forces have rejected it and are continuing with their war. But there are two signs that indicate hope: firstly, the acceptance by the Iraqi president for the first time of the principle of withdrawal from Kuwait; and secondly, the joy of the Iraqi people at what they see as the end of their suffering and the beginning of a return to normal human existence.

The Iraqi president, having accepted the principle of withdrawal from Kuwait, should not dare to ignore the joy of his people at the prospect of an end to the torment of war. That joy arose like a spontaneous referendum, which he should respect and rely on, even if it requires a change in rhetoric or a retreat from obstinacy. It will not harm a leader or diminish his standing to listen to the voice of his people and carry out their innermost wishes. Indeed, what a shame – what a great shame! – if pride leads him to sin in front of his people.

The terms of the communiqué, which the president of Egypt described as crippling, should now be the subject of talks between those sympathetic to Iraq and the Iraqi authorities, and this should happen without delay.

Among the terms, some are indeed crippling, and these should be deleted.

Others constitute demands of the whole Arab community that we never cease thinking about and preparing for, like the Palestinian case, Golan, Southern Lebanon and inter-Arab borders.

The sympathetic should persuade the Iraqi president to withdraw unconditionally, in accordance with the Security Council resolutions and the wishes of the people of Iraq.

At the same time they should ask the Security Council and the concerned countries to commit to finding solutions to the remaining problems, once the withdrawal is complete and legitimacy has returned to the region.

Not a minute must be wasted without action, for with every passing minute, lives and communities are perishing.

18 February 1991

The Wailing Wall of the Arabs

We must concede that every error has its price. Human life is a continuous struggle, at every moment requiring us to exert all the strength and wisdom we have. It is a harsh struggle, which knows no mercy, tolerates no weakness and condones no lapse, and has no room for the inattentive, the careless, the heedless or the frivolous. Whoever makes a mistake must pay its price, and anybody who makes a pact with that person, or is taken in by him, or does not speak out against him, must also share his punishment and join him in his fate.

A tyrant may rule despotically, and in his tyranny bring calamity upon his populace. And we may wonder in lament: what fault is it of the populace? Did he not shackle them in chains? Did he not descend on them with iron and fire? I do not belittle the chains, and I do not make light of the iron and fire, but life in its forward drive does not give any weight to these excuses, and stamps the miserable populations with the offence, places the responsibility on them, and does not spare them the punishment. A tyrant cannot be thwarted without touching his people, and there is no place in the dictionary of struggle for security, patience and complacency. We have had one lesson after another, and after each one we promise ourselves we have absorbed the lesson and changed the adverse situation. Then we quickly forget, the crime is repeated, we submit once more, the mistake is made, the punishment arrives, what is swept away is swept away and the wailing mounts. We appear like innocent lambs – but we are nothing but guilty sinners.

Because of this civilisational negligence, our crises erupt like volcanoes, spewing out disasters. One minute we are as good as can be, we think about building and reconstruction, and we earn a good reputation. Then suddenly some despot fires off a reckless word, or commits a heinous sin or behaves in a brutish manner, and we are immediately tossed about by dissension and hostility, and the world unites in a bloc against us as though we were a gang of outlaws. Our reputation falls apart and disintegrates, and we become a byword for barbarism and corruption.

The political philosophers and the fortune-tellers apply themselves to tearing apart the darkness. They cast the light of their keen insight on plots, scenarios and global imperialism, imaginings that may or may not be true. But why do we avoid putting ourselves under the microscope? Why do we not define our responsibility, when we are the direct catalyst? We have kept silent when we should have spoken, stepped back when we should have acted, exposed our necks to the liars, the swindlers and their like, and abandoned our responsibility and our true heritage of pride and struggle.

And disaster strikes, so let us gather around the Wailing Wall of the Arabs, to spill our tears and curse global imperialism.

21 February 1991

The Tragedy, Real and Imagined

The events that are convulsing us are that an Arab leader invaded Kuwait, plundered it, then annexed it to his country. The result of his action is an Arab rift between those who uphold legitimacy, principles and Arab interests based on freedom and justice, and those who side with might at any price. For the world, the invasion was a threat to their interests and their new ideals, and they issued their resolutions, as we know. Several efforts have been made in both the East and the West to solve the problem peacefully, but these have shattered on the rock of the leader's obstinacy. So it was war. The leader has manoeuvred by every illegitimate means: he has haggled over hostages, tortured prisoners of war, fired rockets at civilians and polluted the environment, and still he threatens further shocking acts to rub the reputation of the Arabs in the dust and make them an emblem of barbarism and evil.

Those are the facts, but their interpretation has split opinion.

Some have found sufficient explanation in the chain of events, the nature of the leader, and the historical background: in the end, the events were caused by a bloody despot who has a history of rushing to war and has been irrefutably shown to be short-sighted and a poor judge of consequences.

But others go beyond the events and the visible to what is behind them. They maintain that the tragedy we are enduring is the result of a plot woven for control over the Arabs and their wealth and future, and that the Arab leader, wittingly or unwittingly, is playing a role in the drama.

The disagreement is only about the explanation, as you see, including how we judge Saddam Hussein. We say he is an Arab tyrant of poor judgement and bad behaviour; they say he is an agent or a dupe.

The strange thing is that while we have gone no further than to call for the return to legitimacy and the withdrawal from Kuwait, and see nothing wrong in punishing him if he digs in his heels, the others are calling for an unconditional halt to the war, which would mean concealing the crime and saving the man their creative imaginations have identified as an agent or a dupe.

They would be better off scrutinising their 'reality' and asking themselves what is saved by this descent into intrigue, what it contributes in confronting a world already heaving with schemes and machinations, or what the system of government will be and what kind of people will sail the ship without sliding into carelessness or betrayal. But they have no concern except saving the criminal and covering up the crime.

Sirs: in spite of the pain and the sorrow, we are optimistic of the outcome. We hope for the return of legitimacy and a solution to the problems of the region under the shade of fine, new international ideals.

But you are pessimistic. All you see in what is happening and what is being said is a repetition of the past, with its coercive colonial tragedies. I do not claim that we are one hundred percent certain in our optimism, so do not be one hundred percent certain in your pessimism.

Let us wait a month or two, and the truth will brightly shine. If it is good, then good. If it is bad, then we may have learned from our past how to deal appropriately with good, and how to deal appropriately with bad.

28 February 1991

The Tragedy

In this period of history, three waves of frustration are giving expression to the Arab world:

First: a wave of poverty and suffering in some countries and social classes, making life an unbearable burden and throwing a black veil across the face of the future, inciting people to protest and rebel.

Second: the Palestine issue. Israel has continued to act harshly and use violence, as we see every day in the Occupied Territories and Southern Lebanon, and these practices have left a deep wound in the pride of all Arabs and caused them to yearn for strength at any price and by any means.

Third: a wave of religious extremism has stopped time at a point that cannot be passed. It seems – according to this – that the Crusades are still going on, that Islam is the target of the Crusader brigands, and that they are still plotting against it with weapons, thought and culture.

Because of all this, a man like Saddam Hussein has found more than a few sectors of Arab society supporting his leadership and declaring their readiness to sacrifice themselves for him with soul and blood.

And who is Saddam Hussein?

He is a man not without inner strength and touches of charismatic leadership, but he is ignorant on both the civil and the military levels, and he is greedy, selfish and bloody. He is a tyrant who does not tolerate dissenting opinions or anyone of independent thought or strength. He took control of Iraq when it was striding firmly forwards, and he took it further, to the point where many predicted a great future for the country. Then suddenly and tyrannically he threw it into a war against Iran, heedless of all Islamic principles, and turned it into a nation in debt and steeped in wounds, before driving it on once more to devour Kuwait, in contempt of Arab ideals and international legitimacy.

The acts of this tragedy played out as we all remember them, and as it has gone on the remaining hidden aspects of his character have become apparent before our eyes. It has become clear that he is an uncouth blusterer, opinionated and boorish, piratical and treacherous. He plays with hostages and prisoners of war, he attacks civilians, he pollutes the environment, he sets fire to oil wells. In short, he is the ugliest face of the Arabs, the worst epitome, the most evil example. Where did this depraved creature come from? Who promotes him? Or follows him? Or sympathises with him?

I come back to the three waves of frustration, which you may think explain it all. But an explanation is not an excuse, and it accordingly makes us ponder our moral tragedy and search out its roots.

We must overcome poverty, solve the issue of Palestine and cure extremism. It is a long road, but it begins with full democracy.

4 March 1991

The Battle for Peace

The coalition forces have won in the battle of the Gulf, and they must now win in the battle for peace. They won under the umbrella of international resolutions; condemning aggression and upholding legitimacy and international law. Now we hope and expect that the pillars of peace will be built on the same principles, ensuring the coalition's honesty and fairness and refuting the view of their opponents, who have warned of their slogans, seeing them as a cover for nefarious intentions to control the region and its wealth. For how many peace treaties have given the victor the revenge they desired over their enemy, and his humiliation and the annihilation of his power and his dignity, only to bring peace temporarily but pave the way for another war that leads to millions of lives lost and billions in financial losses?

The Gulf War is the first experience the world has faced as it works on its transition to a new politics based on cooperation, justice and a comprehensive humanistic view. The success of the world in dealing with it is equivalent to the placing of a foundation stone in the construction of a new world for a new humanity. And as long as the talk is of a new security arrangement for the region, it will achieve stability and development, guarantee the interests of the nations of the region, and put an end to its periodic crises.

The security arrangement will not be confined to the organisation of military forces but requires before that – or at the same time – a solution to the problems that are to blame for generating crises and unrest and exporting disorder to all parts of the world.

We must apply ourselves to solving the Palestinian issue in a way that brings comprehensive peace based on justice. Likewise with Golan and Southern Lebanon. And we must find a final and decisive solution to the problems of inter-Arab borders.

We must throw off all the encumbrances of the past to allow us to begin a new life that will deliver everything we lack in systems of governance and economic integration, and a civilised approach to science and advancement, in the shade of peace, faith and human brotherhood.

7 March 1991

Returning Home

The day after the end of the fighting, the president of Egypt addressed a call to the Arabs, of which the outstanding points are:

1. To restore trust between the Arab nations.
2. To settle the Arab–Israeli conflict.
3. To clear the region of weapons of mass destruction.
4. To settle disagreements between the Arab countries.
5. To concentrate on security and development.
6. To strengthen the path of democracy.

As for Egypt, it must return to the scheduling of its goals and prioritise their fulfilment with serious intent, firm determination and unceasing perseverance. At the head of these goals – to summarise, without going into detail:

1. Strengthening the path of democracy by reviewing the constitution, revoking the emergency laws, and concentrating on respect for human rights and national unity.
2. Concentrating on economic issues and preparing the ground for business and investment, removing all bureaucratic and legal obstacles, and confronting problems with the determination and courage they require.
3. Continuing the revolution in education, with the aim of linking it with development and society, building it on democratic foundations that will encourage free thought and creativity, and applying particular and enlightened care to religious, national and cultural instruction.
4. Paying the necessary attention to science and scientific research, and enabling the scientists to fulfil their role in the planning and guidance of everything to do with matters of society, including the environment and family planning.
5. The complete and absolute sovereignty of the law, and the arrangement and screening of the statutes; this will also take in

the independence of the judiciary and fulfilling the demands of the judges.

6. Launching a war on corruption, drugs and extremism by various scientific, religious and security means.

We hope to be following the news of our progress as we followed the news of the war, with no day going by without a constructive decision or a solid accomplishment.

14 March 1991

Tomorrow Is a New Day

We must get the domestic march forward underway, without hesitation or delay. We must put the decisions of the foreign ministers of the eight states[1] into force in all areas of economic, social and cultural cooperation, so that we can move ahead, strongly and sincerely, with putting our house in order, even while our external politics are fully engaged in global concerns that also cannot wait.

At the head of these external affairs is the security arrangement for the region, which as I see it comprises two parts: one is the political, relating to the near-chronic problems that blow up every ten years in the form of acute crises, unrest and wars. The other is the military, which includes resources for defence, their nature and their concentration.

If the political side did not require a considerable amount of time I would have suggested dealing with it first, because thinking about a defence system for a region that is stable and free of problems is very different from thinking about a defence system for a region exhausted by disagreements and painful memories. It is thus better to treat the two things together and at the same time.

We must begin with the Arab–Israeli issue, which should also cover clearing the region of weapons of mass destruction. And I hope that we can deal with the substance of the matter rather than just the appearances, and concentrate on negotiations between the parties to the conflict, in order to achieve a just and comprehensive peace.

We must also put the problem of Arab borders on the table, and we must not spare any effort to find a just solution that will open the doors to sincere and comprehensive cooperation.

When we look at the military security arrangement, we must see it from an Arab and global perspective: we cannot be allowed to forget that Kuwait was liberated thanks to a coalition of Arab and international forces, so it is inevitable that we should consider the question

---

1 The Damascus Declaration of 6 March 1991 established a protocol of cooperation between Bahrain, Egypt, Kuwait, Oman, Qatar, Saudi Arabia, Syria and the United Arab Emirates.

of security an Arab and global one too. Likewise, it should be accomplished in a climate of cooperation and with due regard to interests and ideals, which is more conducive to the security and stability of the region and offers a better guarantee of a future free of disturbing surprises.

It may be a new world, but it requires a new vision and a new way of thinking.

21 March 1991

The Highest Aim

We have to believe that the highest aim for the Arabs at this period in time is comprehensive development. It represents a civilisational shift from underdevelopment to the modern age in governance, agriculture, industry, the environment, education, culture, health and all the other fields of activity that provide people with a decent human existence.

This is the highest target, and all other aims are means to its end, smoothing and clearing obstacles from its path. The only exceptions I make to this are cases of liberation of the land and self-determination, for these are ends in themselves, neither ways nor means. But the security arrangement is not an end in itself, nor is the problem of Arab borders, nor the clearance of weapons of mass destruction from the region, although these matters become important when they lead to any kind of stability. And stability itself is important only in providing the right climate for advancement and growth – otherwise, what is the use of stability based on ignorance, poverty, underdevelopment and scorn for the respect of human rights?

So comprehensive development is the aim, and it cannot be postponed under any circumstance. We must have faith that anything we do in external politics we do for the sake of this one aim, which means true life to us, just as its neglect would mean extinction and death.

Dealing with external affairs may require time, and may be subject to differences of opinion among the Arabs themselves, or between the Arabs and others, but we cannot allow this to impede us in the beginning of our development, or at least what there is of it.

It may be difficult for the time being for our development to begin in the compass of total Arab integration, but it must begin within the circle of the eight states that are in agreement.[1]

We must vow not to allow it to be affected by the political differences that may face us from time to time. All nations agree and disagree, but economic, social and cultural cooperation must move ahead

1 See note on page 178.

without interruption, since it is the well from which life flows for all, whether they agree or disagree.

Forgive me – waiting has become tedious, after the war had accustomed us to a rapid rhythm that gave rise to events not just with every passing hour but with every passing minute.

28 March 1991

Pessimism and Optimism

We should not rush to pessimism if the post-war world does not bring us what we dreamed of in the manner or with the speed we imagined. Let us look at things with reason and objectivity.

Regarding Kuwait, we are eager for a reward, a favour in return. The first obligation of the Kuwaiti people after liberation was to give us our due deserts and open the doors of employment to our youth. But let us somewhat forget the self, and firmly hold the tongue. Let us think about what happened to Kuwait and its citizens, and the unprecedented catastrophes they suffered. Let us think about the dead and the raped, the destruction of institutions, the fires that consumed property, polluted the air and threatened human life, the lack of water, electricity, medical supplies and food. Do these people not have the right to anger and grief? Do they not have the right to punish those who betrayed them in their time of adversity? Do they not have the right to protect themselves as a minority lost among outsiders who did not respect their sanctity? Take care, sirs: they are human beings, and we must deal with them as befits human beings.

Regarding the problems of the region, perhaps we dreamed that the Security Council would meet the day after the fighting stopped (in fulfilment of their earlier resolutions) and issue warnings to any obstinate party. But the solution we need to all those problems is the fair one that will bring peace and stability. This will not come about without negotiations, the elimination of any differences and the relief of any grudges or painful memories. It is not that simple with the Gulf Crisis, which began with invasion, plunder and defiance, and the response came with equal violence and decisiveness. The problems of our region are old ones that have defied many attempts at their solution. The time has come to attack them head-on, and eliminate them. We must prepare the way for this with whatever suggestions and ideas we may have, and we must not allow time to run away from us or to run out.

Certainly, the Palestinian case in particular is the final test of the sincerity of the new world, but its sincerity cannot be judged before its final position is clear to us.

And up until now, all the signs are that pessimism is not called for.

4 April 1991

Leadership Suicide

There has been a widespread popular uprising in Iraq, but the tyrant has quashed it in a disproportionate and inhuman battle. Through these events some truths have stood out that are worth recording, even if they do not add much to the terrible picture that has settled in the mind.

First: the uprising engulfed all corners of Iraq with proof that the majority of the Iraqi people reject the despot and his regime. For although the regime was victorious, the uprising succeeded in the historic tearing away of Saddam Hussein's mantle of leadership, leaving him a ruined tyrant whose rule stands on pillars of weapons, blood, oppression and hatred. Saddam and his self-glorification and all his fabulous stories and delusions have been annihilated, and nothing is left of him but the awful naked truth.

Second: it has been shown that the tyrant possesses a force equipped with the latest land and air weaponry, but that he did not use it in the defence of his nation. He granted his enemies a startlingly quick victory with no losses to speak of. He exposed his regular army to a shocking defeat in the worst of circumstances, but he only let his real forces out of their bottle for the onslaught on his own wretched people in a one-sided battle with no regard for mercy, national sentiment or human compassion, in the end erecting a throne upon mounds of martyrs' skulls.

Third: just as the events of the war showed up his foolishness, investigation by his opponents revealed his betrayal of conscience and ethics, for under his patronage rape was committed, wealth was plundered and billions were smuggled abroad in his name and in that of his family.

Fourth: the despot has not refrained from threatening people with extermination, after targeting them with his artillery, jets, and weapons both licit and illicit. This was the culmination of the crimes that he began with the destruction of Kuwait and Iraq, with the consequent losses in life and property that are not even partly matched by the results of great natural disasters such as historic earthquakes and volcanoes.

Certainly, if the tyrant and his supporters are not brought to international justice, there is no point in talking about values in this world.

8 April 1991

Examining Memories

The Gulf Crisis erupted on 2 August and reached its climax in a destructive war, which ended with the achievement of its primary goal, the liberation of Kuwait. And now complex historical factors are interacting to bring about a new future.

So what did it do to us in Egypt? And what does it amount to?

The negatives:

1. In economic terms, our financial losses reached 20 billion dollars.
2. Our relations with some Arab countries deteriorated in an unprecedented way, although in Egypt itself Egyptians came together in a sweeping popular unanimity.
3. No heart was free from pain at the destruction that happened in Kuwait, nor at what happened to Iraq and its people.

The positives:

1. Our position on the crisis, which was based on noble principles and the defence of legitimate interests.
2. Our initiative to shoulder responsibility in a coalition with our Arab brothers and international forces, and our honourable performance in the war for all to see.
3. The start of a new Arab cooperation formed of the eight nations[1] to plan for the establishment of security arrangements and economic, social and cultural integration, leaving the door open for others who wish to join.
4. The cancellation by friendly Arab countries and the United States of a considerable portion of our debts.
5. Movement in the East and the West towards a solution for the problems of the region, with a view to deep-rooted stability and comprehensive justice.

---

1 See note on page 178.

6. The participation of all Arab countries in a meeting of the League of Arab States (30 March 1991), which bodes well for the settling of differences, even if it takes time.
7. Increased attention to overall development, as the president made clear in an interview with the editor-in-chief of *Al-Ahram*.

We so much wanted democracy to be given a fresh push, to match its importance in the popular awakening and desired renaissance, especially since the first lesson of the Gulf catastrophe is that it was the bitter fruit of one despotic man and his autocratic regime; and in such matters the door of hope will not shut until all is well.

11 April 1991

The Bush Initiative

The Bush initiative that was recently announced comes as quite a surprise,[1] though a happy one for those on the side of law, legitimacy and a peaceful solution to the Palestinian issue. It heralds the return of rights, and averts from the region the woes of ruin, destruction and death without accountability.

The truth is that nobody supports aggression, and there is no country that has not called for the restoration of rights. The great majority reject war and wish for a peaceful solution, at the head of them all the American people themselves – to the extent that there came a point when it was clear that none of them wanted war except their president and a small minority. If Bush had been an autocrat, or master of his own decisions, things would have been easy and he would have gone his own way, but what could be done when he was the icon of democracy in the modern age? Things progressed, one step after another; the American president visited a variety of countries in both the East and the West; then came the latest Security Council resolution, then the initiative.

And here a question arises: was the initiative a surprise only to us, the readers, or also to the countries that he visited? I hope it was all agreed during his visits, or at the least that it did not come with any retreat from inalienable principles.

I am a proponent of peace, of negotiation, of a solution to all the problems of the region that rock its security every few years, and of an agreement on an all-encompassing security arrangement, but the condemnation of aggression and the restoration of rights and legitimacy are fundamentals that cannot be infringed or neglected.

The Bush initiative is a happy surprise for us, and we hope it will lead to the desired peaceful solution and will establish rights, justice and comprehensive peace in the region.

18 April 1991

---

1 In a March 1991 speech to Congress, President George Bush announced a new push to achieve an Arab–Israeli peace treaty, the first step of which was the Madrid Conference of October 1991.

The Parties

Daily life indicates the presence of the following political currents:

1. The current that brings together democracy and socialism, represented by the National Democratic Party (NDP).
2. The current that stands for democracy and sees nothing wrong with incorporating some strands of socialism, represented by the Wafd Party.
3. The leftist current, represented by the Tagammu Party, the Nasserists, and one wing of the Labour Party.
4. The moderate Islamic current, represented by the Muslim Brotherhood and a selection of enlightened Islamic thinkers.
5. The Islamic groups, characterised by extremism and violence.

These are the currents that one comes across as one moves around, or whose news is spread through their publications and talks. Consequently it is these that could become parties if the freedom to form parties were applied and if political rights were respected, and they might at the same time find different popular bases in their strength and scope.

Reality demands – and the public interest requires – that the NDP, the Wafd and the Liberals merge into one party, as should also the Tagammu, the Nasserists and the Labour wing. Thus the real parties would look like this:

1. A party comprising the Wafd, the NDP and the Liberals.
2. A party comprising the Tagammu, the Nasserists and the Labour wing.
3. The Muslim Brotherhood.
4. The extremist Islamic groups.

The establishment of a religious party does not mean the exclusion of piety from the other parties: the current NDP government bases its legislation on sharia law, has designated a ministry of religious affairs, and devotes great attention to Islamic instruction in its schools and in its media organs, besides being the guardian of national unity and social justice.

Complete and long-lasting stability will not arrive until these parties are established and are legitimately active among the population under the umbrella of liberty, law and respect for human rights.

Everything is possible if we move beyond historical memories and personal pride and raise the banners of the public interest.

The battle is coming, and all the better if it comes within the compass of liberty and law. And let us accept the will of the people, however it may be.

25 April 1991

Towards a New Vision

We came into a world torn apart by struggles, divided between competing empires and menaced by global and local wars, its relations based on the mastery and exploitation of the weak by the strong. Our aim was to gain independence, then to hold onto it, being wary of all that was foreign, and fearful of its evils.

Today we turn to meet the rising of a new world, a world of rapid communication and ready information, a world whose fringes are coming closer to each other, whose dimensions are merging, and whose views and traditions are melting together, a world that heralds a geographical and civilisational unity.

The miracle of a congruence of ideologies has occurred in this world, almost to the point of conjoining to give birth to something new; putting an end to the Cold War and allowing a global symbiosis to replace it that has cooperation and dialogue as its goal.

What calls for further cohesion and coordination is that it is a world threatened with natural disasters such as pollution, climate change, incurable diseases and drugs, which can only be confronted on the global level with the effort of all humanity.

We must think patiently and objectively about our choice of the best means to contribute to this new world, to find our way to a role that suits both us and it. We must put our old world view under the microscope of critical examination: we must welcome give and take, we must rid ourselves of our complex of fear and introversion, and we must find ourselves a place in international action in keeping with its principles and directions. We must not make our proud heritage an impediment to progress or a basis for conflict that can be resolved by other means, instead making of it a gift that we can contribute to the raising of a new edifice.

It is our goal today to rid ourselves of the restrictive entanglements of the past, and carry forward its eternal, overarching, driving principles into the present and the future.

25 April 1991

In Defence of Liberty and Dignity

Iraq's popular uprising has been subjected to a monstrous suppression in which thousands have perished, impelling the entire population towards extinction. At first, reaction was limited to perplexity and indignation, then came an operation to deliver food and medical aid to the victims, and finally forces were dispatched to take in the refugees and give them protection.

While many called on the coalition forces to intervene to save innocent lives, some had reservations, believing that this would constitute interference in a state's internal affairs, which could set a dangerous precedent that would be difficult to negotiate in the future.

We recognise the right of every state to independence in its internal affairs and the defence of its legitimate regime, allowing it to fulfil all its national obligations. But we also see that a state's rights must be exercised within certain bounds and limits.

Any state has rights, no doubt, but it also has obligations.

Its rights include sovereignty and the implementation of laws, the fulfilment of safety and security, and the defence of its regime and its country's borders.

But its obligation is that these things be done within a civilised compass, in a humanistic framework, with respect for human rights, and under whatever commitments it must adhere to as a member of the United Nations. So it does not have the right to institutionalise discrimination, or to persecute political or religious minorities, or to use its heavy weapons that are actually designed for war and defence in the suppression of popular movements, killing women and children and destroying cities.

We live in an age of lethal weapons that are capable of obliterating cities in days, and people cannot be left at the mercy of tyranny, megalomania and insane despotism.

If a state diverges from the fundamentals, the international community has the right to send fact-finding missions, and if wrongdoing is proven, then appropriate measures must be taken, such as economic sanctions and other deterrent means. In the end this is no more than the defence of human liberty and dignity.

2 May 1991

A Picture of the Arabs

The Gulf War revealed a picture of the Arabs that, even if it did not reflect the reality of all of them, did so for a considerable faction of them. So let them scrutinise this picture honestly and objectively if they truly want to have the hope of a better future.

The picture tells us that some of them, when strength and might held sway, rushed to solve their issues with their Arab brothers through invasion, ignoring all means of peaceful understanding.

It also tells us that in their invasion they paid no regard to brotherhood, nor to the weakness of their adversary and their inability to defend themselves, nor to the international conventions of war, as they killed the innocent, violated women, plundered property and destroyed livelihoods. It is true that these crimes aroused the anger of parts of the Arab community, but many demonstrations were held in support of the criminal, arousing the alarm, shock and disgust of the civilised world.

And it tells us that when the war led to a battle between actual forces, the offending party crumbled and his arrogance fell away to reveal ignorance, cowardice and impotence. He abandoned his troops in the worst circumstances, to be killed or captured.

And it tells us that when the defeated coward faced his own angry people he caught his breath, turned into a lion, and brought out his forces – which he had held back from using in the defence of his country – to kill unarmed civilians, women and children, and to toss them all into the abyss of annihilation. The civilised world was outraged at what was happening to the people of Iraq, and rushed to help and protect them, while at the same time there was not a single demonstration in an Arab country in protest against the slaughter. It was as though all the tears had been already used up in sympathy with the criminal, so there were none left to shed for his victims.

Look carefully at the picture as it has been revealed by events, and do not put its ugliness down to original traits in the Arab character, for it is nothing but the inevitable consequence of civilisational backwardness and the failure of some forms of government. The truth is that great numbers of Arabs live under the oppression of ignorance, fiction and coercion, living and dying without the slightest say in the determination of their destiny, or seeing even an atom of human rights. Their dignity has no weight, and their very lives have no value.

Indeed, let the Arabs look at their picture honestly and objectively, and summon up the resolve to throw off everything that stands in their way towards a more exalted life.

3 May 1991

The Reality and the Dream

The wheel of events turns around us. We follow these events with the passion of those who look to a better tomorrow, and we do not want them to cease. We should participate in them with all the reason and will at our disposal. The US secretary of state[1] is working assiduously to push forward the peace process. The authorities are researching security arrangements in the Gulf. And conflicting opinions are flying about in the air.

We follow all this alertly and with interest, but what concerns us more is what is happening domestically, or what we may expect to happen. Anything else ranks second in relation to our overall development, our modern revival – the life whose cornerstones we are constructing with our minds, our hands, our proud heritage and our patriotism. Which is why I run breathlessly after news of the IMF and the Paris Club,[2] and scour the newspapers for what has happened between us and Libya in the fields of cooperation, economy, culture and media. I was most excited by what was reported about the setting up of an Arab agricultural production authority between Egypt, Syria, Libya and Sudan.

In addition to that, we have been promised an administrative leap forward and more harmony of thought and action in the drive to production, along with a conscious, purposeful movement in business leadership. The general feeling is that we are entering a period that will be both active and crucial at the same time. Not the cruciality that leads to collapse, but the cruciality that one passes through from hardship to relief by way of willpower, thought and creativity; the true victory that one wins over one's own self by defeating its negative side and the elimination of the obstacles of misfortune that stand in one's way.

I have not yet come across a word about political reform and the

---

1 James Baker, US Secretary of State from 1989 to 1992.

2 The Paris Club came into being in 1956, and works to find financial solutions for debtor nations.

rebuilding of democracy, so I pray that we do not forget that our first mission in the region is to put in place a model for political life suitable to be followed by whoever is looking for a good example of liberty, social justice and respect for human rights.

9 May 1991

Coming of Age

The more one is surrounded by the troubles of the present, the sweeter it is to return to memories of the past. This is why we retrieve it from the gloom of time, wrapped in nostalgia and happiness and conveniently forgetting its sufferings and pains. How many people talk about the past in this romantic way, in all sincerity, unaware of the deception of time? They tell you about the amazingly cheap prices, about the small salaries that satisfied the needs of a large family. They tell you about Cairo and how clean, quiet, beautiful, peaceful and unpolluted it was, and about its guardians, the policemen who patrolled day and night. They tell you about strong family ties, their deep-rooted traditions, their customary good manners; about the perfect schools, their venerable teachers, and their polite, hard-working pupils. They tell you about the freedom of thought, the flourishing of literature, the liberty of the press, the diversity of the political parties, the enthusiasm of the workers and 'what a wonderful life the farmers had!'[1]

Without doubt they are sincere, and we could add many more to their examples, but in the face of the gloomy present and its difficulties they forget that the society of the past was a society of a privileged few and a deprived, toiling majority, and that it was backward when measured against the age of its civilisation. It was ruled over autocratically by a king; it was occupied by a foreign army; it was manipulated by despots on account of the king at times, of the occupying army at others; and it was governed by people who did not have the right to govern. Its development was limited, its hopes were modest and its problems consequently small and obscure.

Despite our current innumerable difficulties, and our sufferings for which the demons pity us, despite the corruption, the debts, the housing problem and rising prices, Egypt today is embarking on a period of transition. It is enduring labour pains, and is setting its sights on great hopes: how many schools! How many students! How many

---

1 Echoing the 1939 song *Ma ahlaha 'ishat al-fallah*, sung by Asmahan, words by Bayram al-Tunisi, music by Muhammad 'Abd al-Wahab.

universities, cultural and scholarly institutions, factories and businesses! How wonderful the international dealings, the desert development and the interaction with all avenues of thought from right and left! By my life, the torment of struggle is better than the ease of apathy, so forwards ever and always – we will take the pain and suffering along with the blessings of life and progress.

16 May 1991

The Late Muhammad 'Abd al-Wahab

Most great people achieve their missions through sweet and bitter experiences: victories and defeats, gains and losses, joys and sorrows – these are the ingredients that accompany every significant change in life. But it is different for the great figures of art, for they manufacture happiness, and they donate it unreservedly and unconditionally, devoting their lives to making others happy. Whoever accepts all of them, good for him; whoever does not accept them is perfectly free to do without them for now, or for ever. They are truly and honestly the masters of happiness in this life. When one of them dies young he leaves behind the sighs of grief; when one dies in old age he leaves behind the sighs of beautiful companionship and pleasant memories. They are friends to all, which is better than any individual relationship. For they are in our deepest feelings, whether or not we have been fortunate enough to be personally acquainted with them for an unforgettable hour.

When I was in the primary or the early part of secondary school, there drifted into my hearing as I walked along the road a new voice singing a lovely song on a record being played in some house or other. I was strongly drawn to it, and I asked whose voice it was. Thus began my history of listening to Muhammad 'Abd al-Wahab, and thus was confirmed to me what I had heard about him, that he was the student and successor of Sayyid Darwish.[1] After that I followed his output and saw many of his concerts, and his compositions went on accumulating in my consciousness. They carved out a renewed history in the public and private life of Egypt, reflected its joys and sorrows, and interpreted every heartbeat of the street, the home and the fields, as well as of reality and dream, man and woman, old and young. And all of this was blended into pleasant melodies that combined innovation and experience, knowledge and intelligence, and an extraordinary mastery

1 Muhammad 'Abd al-Wahab (1910–91) was one of Egypt's leading popular composers, who also sang and acted in many films. Sayyid Darwish (1892–1923) is widely considered the father of modern Egyptian popular music.

of composition. He was the writer, the scenarist, and the director who could present an open buffet to East and West; he was the one best able to represent the state of Egypt from both worlds, from heritage and modernity, from originality and legitimate adaptation. His melodies together flowed like a diary of private and public life. When a tune spilled out, it drew behind it thoughts of nationhood, politics or economic life; or it brought back from oblivion a personal feeling and preserved it beautifully in the sweetest of forms: encased in melodies and harmony, performed by the most beautiful voices and connected with the heart.

Dear departed one: death has taken what it can of you, but it has left with us what it cannot take.

23 May 1991

Changing Positions

The president was asked about the position of the council for cooperation between Egypt, Iraq, Jordan and Yemen, and he replied that it was currently on hold. From which I had the impression that the hold may be temporary and that it may disappear with the disappearance of its reasons.

I read a day or two later about a likely improvement in relations with Yemen, Jordan and Sudan.

And I heard someone who comments disapprovingly on this and that saying: 'We don't stick to one position, and we are oblivious of our mistakes, even our offences. We come together later in embraces and kisses, as if we had not painted our faces with all the abuse, calumny and scorn in the dictionary of wrath. And they are left wondering: how can we believe what is said after this? How do we distinguish between right and wrong?'

In my opinion, political life has a particular stamp to it that refuses consistency and does not abide by permanence. Immutable decisions do not exist in its sphere. But mature countries always look into the distance and focus on the greater goal, and thus differences are contained if their reasons dissipate or if their conditions change. There are always higher interests that must have an effect on considerations, whatever the sacrifices and whatever flexibility, self-control or cheek-turning is required.

Relations between us and any Arab state have never been as terrible as they were between Germany and France, or between France and England, or between America and Japan. Yet here you have the European countries leaving their bloody past behind, and heading towards solid cooperation and stable unity.

Let us learn from politics how to be angry when anger is needed, and how to forget when forgetting is necessary. It is not a matter of emotions or brotherhood or historic dreams, but of tireless, attentive work to build a better future, based on economic integration, cultural unification, participation in the modern age and the sanctity of science and hard work, under the sovereignty of noble values and complete respect for human rights.

In this way, we will accept any change, welcome any thinking, and rid ourselves of a multitude of cruel experiences, to face the future with hearts beating with progress and higher ideals.

6 June 1991

Excitement and Worth

Our modern history has taught us to pay the most attention to dramatic events, and we have located our grail in great dreams and lustrous undertakings, as though we are seeking refuge in an escape from our grim reality, our slow development and our critical problems. It is as if in missing excitement, adventure and miracles we imagine that our life is empty of any aim that we can wrap ourselves around or to which we can apply loyalty and determination. I am astounded by people who suffer from the problems of overpopulation, pollution, rising prices, corruption, unemployment, oppression, emergency laws and terrorism – I am astounded by people who suffer from all this, who at the same time are searching for a goal for their society in history, in thin air, or in empty slogans. This is why I hope that we give economic reform the attention and sacrifices it deserves, that we follow the promises of administrative reform with vigilance, hope and active scrutiny, and that we encourage every movement that aims towards the political reform we desire. For these and similar issues are the fabric of our true life and the first priority of this generation, who consider any other aim to be secondary in comparison.

Perhaps it is good to invite you to join me in celebrating the following pieces of news:

The first is: Egypt and Libya have taken a new step on the road to mutual integration. They are in the process of finalising an agreement to establish agricultural communities. This is a genuine labour that will create when it matures a genuine unity, based on work and shared interests and the advancement of both our peoples.

The second is: a delegation from a giant American company has been examining the capabilities of the Arab Organisation for Industrialisation (AOI) and has found it to have surprisingly outstanding potential, leading to the awarding of two contracts to the AOI for the manufacture of spare parts for the American company. How we need news like this once or twice a year to restore our spirit and revive our hopes!

The third is: Dr Muhammad Hilmi Murad sent a message to the

great writer Mustafa Amin, letting him know that a national committee has completed a draft of a new constitution in preparation for presenting it to the people. It is a novel work that turns the opposition into a 'shadow cabinet', so long as a change of government is impractical in the circumstances of the time.

Now, do these pieces of news not deserve our celebration, our appreciation and our admiration?

13 June 1991

Reading for All

The Reading for All project sponsored by Mrs Suzanne Mubarak is a great cultural achievement in all senses, a project that must develop, continue and spread; and must always be supported with care, attention and enthusiasm in order for it to reach its goals and harvest its fruits. In the field of culture, the first mission of society is to concentrate on the creation of the cultured citizen, the citizen who loves knowledge and adores beauty in all its artistic and natural forms. If a foundation could be put together of a reasonable number of intellectuals, it would be able on its own to provide the solution to all cultural problems, without the need for state intervention, except in what concerns legislation, awards and involvement in family relations.

If this foundation existed, it would solve the problem of publication for established and new writers alike, because private-sector (more than public-sector) publishers would strive seriously to discover and embrace new voices, and beginners would face no difficulties beyond their need to study, prepare and develop their talent.

Similarly, it could solve the problem of the arts pages in the newspapers and magazines by assuring the right attention is given to them, with respect to their wide range of readers, as with the sports and other pages.

The television and radio should redouble their focus on serious cultural programmes, to satisfy their not inconsiderable audience and their wishes.

And interest in art exhibitions, classical music concerts, genuine theatre and creative cinema can be increased.

The making of the cultured citizen is the most important achievement to be offered in the field of culture. This truly is a great project that must continue and succeed. To its sponsor, our appreciation and thanks.

20 June 1991

Clarity

What would a neutral observer make of the serious legislative decisions that have been announced one after the other, which have provoked arguments, caused significant unintentional damage and sometimes threatened results that contradict the expressed policies of the state?

Policies should be transparent to all, their goals defined, and legislation should not contradict them, indeed it should support their course and act towards their establishment, consolidation and success. We have frequently heard the repeated call for investment and its promotion, which should have been followed by the provision of the right climate for investment and an understanding of the requirements of business. We know what has been said about the capital of Egyptians abroad, their readiness for business and their needs: we must verify what has been said and move forward in our understanding of what will bring us a real economic boom, without the need for loans, and open up the arena of business for Egyptians at home.

The goals must be clear, the determination sincere and the consultation comprehensive. This did not happen with the sales-tax law, as far as I know. Suffice it to say that it was applied before its implementation schedule was published, and it is enough to note the errors that have been made in its name and the protests, cries and anguish that we have read about in the newspapers. The people, before all else, are respectable citizens, not laboratory mice for hasty legislation.

And then there is the legislation on credit for the banks, to which bankers and businessmen have put up such an opposition as to make the neutral observer believe that it was formulated in complete isolation from them, while it is they who have the most direct interest in it. Did this ruling not require consultation before it was issued, rather than afterwards?

We want transparent politics, clear goals, consultation and flawless legislation.

27 June 1991

Egypt the Safeguarded[1]

The esteemed *Al-Ahram* has broken a frightening story about the future of the Nile Delta: some scientists announced at their meeting in Rome that Lake Burullus will increase in size and that by the year 2100 the level of the Delta will have dropped an average of seventy cm.[2] There are several factors at work together that will make this expected catastrophe happen: the slow rate of water discharge, the lack of silt accumulating on the land, the extraction of gas and artesian water and the removal of topsoil in places.

And we have already heard about the delta that is being formed from silt deposits south of the Aswan High Dam. The two events together mean that Egypt's essential existence is now under threat.

How are these reports and warnings to affect us?

Are we to meet them with indifference and silence, as though they were some account from history, or a curious prophecy about the distant future that we will never see? Are we to be numbed by indifference and apathy, and be satisfied with immersing ourselves in the worries and problems of the present?

I have not perceived any effect on people commensurate with the news, as I did with the sales tax, or even with the limited cabinet reshuffle, or the news of a football championship or a TV drama series. This cannot be explained by the very existence of Egypt meaning less to people than these other things, but it seems that we no longer pay the requisite attention to what science and the scientists tell us. For quite some time our minds have been swimming in a sea of fiction and fairy tales, and deep down our faith in science and scientists has been shaken.

Even so, I hope that I am not correct in my doubts, and that the disturbing news has in fact aroused the attention it warrants, and sharpened our resolve to think and act.

And I am not asking too much if I request that the state appoint a

---

1 Misr al-Mahrusa, a common epithet of the country.

2 Lake Burullus is a shallow, brackish lake some fifty km long, within the Nile Delta.

committee of specialised scientists to research the entire matter, to reveal the full truth behind it, and to recommend what they see as necessary for us to begin doing now, relying on our own capabilities and requesting help from others if our capabilities fall short.

Egypt's existence and future are now threatened by a delta forming in the south and a delta drowning in the north. Life on this earth is kind only to those who deserve it.

4 July 1991

'When One Is Tested ...'

The development of events between the Socialist Bloc and the West have heralded for us the birth of a new world, one built on the shunning of violence in resolving its problems, its vision resting on the support of liberty and justice. We have previous experience here, as with the League of Nations, which suffered failure, and the United Nations, which has achieved moderate success – true, it was not able to bring an end to the struggle of the giants or to their manipulation of the fates of smaller nations at times, but under its auspices many peoples have gained their independence and sanctions were imposed on South Africa, while it has spawned organisations that perform genuine services in education, health, culture and development. Under its roof too, the world has found a palpable voice of public opinion and a global conscience that cannot be ignored.

So we have high hopes for the heralded new world, and we refuse to jump the gun with doubts and misgivings under the influence of a long history full of sadnesses and disappointments. Fate decreed that our region, the Middle East, would be the first test for this new world. An evil aggression occurred here, challenging the highest principles and threatening the most serious interests. The world condemned it and called for a peaceful resolution, but when there was no other way, it resolved the situation with force and liberated the conquered people, secured global interests and punished the aggressors.

But the work is not finished, and the Middle East still holds a serious test for the new world, perhaps more important than the first, for the construction of the pillars of peace may be more difficult than the war itself.

Today the world is confronting the problems of the region, first among which are the Palestinian issue, Arab–Israeli relations, non-conventional weapons and the matter of security and development.

We need not mention the persistent efforts that have been made and are being made, or what we perceive of a general plan for a solution to the problems. I cannot imagine – or I do not want to imagine – that the global effort will cease or retreat if it faces a trench filled with obstinacy and selfish interests. I cannot imagine that it will accept failure in the test, and sacrifice the dream of the new world.

It is a true test – and as the adage avers, 'When one is tested, one is treated with honour or held in contempt.'

11 July 1991

The July Revolution and 1991

The July Revolution took place in 1952. It arrived resoundingly amid national pride and a halo of promises of justice, honour, integrity and democratic strength – and the people received it as would anybody who had long looked forward to justice, honour, integrity and democratic strength. In its shade they lived and dreamed of utopia, of glory and of prosperity, and they saw great advances in their spiritual and material lives and in their political ambitions both domestically and globally.

By 1991 the expectation was that the utopia would be well and truly established on the land; that the pillars of glory would be deeply rooted; that prosperity would be blowing like a zephyr on a cool day; that liberty would be shining like the rays of the sun; and that justice would be as firmly embedded as the Great Pyramid.

How could it not be so, when Egypt now belonged to its own people, with no foreign occupation, no rapacious enemy, no class privilege? Our rule was wholly Egyptian and purely national, minds were wide awake, hands were vigorous, hearts were beating and intentions were good. And behind it all was an energy that came from planning and hard work.

But in reality, 1991 is the year that witnesses the strenuous effort of our leadership to reduce the pressure of the debts in which we have been drowning. It also sees us taking the first steps at the beginning of the right path out of a totally suffocating crisis.

I will not repeat the story of the tragedy, nor enumerate the mistakes, nor note the disasters, the defeats, the negligence or the corruption, since all these are permanently engraved deep in our sad hearts.

I would like to focus on one matter:

This land has had two revolutions: the revolution of liberty and the revolution of social justice.[1] And what happened, happened. But we

1 The reference here is to the 1919 revolution against British rule and the 1952 revolution against what was seen as a corrupt royal regime and an unjust social system.

must not squander their message – so let us start again, with a new determination and following the lessons we have learned, without delay.

We have been betrayed by thieving, mad and despicable people, but there are honest, intelligent and high-minded people left among us.

Let us work and build to achieve the nation of the two revolutions: the nation of liberty and justice.

18 July 1991

An End to the Nightmare

We truly hope that we have found the right path. We hope we can wake from the nightmare to greet a proper return to consciousness, with good omens and the promise of salvation.

It has been – and still is – an oppressive nightmare.

Ask any member of the public you like about anything, and you will receive only one answer. Whenever a mishap occurs, of the kind that happens in any society, it exposes an underlying disease or a disintegrated value, and a fire breaks out in the building to reveal a disgraceful chain of wrongdoings that shame the law and show contempt for security and people's lives.

Investigation is going on in a case in which documents reveal shocking corruption involving leading figures in authority and in government, who have been trading in the interests of the public.

And an incident has come to light in the world of education that unveils unbelievable cheating practices in the most respectable corners of the country – its universities.

These are examples, but close examination reveals more, and worse.

What has happened to Egypt? We were never this bad before. True, we have not been an ideal people, but we have also not been a gang of scoundrels. How are we to face an age that demands perfection of its citizens in learning, work and values?

This degeneracy does not come from our original nature, but from wars, from the economic crisis, from going back and forth between eastern and western models, and from the convergence of afflictions on the best of us – those we label 'low-income' citizens – that have burdened them with more than they can bear, and torn their principles and their loyalty away from them. They and others are victims of totalitarian government, which harasses society and neglects the individual – totalitarian government that only recognises the individual when it asks him to make sacrifices, without setting a guiding example and while provocatively and unconscionably enjoying the good things of life.

In the midst of all this gloom we truly hope that we have found the right path. We hope we can restore our equilibrium, even if it takes time. We hope Egypt can regain its health and well-being, return to its faith in learning, work and values, and preserve its national unity in order to resume its role in the building of civilisation.

25 July 1991

Towards a Modern Education

Education is a vital general responsibility, representing fundamental elements in the building of the human character. So we must give it due attention at all levels, as well as through the media, in order to establish a solid foundation for individuals and a human basis worthy of life in the present age. We give religious and national instruction the attention they deserve, but there should be additions to these, which can be included as elective studies, or in reading-books and other modern channels of communication.

At the head of the list is cultural education, which aims to create citizens with a love of knowledge, excellence and beauty in all its artistic and natural forms. This requires the spread of libraries in schools, as well as magazines and clubs for theatre, music, poetry and public speaking. And it is important to display the history of civilisations, to elucidate the spiritual and material advances that each of the peoples of the world has contributed to humanity, so that the variety in cultures can be the gateway to mutual understanding and the exchange of esteem, in place of alienation and misunderstanding.

Our children must also be acquainted with the simpler principles of scientific methodology, not only as a door to success in science and its achievements but also as the correct path to unimpaired thinking; guaranteeing a sound mind and its preservation from the aberrations and scourges that subject it to the influence of emotionality and fanaticism, and freeing it from the grip of the superstition and nonsense that falsify facts and impede progress.

Last but not least, special attention must be given to human rights in thought, belief, behaviour and treatment, to instil in our children respect for themselves, for their fellow citizens, and for all people, so that every individual may attain the respect and sanctity that he deserves.

Caring for these values means caring for people and for humanity, caring for reason, thought and true democracy as it flows through our daily lives, and finally caring for civilisation, for which we must prepare ourselves in the modern world in order to be in tune with it and earn the ability to live in it with success, happiness and dignity.

1 August 1991

Farewell Yusuf Idris

A revolution was his literary birthplace, and his whole literary life was an ongoing revolution, a rebellion against the rules of art and of society. He plunged into everything with courage, applying himself without restraint, raising storms of agitation and excitement around him, heedless of anything except the dictates of his inner sentiments or the aspirations of his dreams.

He attracted attention from the first word he published, and for the last forty years his name has been on people's lips as an example of rare originality and great art. He wrote with amazing particularity in his content, his composition and his language, taking pride in his extraordinary ability to create and innovate.

Thus he produced his output of short stories, novels, plays and newspaper columns, excelling in everything he did, stamping his distinctive creations with his unique talents. It is almost unanimously agreed that he attained the peak of his creativity in the short story, an exact and deceptively simple art, and if universality and depth came easily to him, he achieved what can be considered miracles in the world of literary innovation. In all his writing in the field of short stories can be found the choicest and finest of global literature.

He is one of the rare writers who have influenced both his own generation and the generations that have followed. His devotion to his art was such that it gave him everything he cherished, and for its sake he forwent everything precious. His art was his passion, and excelling in it was his dream, and for this reason he spared no effort and let no social conventions or anything else stand in his way. Art first and last, and come what may! So his happiest days were those when he had something to give, and his most wretched days were those when he was waiting for inspiration. He was even perfectly prepared to accommodate and accept illness and adverse times if they gave him new material, or opened a closed window for him, or blessed him with one of the hidden truths of the universe.

Such is the great artist. But his merit is measured by the quality of his legacy, and his is a great legacy that generation after generation will enjoy. His favour, past and future, will prevail, and there is nothing left for a rival to say but to ask God to grant him mercy and forgiveness.

8 August 1991

Between Love and Hate

One of the curious studies carried out by the US Department of Justice is the monitoring and recording of crimes committed in America motivated by hate. Behind this is certainly a sensible desire to understand society and what affects the relationships between its members and its groups, in order to develop legislation in the future to bring it in line with its reality, to treat its maladies, to reform its behaviour and to uphold the affirmation of its humanity. This study will reveal the extent of the real effect of racism, religious discord, class differences, culture clashes, sexual and emotional frustrations, economic conflicts and intergenerational disputes.

It is true that social coexistence has long been a human goal, which is essentially built both on and for the sake of cooperation in whatever brings us safety, security and progress, sets down our responsibilities and rights, and lays the path to our creative ability and upward development. But selfishness, competition and missed opportunities leave a wide space open for unfairness and injustice, oppression and ruin. These have been counteracted throughout history by religions and belief systems, which aim to achieve justice, equilibrium and compassion, and to fight iniquity and corruption. The only degree of happiness available to humanity is the fruit that we win in the battle between good and evil, or between law and chaos. Yes, human behaviour requires continual review and watchful vigilance, and these find expression in religious movements, innovations in belief and the triumph of ideas. We are in constant need of whatever will unleash our mental capacities, strengthen our will and kindle our love for good. We always need to conquer our emotions of hate and evil, and to nurture our emotions of good, and of love for our fellow citizens in particular, and humanity in general.

If only each one of us would ask himself before he sleeps what love has done for him and what hate has done for him, in order to know what kind of person he is, and what kind of path he follows.

This is the eternal human battle, and this is our fate.

15 August 1991

23 August

Tomorrow is the anniversary of the death of the two great nationalist leaders, Saad Zaghloul and Mustafa al-Nahhas. True, our concerns about the present day and its challenges have left us no time to celebrate fine memories, but the remembrance of these two leaders is no longer merely a historic occasion on which to pause, learn and show respect, or to stand in pride and glory; it is an eternal memory that by virtue of contemporary history and recent global events, through which a new world is being born, has been turned into the mission of today, a future vision and a firm foundation for the building of our modern life.

The 1919 revolution was the revolution of independence, and that was achieved, praise be to God. But it was also a revolution of Egyptian nationalism, of national unity, of democracy, of human rights, of national capitalism and the free economy, of women, of thought and of art.

Today we are plunging into a sea of challenges in order to establish our identity and play our appropriate role in the Arab region; to promote a unique model of democracy and respect for human rights; and finally to prove our ability to participate in the building of the new world, to understand it and engage with it.

This contemporary orientation is what has stirred up life once more in our great heritage, the heritage of our popular revolution in nation-building, governance and economic awakening, and in the necessary concord with our Arab nationhood and the modern world around us.

We must make of Egyptian nationalism a foundation for Arab nationhood, without one contradicting the other, and we must reconcile our national unity with our religious revival, so that it becomes a revival that is both comprehensive and humanistic.

We must reconcile our launch into a free economy with the preservation of social justice.

And we must be firmly determined to solve the problems of the region, however much patience and effort this may cost us.

The greatest popular experiment in our lives has not been buried by history, nor has it been added to history's museum of fine memories, but global development has placed it at the forefront, where it should be, and it will remain a reference point that supports us in the renewal of our life and our trajectory.

22 August 1991

Gorbachev

The hearts of liberals everywhere beat with sorrow at the removal of Gorbachev,[1] who was not only Soviet president but was – and will remain – a global leader and a symbol of liberty, peace and courage. His name will be the first to be mentioned in the headlines of the new world that humanity is dreaming of – if this world is destined to exist.

He set out a great project for the reconstruction of his country, including new foundations for the building of new relations with the world. But his policy for the implementation of the project was not without its critics inside and outside Russia, and many predicted that he would be a noble victim in the great battle that he had unleashed in this unprecedented attempt to create a better humanity in a happier and better world. The predictions were correct, and reactionary forces have overthrown him with their usual methods in a violent struggle that will not end today or tomorrow.

The issue is not a struggle between men: the reactionary voice may be in the ascendant for a while, as the wave of liberty meanwhile retreats, but in the end the issue is the struggle between values in the vastness of a particular time. One man may be defeated, but his defeat may declare the victory of his values. So it is not a question of Gorbachev's applied politics, because the price of liberty is not inconsiderable and the price of economic transformation is likewise heavy, and reactionism exploits the suffering of the people and pounces when the time is right. But all these things are incidental in comparison to what is really on offer to the people and the age, which can be summarised in one small but great question: is this modern age suited to dictatorial rule, bureaucratic centralisation of the economy and unjust suppression of human rights, or is it an age of liberty, democracy and respect for human rights and international legitimacy?

Gorbachev is a great man, but his values are greater. He is a man

1 Mahfouz is reacting here to the coup by hardliners of August 1991, when Mikhail Gorbachev was briefly held under house arrest at his rural dacha; the coup failed, and Gorbachev returned to power in Moscow.

who will not be forgotten, but his principles are better and more lasting. No power will be able to remove him from his leadership or to essentially undermine his call for freedom, peace and human rights. The tank may triumph over a target, but it is defeated when faced with human will and with time.

29 August 1991

A Return to Cultural Invasion

The case of what is called cultural invasion deserves the attention of everybody, whatever their position or orientation. We can summarise it as follows: how can we deal with the civilisations and cultures that we share this age with around the world? It is a case whose dimensions can only be known and whose consequences, positive and negative, can only be assessed in the light of the modern age, its capabilities and the nature of its life.

In the old days, some would call for the opening of windows onto a superior civilisation, and unconditional submission to it. Others would call for the windows to be closed – except for scientific necessities – to preserve their own heritage and chosen security. A moderate faction aspired to choose what was useful to them and reject what was harmful or did not suit them. And it was possible, at that time, to keep in place a pattern of politics agreed on through deputations, translation, education and media.

But today we live in a new age, an age of rapid transportation and travel, and of modern media that plough ahead without supervision or control. It is an age that deals with the margins as though they are part of a single body; it is an age that promises unification, commingling, blending, the breaking of barriers and the removal of spiritual and material borders.

In the light of these facts we must review the issue, because we cannot rely on censorship or on force, and every opinion, every tendency, every taste and every practice will echo through every house openly and clearly. There will be an enormous struggle to create a single civilisation and a single culture, and everybody will bring all their knowledge and intelligence to bear in this struggle.

Unity of civilisation and culture does not necessarily mean the elimination of identity and individuality, for even in a single civilisation in a single country, this has not prevented the existence of differing cultures in the various provinces.

And even if we lose the familiar means of censorship, it is possible through judicious education to replace it with self-regulation that is dependent on critical assessment and the ability to make choices. Yes, there is a need for democratic education based on freedom, independence, discussion and dialogue.

So all we have to do is to give our children a sound, rational upbringing, so that they are capable of facing anything new, without prejudice or bigotry on the one hand, and without being dazzled and drawn in on the other.

And what remains will be determined by what is most suitable, most practical and most beautiful.

5 September 1991

The Sacred Trust of Democracy

The democratic current in our country is frequently described as weak in comparison to other currents. This judgement in my view is mistaken, and is the result of the negativity of the democratic masses, who are exhausted by crisis and the demands of making a living.

The mistake was confirmed by the dispute that broke out between the government and the opposition over the opposition's constitutional demands, which created the impression that the opposition is the only representative of democracy and that the government represents a different system.

For the truth to become clear in all its dimensions, we must note:

First: there is true democracy in our country, as shown by the multiparty system, the existence of the opposition, the freedom of the press, the upper and lower houses of parliament and the independence of the judiciary.

Second: what is achieved by democracy comes not as the fruit of a popular revolution but from the response of the government to the requirements of the people, a judicious reading of its pulse, and by learning wisely from the errors of totalitarian rule.

We can conclude from this that the government represents democracy just as much as the opposition does, and that the dispute over constitutional demands was between two factions who belong to one democratic family and who agree on the concept and the goal but disagree on the steps for implementation.

Based on this, we can say that the democratic current is a prevailing majority, despite the negativity of the masses and their differences, which will vanish with time.

The opposition may have gone ahead of themselves somewhat with their demands, but did the majority party not delay things with its slow progress and excessive caution?

The majority party must understand its democratic mission, and follow it with vigilance and determination.

Its recent political decisions went beyond some clauses of the constitution and made of the emergency laws outdated customs, unsuited to the modernity of its recent thinking. It should review its reading of reality in order to prepare the ground for enduring stability, international legitimacy and participation in the birth of a new world.

You have begun to face towards democracy, and you must continue on the path until the peak of perfection.

12 September 1991

The Model of the Age

All civilisational fields of endeavour are important and essential, indispensable to humanity in its arduous journey wreathed with strife, tenacity and sacrifice. Each endeavour has ascended the throne of sovereignty and relinquished it over the course of time, while not relinquishing its importance and remaining crucial to both the present and the future. This has been the case with chivalry, literature, the arts, agriculture, industry and many other things: every field is important and essential, whatever its position in the civilisational ranking. But we must not lose sight of the focal point of our age, to which we owe our direction and orientation, which is so well provided with the means to excellence and progress, and on which the present depends and to which our future aspires – and that is science.

Ours is an age of science and scientists – as I have said – since science plays a central and fundamental role. This, though, is not to reduce the importance of other fields, without which science itself and its achievements lose any real benefit and fail to bring completeness and contentment to humanity.

The education system must take this understanding into account as it plans our children's development, their models and their motivation in their orientation towards the right path.

Our children's imaginations must be filled with the dreams of science and scientists and the broadest possible familiarity with their accomplishments, with the service and achievements they have given to humanity, and with how they battled the armies of darkness with the lights of reason and intellect.

This must be followed and backed up by continuously and liberally throwing light on local scientific research and researchers, and presenting the most distinguished of them in the media as true haloed heroes and models of enlightenment, so that they receive their due in relation to their worth and the significance of their work alongside the stars of the arts and of sport. This is not only a matter of proper appreciation but at the same time an elevated form of education, spreading the first value of our age in the souls of our children and pointing the ascending generation in the direction of the straight path built on reason, hard work, love of knowledge and faith in humanity and its happiness.

19 September 1991

The Russian People

The Russian people have written a shining history for themselves in the experiment of human civilisation.

In the recent past they embraced a momentous revolution unprecedented in its violence and excess, a revolution that wanted to rid the old world of all its givens, its conventions and its constructs in order to establish in contrast a world that was new in every sense of the word. The Russian people drove this revolution, undertaking the realisation of the dream of millions to create the desired paradise in this life. They certainly had to endure persistent hardship, suffer immense sacrifices and be satisfied with the least that life had to offer, at the same time doing without human freedoms, human rights and the happiness that many enjoy who have less than they do in the way of civilisation and hopes.

If success had then been granted to them, they would have led humanity to its new life, but the experiment brought sweeping failure. So the Russian people instead became a warning to all humanity to avoid vainly slipping into a sparkling dream and to safeguard themselves against the calamity of a failed experiment and immeasurable losses. But if they missed being the pioneer, they did not miss being the warning, and the warning is no less of a waymarker than is the pioneer in the vastness of the civilisational experiment.

If the Communist project had been founded on a democratic system, it would have been established in an atmosphere of liberty, and would have benefited from the successive criticisms of its economic and philosophical systems and followed a beneficial development, cleansing it of all the negative aspects that brought it down.

Communism could be the last failed experiment of human life, if nations take care to follow democratic freedoms and respect for human rights, and their experiments set out boldly in that free human atmosphere in which no viewpoint is enforced or policy imposed, and no perversion can grow through power or coercion. And we must not forget in this happy moment in the life of humankind, in which freedom has scored a decisive victory that we hope will be permanent, and oppressive government has suffered a defeat that we also hope will be permanent – we must not forget the heroic role played by the Russian people in the experiment with its two sides, negative and positive, and we must always remember their sacrifices for the sake of human civilisation.

26 September 1991

Progress, Power and Liberty

Communism has fallen in its homeland. It has fallen when it possessed unassailable power. It has fallen without war or enemy attack. It has fallen by itself, meaning that it had no reason to abide, and whatever has no reason to abide is doomed to extinction by and of itself.

It has fallen because its philosophy was incompatible with human nature, and because its economy ignored the laws of business and society. I do not deny that at its beginning it achieved great success, but that was thanks to the zeal of the revolutionaries and their sacrifices: when things stabilised and people settled down, the cracks and faults began to show.

Human history has known not a few idealistic enterprises, originating in the dreams of great men with fine intentions, but these were presented as plans, and people were invited to embrace them without coercion. They addressed hearts and consciences, and respected people's liberty; they were practised by a capable elite, and the majority saw them as guiding beacons towards enlightenment and comfort. Thus it was with utopia, and thus it was with Sufism, and if the promoters of these movements had used force to impose them on people with iron and fire, ignoring human nature and the way things work, they would have suffered the same sad fate as befell Communism in Russia. Our ancient history knew a glorious, beautiful dream, propagated by King Akhenaten, but it depended on power and the throne for its dissemination, and it suffered a sorry and bloody end.[1]

Indeed, there must be enterprises for humanity to walk the path to maturity, but dreams can only succeed if they respect human nature and comprehend the secret workings of the laws of society. This task is not granted to one person or one group. There must be full democracy in which all views are incorporated, all voices are listened to and all human rights are respected.

---

1 In the fourteenth century BCE, Akhenaten attempted to replace the traditional pantheon of Egyptian gods with the worship of a single deity, the sun disk. The old religion was quickly re-established after his death.

Full democracy is the best climate for progress, and the greatest guarantee of success.

3 October 1991

In Search of Lost Time

Egypt is very rich in conferences and meetings that bring together scientists and experts in various domains and disciplines. For a long time it has also had a permanent, extremely active and diligent congress of experts and scientists, which is the Assembly of National Councils, and there is also the Ministry of Scientific Research – and hundreds of university scientific theses.

The handling of scientific research takes many forms. It may end where it begins with the opening speech, the reading out of the studies, the exchange of views and the awarding of grades. Or it may begin like that and then be extended in the shape of direct application or planning for the future, and at this point it is transformed, and we are transformed with it, from a Third World nation into a nation of the modern age in terms of production, thought, problem-solving and progress on all levels.

I do not know how we deal with what we have available, and the way we deal with it may not be as would be wished by a person who loves his country and is earnestly concerned about its future. But whoever follows our slow steps to progress will doubt – or has the right to doubt – the extent to which we make use of the ideas and research that we have.

The matter requires coordination, study and follow-up, and it may be that each field has a focal point for gathering its interests, for its study, and for working on its application; but overall coordination will only be achieved if it comes out of one centre, and perhaps there is no better place for this than the Ministry of Scientific Research, whose mission should be:

1. To gather together researches from their sources in the national councils, in conferences, and in university theses, so that nothing either great or small is overlooked.
2. To maintain contact with the competent authorities, and to consult on what can be accomplished through them.
3. To work on initiating the application of whatever is not held up by impediments of finance or structure.

4. To make a plan, in collaboration with the Planning Authority, for whatever needs to be done in the way of financial subventions and procedures.

This is the least we can pursue, to protect ourselves in this modern age.

10 October 1991

Honouring Those Worthy of Being Honoured

Honours bestowed should be sincere, and they should be to the benefit of the honouree, to the benefit of the rising generations, and to the benefit of our highest values.

During the lifetime of great figures, light should be shed on their achievements and they should be encouraged with monetary awards. After their death, their lasting legacy should be preserved as a lesson and an example for succeeding generations. But beyond that, celebrations, medals, statues and names on streets are a fleeting salute with no real value, quickly disappearing in the course of time and leaving behind nothing but names and pictures without meaning.

True tributes achieve two aims: first, they unfold strength and life in the person as he labours. Second, they educate our youth and provide them with sound models, spurring them on to work and innovate in the service of the country and humanity. The media are best placed to carry out this honourable task, by spreading their bright light on beneficial and beautiful works in the fields of science, business and the arts, as they already most competently do in the field of sports.

Monetary awards must be generous and appropriate to the time in which they are given, both to allow the recipient the freedom to continue creating and to compensate him for the extraordinary efforts exerted in works of great influence on human life, regardless of the triviality of the material fruits they earn for him.

This is what is required for the honouring of great figures in their lifetime and after their death, but it does not mean that it should be restricted to the honouree alone; more importantly, its effect should be extended in the form of educational and cultural movements for succeeding generations, and should contribute powerfully to the shaping of society's culture and the renewal of its strengths and loyalties.

In truth, it can be said that the honouring of great figures is in the end no more than the honouring of science, politics, the economy, literature, the arts and all our highest values.

17 October 1991

A Period of Transition

We are living in a period of transition and at a crossroads. But this can also be said of the entire world, with its differing degrees of development. You only need to recall what is happening in the socialist world, in Europe and in Asia, quite apart from the Third World. Transitional periods are extremely difficult times, chock-full of pains, as they are in the lives of individuals at the transition from infancy to childhood, or from childhood to adolescence, or at the decline into old age: across all societies, people are generally torn between radicalisation on the one hand as a means of confrontation right and left, and apathy on the other hand as an escape from the burdens of confrontation and its troubles. And between this group and that, others fall into crime, or drugs, or dissipation and egoism.

It is not easy for us to leave our Third World for the developed world, and it is not easy to find a solution that reconciles straight patrimony with straight realism; or a fair balance between the authority of the state and the authority of the people; or between the arrogance of power and the judgement of the law; or between unruly passions and a scientific, rational platform; or between introversion and the globalism that is about to engulf us in our family sitting-rooms. And we will not be left to the course of time alone or to the flow of history, because we carry the extra burdens of mountainous problems including overpopulation, debt, unemployment and revenue shortfall.

Thus if a person is well aware, he will fall prey to confusion and depression, and if he is unaware, he will drown in his own self, dying while alive or living while dead.

It is a transitional period, a period of suffering, but it is also a period of work and effort, the cause of creation and innovation, the birth of leadership and heroes. It is the historic test of ardour and will, and nothing but success is possible, because the alternative is death, and we were not created for self-destruction.

24 October 1991

The Greater Nation

The world today is rolling with contradictions. Science is leading it to wonderful horizons of knowledge and achievement, taking it to vistas of progress, enlightenment and strength, from the centre of the earth to space, in a march with humanity and with animals, plants and minerals. At the same time it is assailed by terrible perils such as pollution, drought, disease, drugs and terrorism, which are on the point of wrecking it, or afflicting it with blight. Every nation has its share of progress and peril, according to its place in civilisation, and is required to confront its problems by every means within the limits of its energies and talents.

But our age is distinguished by a new situation, which is that it is headed towards rapprochement and unification, so that the positives and the negatives now flow through it as one, admitting no boundaries. It is an age of exchange between extremes, of merging in larger groupings, of sharing good and evil, and evil more frequently than good. It only rarely has secrets any more, and perhaps the secrets will remain hidden only for a time before becoming known. We are in a time of public knowledge, global trade, an international economy and the dialogue of nations. We are brought together by values such as human rights, we meet in organisations and conferences, and we face the same threats that deepen our feelings of unity and the necessity of comprehensive cooperation.

There is no way a problem can be solved, no matter how local it may appear to those faced with it, unless from a collective standpoint, in true cooperation and general human fellow-feeling. People have moved beyond the traditional limits of the old boundaries of selfishness, and the interests of the selfish ego.

Those who live in this world with fossilised minds, selfish visions, discriminatory passions or fanatical tendencies, or who are prisoners to pettiness or transient spite – these are the outsiders now. We have taken account of the mistakes we made in the days of isolation, of the copious blood we shed, and we have prayed to God not to let us miss the chances of salvation, and not to let the feelings of human obligation stumble in our inner souls.

7 November 1991

The Inescapable Battle

Whoever has contact with the people will be engulfed by their complaints like the flames of a fire. There is nothing that can be done except to offer comfort to this enormous multitude of humanity, who live in the grip of a nightmare that must be driven away in order for life to take on a new face. I listen to it all with a gloomy heart. And as much as I concur with the efforts of honest leaders and the many comprehensive reforms they have achieved, I cannot help thinking about important and urgent things like the following:

1. The fulfilment of the people's liberty and respect for their rights, so that they can enter their life's battle proud of their dignity, reliant on themselves and shouldering their responsibility. As a first step we must begin by lifting the restrictions on the formation of political parties, to remove the gatekeeper from this most important political right, because economic reform must be supported by political reform – a bird cannot fly with one wing.
2. The collection of public wealth, especially taxes, with the running of a complete count of taxpayers, and the pursuit of tax dodgers. Here we must acknowledge the considerable effort made by the Tax Authority, as we must laud their adoption of new practices that marry respect for the public with concern for the public interest.
3. The sanctity of work and respect for time and organisation, focusing on production, rewarding the diligent and rapping the knuckles of the careless and the slothful. Leniency today leads to laxity, which contributes to destruction.
4. The call for a general policy of austerity appropriate to a nation burdened by debts and stumbling with its repayments, provided that the austerity begins with the state and then extends to those who can bear it, and that it applies to food, clothing, celebrations, festivals and all displays of ostentation.
5. Vigilant attention to exports, even if this means going without

> many luxuries, since in the end it is the respectable way to curbing our debts and the prime factor in raising production by modern scientific methods.

There are many things we could consider, but first we must begin, and with a new determination.

14 November 1991

What the Years Promise Us

The anniversary of the beginning of the rule of President Hosni Mubarak was an opportunity to count the achievements of his time in office.[1] These achievements are many, real, and varied, both domestically and internationally, and represent an outstanding human effort. If they had been accomplished in any country that had already begun its revival, they would have brought about a tangible change in its circumstances and propelled it to the heights of progress and development. But most unfortunately, our revival was starting from zero, or below zero, in a country exhausted by successive wars and whose fundamental structures had deteriorated to rock bottom. Development had ceased when we were most in need of it, and the country was in the grip of despair, apathy, inflation, the scourge of fanaticism, drugs, unemployment and the selfishness of the profiteers, and was surrounded by dead ends. What had we done to ourselves? How had life brought us to this? But what is the use of returning to the events of the past, with their sorrows and their errors?

It is enough for us to know the disease whose consequences and complications we are suffering from, and to know the road to deliverance, however long and uneven it may be. We know and believe in the value of work, even if we have not exerted the effort on its behalf that we should have done. We know the meaning and necessity of production, even though we are still hesitating to set our public sector straight and incentivise the private sector. We know democracy, human rights, and the wisdom of relying on the Egyptian people and awakening their potency, even as we dread embarking on the decisive steps to break the chains and set loose the freedoms.

We know the meaning of justice and the sovereignty of law, even if we have not yet responded to the demands of the judiciary or abandoned our ugly habits of nepotism and favouritism. We hope that by the time of the next new year of the president's rule, the side of good

1 Hosni Mubarak came to power after the assassination of President Sadat on 6 October 1981.

will have become enriched by wonderful accomplishments, and the side of bad, with those who serve it, with its habits and with its out-moded practices, will be in retreat.

21 November 1991

Life without Duress

There are choices that on the surface appear simple and straightforward, but that entail secrets that are difficult to construe. They may be characterised by unique features that inspire multiple ideas, notions and views, like rich symbols whose interpretations are greater than they appear. Their echo may ring in many hearts that have been lulled into a long sleep by negativity, and which suddenly shine with longings and hopes.

Unexpectedly, and optimistically, a voice asked how we are to begin reform, and went on to say that every individual must begin by himself and must do his duty in his own field as is expected of him. Another voice interrupted him, saying that relying on the individual was not enough, and he gave the example of himself, of how he had been determined to achieve his dream in his situation and how he had been obstructed by a network of tangled relations, obsolete customs and the decay of a stagnant system, and that change on a greater and more comprehensive level than the individual was essential. Then a third asked: does this mean that we must surrender to reality, and get on with it because there is nothing better? Why doesn't every individual do what he can? And why doesn't he then come out of his shell and join any national grouping that suits him, to add to their strength and to his own?

I followed the discussion with great pleasure. Here was the first indication I had seen of a rebellion against negativity, and there is nothing more damaging to a people than negativity – some have considered it the death from which there can be no resurrection. A person may fall and lose his splendid merits, but this does not last, and cannot last. There live deep inside us two natural impulses, side by side, one to live and one to die, and a person will inevitably regain his equilibrium sooner or later in response to a wise choice, a good deed or a kind word. Hardship has reached its peak, and only work and hope are left.

28 November 1991

The Guide in the Darkness

Reason is the greatest gift that has been bestowed on humankind, and we should understand that it was not given to us for no purpose, but to be a guide to life, as instinct is for animals. Yes, there are domains that can be approached only through feeling, taste or inspiration, but in the rest of life – social, political, economic, everyday – we must rely first and last on reason. There must be a planned, knowledge-based approach, and a comprehensive view based on specialisation and scholarship that avoids arbitrariness through objectivity and liberation from old ideas. It must act in complete freedom in conception and execution, and without any limitation beyond general human responsibility and an individual's choice over his situation and destiny.

We can measure the degree of civilisation by the size of the role played by reason and the respect given to it, and on this basis our gains and our losses can be defined. Let us present two testaments from our life:

1. The case of Palestine. We plunged excitedly headlong into it, some of us ignorant of its dimensions, others ignoring them, and until today we have not accepted the real situation. If we had accepted it at the time we would have saved countless lives, measureless property, and enough time to build a nation.
2. The case of Salman Rushdie. We dived into this emotionally, with demonstrations and fatwas, paving the way for the book to spread like wildfire, and exposing Islam through our behaviour and our speech to every critic and anyone looking to find fault. Meanwhile, all that was needed was to ignore it, to shun the ignorant, and to continue on our way, or to discuss the text with analytical critics, and then leave the book to join the hundreds of other books that have attacked Islam from the Middle Ages until today, while Islam itself has abided, and grown and stood firm.

Reason, sirs, is a sublime gift, and we can care for it in the schools and in the media, but first we must believe in it.

5 December 1991

The Other Side of the Picture

In the midst of the darkness appear shimmers that sparkle with light, and these we should take as beacons to illuminate the path that leads to deliverance and salvation. Our life is not just debts, inflation, corruption and suffering; there is also a panorama containing symbols of victory, embodying excellence and determination, and recording the names of martyred soldiers and officers of various ranks. How many are your martyrs, Egypt! And if we add to them the martyrs of the June 1967 War, the 1956 Tripartite Aggression, the North Yemen Civil War of the 1960s and the 1919 Revolution, as well as those who fought for the constitution and democracy – if we add them all together they make up a nation of the righteous that I wish could be gathered in one picture to be fixed in every heart, to help it beat and to fill it with love and the spirit of sacrifice, courage, strength and toil.

The picture makes clear that this is the time for export production, which will put us on the right road towards economic equilibrium and debt repayment. It represents unity in precision production, for the sake of deliverance and development before consumption and pleasure.

It also reveals our wise foreign policy towards the Arabs, the Africans, and the world, keeping one eye abroad with the aim of lofty human engagement, and one eye at home on the reaping of our legitimate fruits, on the strengthening of the ties we need, and on comprehensive and just accomplishment, relying on cooperation and brotherhood.

And it shows the veritable achievements in various branches of production and services, as well as the excellence of our scholars at home and abroad, filling our hearts with confidence and generously painting our future rosy with the wash of life and learning.

Let us remember the hard times in order to arouse in us the spirit of defiance and fortitude, and let us surround ourselves with accomplishments that will show us the way to the beacons of hope. And your martyrs' blood will not have flowed in vain, Egypt.

12 December 1991

The Devotees of Zionism

There lives among us a group of people who imagine themselves to be the prime opponents of global Zionism. They lie in wait for it, they expose its secrets and hidden agendas, reveal day after day its concealed forces, and bring to light its tentacles that extend east, west, north, and south, despite the tiny number of people that it represents. They do not believe in reconciliation and do not call for peace, eternally raising the slogan of struggle and battle.

Look how they view Zionism. They see it as a tribal force that with cunning and planning controls the United States, the Soviet Union and Western Europe, driving all of them along the road that will fulfil its own identity, its interests and its aims both overt and covert. They see it as the force that has shaped human history, disguised in every age behind the mask that suits it: it sparked the French Revolution and the Russian October Revolution, and was even behind the Arab Revolt, the 1919 Revolution in Egypt, and every other historical movement.

The First World War was nothing but a Zionist conspiracy, the Second World War another one. And there is no scientific, literary or artistic organisation or psychological or social theory that does not have the Zionists as its engine, its guiding force, its front and its arbiter in what must happen. So the planet is the object of its aspirations, a plaything in its hands, an enterprise among the effusions of its ideas. It may right now be looking to master the universe, its hidden forces and its eternal destinies.

This is the picture of Zionism as it is represented in the minds of its valiant opposers. They have elevated it to a status of divinity and they unwittingly worship it. If this is right, would it not be better for humanity to submit to it, and call on it to lead us and show us the way out of the shadows and into the light?

O devotees of Zionism, we do not worship what you worship, we do not wallow in delusions, we do not carve idols, we are not debased by feelings of inferiority and degradation. We wage war and we make peace and we reconcile, and we have confidence in people and in humanity and in God Almighty. We ask God to cure all the afflicted.

26 December 1991

The Right Way of Life

Life does not stop: its current always rushes on, bringing something new every day. Then the new becomes old, and the next new appears. So whoever wants to live in its rushing current must be endowed with a broad and constant consciousness, one that comprises soul, reason and will, and confirms liberty as a successful way and an exalted human objective.

By liberty we mean the freedom of thought, of imagination, of behaviour, of choice, of experience. And while we know that all this can be practised in a human society under the shade of common law, principles and customs, we also know that law, principles and customs must not lag behind the rushing current. Their vision, mode and language must be renewed and enriched, and their conduct must be interactive with the movement of life, and look forward with it to a better tomorrow. The dry, yellow leaves must fall in order for the fresh, green leaves to sprout in their place, full of the water of life.

For this to happen, we must exert ourselves in effort, arm ourselves with courage, and be enlightened in our mind and our spirit, even if this means giving up our comfort, security or life. We must rebel against fear, rise above resurgent desire, consider death a part of life and accept the indisputable seriousness of the sacred trust. Any force that stands in the way of humanity and attempts to contain our honourable yearning for knowledge, science, creativity and innovation is a force of darkness and destruction and an ally of the Devil and oblivion. And whatever group of people merits this description can stand back, or be lenient with the challenges of darkness, or else be satisfied to fall prey to the Devil's claws. We had hoped that all our energy could be brought together for construction, development and innovation, but we can take some comfort in the fact that confrontation of the agents of destruction is a kind of construction.

29 December 1991

Balance

When will we regain our balance? When will we regain our economic balance, our moral balance and our psychological balance? How and when will we exit this chain of troubles and disasters?

The medicine I suggest is to raise the salaries of government and public sector employees to the level of genuine security, so that they return to material and psychological stability and are reassured in the face of the challenges that life presents to them and their families, and are not concerned by the ogre of inflation and the uncertainties of an unknown future.

It may be that this is what the authorities would like to do, but of course they are asking themselves where sufficient funds would come from. And if they use the money for this purpose, what will be left for development, especially as this would be an expenditure without profit or return?

The problem is that it is these employees who carry out the work in all the important fields of production and services, and their administrative and psychological deficiency resulting from their low salaries is forcefully reflected in that production and those services. Not only that, it has added an unfortunate stamp of negligence, laxity and indifference to our life in general, and has perhaps contributed to the rise of serious deviations such as extremism, quite apart from the fact that it is in itself an injustice that is unacceptable to both mind and heart.

I do not believe that assuring them their full due would be simply a financial loss with no benefit. On the contrary, its results may be more important than most people think. I can cite some of these by way of example:

Firstly, it would restore financial and psychological stability to a not inconsiderable number of citizens, who, if we add their dependents, may be as many as twenty-five million.[1] And delivering happiness to this number of Egyptians would be a great achievement. The ultimate

1 The total population of Egypt at the time of writing was around sixty million.

aim of any development is no more than to ensure the contentment of the citizens and to raise their spiritual and material standards.

Secondly, with the restoration of the equilibrium of the employees, they might occupy themselves more fully with their duties in the government and the public sector, engage in their work with a new appetite and increased commitment, and deal with the public in a new manner marked by respect and cooperation. The expected result of this would be a rise in production that would be recompense for what they had been given, and a reduction in the suffering of people getting their business attended to in government offices.

Thirdly, the state would regain control over its employees, demanding its full due in return for the full due it had given to them, so administration would improve, the voice of the law would be elevated and the prestige of the state would be consolidated.

Fourthly, all this would have its beneficial consequences in a rise in moral standards, patriotism, culture, health and resistance to extremist tendencies. God be with us, in all cases.

9 January 1992

Algeria's Experience

In the first round of the Algerian elections, the Algerian state presented itself as an example and a model of democracy and integrity. The opposition won by an overwhelming majority, just a whisker away from an absolute majority, and the ruling party suffered a defeat that would usually only be allowed in an Arab country that enjoys a level of civilisation and freedom. We said this was a good thing, a promising omen for all the Arab countries looking towards liberty and human dignity. Then came a convulsive setback to strike the newborn democracy in its cradle, and joy was drowned in disappointment and dejection, as despotism returned to loom with its horns and its monstrous gaze, as though what it had already done to the country was not enough in taking it to the brink of bankruptcy and shedding the blood of so many of it citizens.

This setback has revealed a strange truth, which is that some dictators move in the direction of democracy not through any real faith in democracy, but in the hope of adding popular legitimacy to their authoritarian rule. So if democracy fails them, they bare their fangs and savage it, withdrawing the veil from their ugly face.

Democracy is nothing more than sincere dialogue, respect for the opinions of others, and acceptance of the view of the people and their free choice. Of course it is true that the defeated party will see in its opponent's victory the end of the world and the ruin of the country, and that many will put it down to the ignorance or naivety of the people. But every people – even the simplest – knows what is in its best interests. So many dictators have set themselves up as the custodians of their people, when it turned out that it was they who were in need of custody – we have probably not yet forgotten Hitler, Mussolini and the emperor of Japan, though we do not remember their mistaken popular support. But supposing the Algerian people have made an error – why don't we just leave them to bear the responsibility of it and allow them the opportunity to correct it?

If this latest electoral experience had been a success we would have found something of an excuse for anyone who wanted to return to it or to its like, but it was a failed, corrupt experience that denied human rights and dignity.

If Algeria is fated to be ruled by a new dictator, he may find many justifications for his policies, but he will never be able to claim that he rules in the name of the people, who gave their answer loud and clear.

16 January 1992

The Importance of Peace

The peace conference is an open opportunity to change the face of life in our Arab East, as it promises a solution to the problems that have been almost stricken by time, and prepares the ground for rapid development towards a better life for all.

The two sides – Arab and Israeli – attended it on an unfavourable and far from perfect basis. Israel appears grumpy, as though it were being driven grudgingly to peace. It has let its strength fall over its eyes like a curtain, and sees nothing but what is in its hands, not looking into the distance. And the Arabs may have a single language but they have scattered hearts, and have not yet cleansed themselves of the tragedy of the Gulf War. Some of them still live in the depths of the past, in denial of the passage of time. The truth that should not be in any doubt is that peace is a boon in the interests of both parties. I do not think that Israel is unaware of this truth, and I even imagine sometimes that it manufactures its aversion to it in order to hide its strong desire for it.

As for the Arab side, I don't think they need anyone to remind them that any negotiations look for a middle solution, that there has to be flexibility around the defence of their legitimate rights, and that the future may hold possibilities that are withheld by the present. You should keep in mind that those with the will may achieve in peace what any war fails to bring about, and do not forget in this respect the two examples of Germany and Japan.

The Arabs as a whole need peace no less than the frontline states do. The excuse used by every despot or straggler in the region must be abandoned: we want an Arab East with no pending issue to consume its wealth, wipe out the souls of its progeny and throw up excuse after excuse to avoid peace. We want an Arab East where the sound of battle does not drown out the voices of its children calling for human rights in governance, in scholarship and in culture, as we call for a standard of living that deserves the name.

In the wake of peace there will be no battles but the battle between tyranny and freedom, between underdevelopment and civilisation.

Following peace, the epic of the new Arab heroes will begin.

23 January 1992

The Lifeboat

There is talk here and there about a downturn that is threatening the global economy in general and the American economy in particular. This has led to voices being raised in the United States, calling for the American president to turn his attention from international to domestic affairs and confront the economic crisis, especially as he is entering an election year. Now this president is embarking on a trip to Asia and Australia to open new markets for American trade.

This crisis and the results that may follow have shaken our hopes for the world and for Egypt, because we are watching the birth of the new world with close attention, praying that it fulfills all it has promised humankind in the way of respect for justice and human rights. And in spite of all who mock these promises, we have avoided rushing into doubt and misgivings. We prefer to resort to optimism, holding on to it until we are convinced of the contrary, and not before. Until today we have seen nothing in American politics to cause us to change our minds, and the close alignment of interests and principles in it has boded well.

But today we fear that the economic crisis will inflict a setback on that promise, which could take the world back to the fever of competition, threats, and wars cold and hot.

As for Egypt, I am reminded of the wise saying: 'Nothing lasts forever.' We are a country that enjoys considerable American aid, and beyond that we depend for our life on grants, loans, and sovereign resources such as oil and the Suez Canal. I say we must be more cautious about the future. Any economic tremor could lead to a loss of aid and close the door on loans. Even sovereign resources are not secure: oil reserves are finite, and we have not yet forgotten what happened to Canal revenues and to tourism during the Gulf War. The one foundation that we must trust in and rely on is work, which means production, proficiency and innovation. We cannot be certain of current concessions, and it is always useful to remind ourselves that they are temporary. The target we should be aiming for is to depend on ourselves, and the revolution that this demands in education, training and civic instruction. Our true hope resides in our human capabilities and self-reliance.

I hope we do not fall into a false sense of security, and that we prepare for the future before it happens.

30 January 1992

The Right and the Left

'The Right' is applied to groups that preserve whatever in society relies for its strength on past customs or outdated revolutions in the fields of politics, thought, the arts and different ways of life.

'The Left', meanwhile, applies to groups that strive for progress and follow the flow of history to what is new, which is their dream.

There have been radical shifts on the world stage over recent years that have turned things upside down, which has led to a process of replacement and exchange among the original alignments as people have known them, necessitating a definitive change in names and labels.

For after the seismic events that have destroyed the world of both the Left and the totalitarian regimes, after the almost general trend towards political and economic democracy and individual liberty, after the new direction taken by the course of history – after all this, reality demands that we take a fresh look at what we consider to be the Left and the Right in politics.

The course of history has taken a new direction towards a tomorrow that promises democracy, liberty and respect for human rights, including the right to social justice.

Likewise, totalitarian and Communist rule have become outdated revolutions: the experiment has proved a failure, and its rosy dream has become a nightmare.

On this basis, it is right that we apply the label of 'the Left' to the democrats, the social democrats, the Islamists, and the moderates, as we may apply the label of 'the Right' to the former Communists, the Nasserists, and the extremist groups.

It is not a matter of playing with names and labels: it is more a case of correcting the vision and adhering faithfully to reality, knowing that we do not mean it as propaganda for one side or a dismissal of the other, because we respect everyone's opinion and see that society cannot do without both Right and Left on its path to the tomorrow that we hope for.

1 February 1992

The Road of Justice

We reject and condemn terrorism. We do not excuse it for any reason at all. This is our position on it, whatever its source, whether political or religious groups, or Arab or non-Arab states. It warrants the expulsion of whoever is shown to be guilty of it from the human community, and this person deserves whatever just punishment the world deems appropriate for the loss of the innocent lives of women, children and men.

We have all heard the news of the accusation that the United States has directed at Libya, and the demand that it hand over two Libyan citizens to be tried for the downing of an American plane and its innocent passengers over Scotland.

The United States has the right to accuse any person or organisation if there is sufficient evidence or suspicion to support the accusation. But the demand for the accused to be handed over to them for trial is something we have never heard of before. Every state has laws that prescribe the ways that its citizens may be prosecuted if they are accused of something, but there is nothing among these laws that allows them to be handed over to a foreign state to be tried there.

This is why we were astonished by the US demand, and we were more astonished by its insistence on its demand, and more astonished still by the Security Council resolution on the matter. It even came to our minds that there might be details that are missing from the news reports.

Against all this, we find the position of Libya extremely clear, and its desire to find a solution to the problem far from provocative, and within the frame of international legitimacy and justice. It has not objected to a trial, or to the surrender of the accused, so long as these take place under the protection of neutral investigators and judges, so that the opposing party is not the arbitrator.

This is a very flexible response, which reveals a genuine desire to learn the truth and to bear responsibility, and which is perhaps also not without a degree of self-assurance and a sense of innocence.

Up until the time of writing these lines, we do not know how the situation will be resolved. All we ask is that the voice of reason and justice prevail, and that the solution reached in the end matches the heralded expectations of a truly new world, so that we do not lose both justice and hope.

6 February 1992

How to Preserve Our Identity

Someone asked me: 'How are we to preserve our identity?' It is a timely question, for several reasons, including the ongoing debate in our country about heritage and modernity, and the direction the world is moving in towards connectivity by various methods that have rendered time and borders ineffectual, making the individual a feather blown about in the winds of opinions, beliefs and cultures.

When we are born our identities come into existence with us, and they continue to develop through family, school, society and culture. If we imagined it possible to erect a dam between us and the world, we would retain this identity with peace of mind. Time would run on and leave us behind as a relic, with an identity that has a little that is useful in every age, and much that is outdated.

Because of this, the real question is not: 'How are we to preserve our identity?' It is: 'How do we enrich our identity with the wonders of the age, without losing what is good in our original identity for every age? And how do we embody that in our self, in such a way that the marriage of the two can produce a unified whole, without contradiction or confusion, so that we can truly call it our new identity?' There is nothing wrong with having a new identity in this way, indeed there is nothing wrong with having a new identity to suit every age. The only wrong thing is to lag behind the age and become one of the memories of history, with no place in it but its museums.

The way forward is to make thought an obligation, and idleness a sin. For it is idle to continue in a habit or custom or idea whose time has come to be developed or changed. And it is idle to keep your thoughts, your choice or your criticism to yourself when you come across opinions, views or behaviours in which you may find the best of goodness, the most of progress. Real civilisation is nothing but understanding, acceptance, choice and generosity. And this comes with constant motion, outstanding courage and universal human exchange. And all woe to him who stops moving.

11 February 1992

Thieves and Thieves

One news item that I have read in our papers says that 90 per cent of Third World loans go back to the rich countries to be deposited in the secret accounts of prominent figures who have control over the wretched, indebted, poor countries. I may have seen this repeated more than once, in more than one newspaper or magazine – and at wide intervals – and attributed to sources that like to talk about such matters. It is so strange that it makes the head spin, shocks people and arouses outrage and sadness. As if these countries had not had enough with what colonialism did to them, and the poverty and underdevelopment that have beset them. They now suffer because of a small band of their own who, without morals or conscience, pounce mercilessly and exploit them in the worst way, then leave them as they were, poor and underdeveloped, not to mention the bonds of debt and its humiliation.

How did these scoundrels gain power in their countries? Did they cheat their people, who had a confidence in them they did not deserve? Did they impose themselves through force and terror? And how did their hearts become empty of any patriotic or humanistic feeling, hardening and turning to stone, as they allied with misfortune against their miserable countries?

Then on 20 January *Al-Ahram* reported that two British thieves returned food and clothing they had stolen from a warehouse in Yorkshire once they knew it was destined to be sent to orphans in Romania. Police sources noted that the two thieves also donated £10 and apologised for their dishonourable act.

This is also strange news when compared to the first piece, striking us with unbridled astonishment.

Certainly all are thieves, but what a difference between one variety and the other! One kind has lost all human feeling in their conscience and filled their heart to overflowing with selfishness and depravity in spite of their position of authority and responsibility. In the other case, the loss of their conscience has not prevented them from displaying a degree of mercy and decency, and a sense of obligation to humanity.

So although time has begrudged some Third World countries honest rulers, may it not begrudge them thieves of the same clay as these two thieves from Britain.

And finally let us remember the benefit of democracy in the choice, oversight and dismissal of rulers. Let us remember too that the tragedies of plundering and looting all happened in times full of despotism and darkness.

13 February 1992

Talking about Disasters

We must not forget our disasters: the flood, the fire, the ship that sank. We must not forget them, not for the sake of holding onto sadness and more tears but in order to know the full truth.

So much talk, so many stories, all of them at the time accepted and welcomed, either as a response from people shaken to their core by disaster, their hearts bursting with grief and distress, or as a manifestation of political resentment and a dismissive attitude towards the ruling regime. But we want to know the whole truth, and all the disasters must be referred to investigation. We must beware of the tears drying, the bad memories vanishing and the investigations disappearing into the corners of history. We want to study the results of the investigations in all their details. We want to know the role of destiny and fate in what happened, and at the same time to determine human responsibility, if there is any. We have no wish at all to treat anyone, great or small, unfairly – but we also do not wish to be unfair to ourselves by squandering people's rights to life, justice and dignity. This should all be followed by a just accounting, or by the reform of regulations and procedures.

Souls should not be calmed and hearts should not be eased until the results of the investigations are announced publicly, responsibilities are determined, and justice is served. Forgetting about these disasters before that point would be a disaster as big as any of the original ones, while taking the matter to its just conclusion will have beneficial lessons, perhaps reducing our pains and permitting us to quote the proverb: 'Every cloud has a silver lining.' The prime minister's announcement before the People's Assembly raised our hopes of learning the truth, of a fair investigation and of reform.

After this, and not before, it may be possible to forget the disasters in the course of our life, which is so full of accidents. Indeed, we must forget them and not allow pessimism to throw its heavy shadow across our souls. Life brings many disasters like those we have suffered, or even immeasurably worse. We must reconcile ourselves to facing every adversity, without despairing of reforming ourselves and our situation, and rectifying all negative aspects on land and sea, and in our will. Calamities destroy only weak defeatists. But they strengthen the ardour of the able and of those who appreciate the blessed grace of life.

20 February 1992

A Sacred Struggle

There are two fronts that are destined to be in constant conflict, and there can be no hope of compromise between them, nor would there be any benefit in compromise were it possible. They are tradition and law on the one hand, and liberty on the other.

The spirit of conservatism is the symbol of existing tradition and law. In the heat of debate it is labelled reactionism, and it is supported by people who display a boundless fidelity to society as it currently stands, safeguarding its stability and permanence, and holding sacred the traditions and laws that protect it. These people are agitated by any movement at all in thought or behaviour, seeing this as a summons to depart from stability and permanence, or a warning of change, and they wage war on it with force and without mercy, for they are the enemies of change – and their opponents consider them the enemies of progress and captives of the outdated past. But at the same time they are an indispensable necessity, a side in the struggle that performs an important role in discipline, in the checking of anything new, and in preserving us from impulsiveness and error.

On the other side stands liberty, supported by those who look forward to a better tomorrow, and who dream of a more beautiful utopia and a deeper humanity. They see a tradition that is outdated, or a law that has turned old and bitter, and leap to declare war on it, calling for development and revolution, plunging into a fierce battle with the forces of conservatism, and exposing themselves to infinite hardships, with the battle perhaps even ending in the sacrifice of life itself.

And through the struggle of these two forces, society moves forward and changes, and new horizons open up before it for heart, mind and will. It is an eternal struggle and a continuing battle to which we wish no end, agreement or peace. History and the present witness their martyrs, both individually and communally, and society takes refuge in silence and patience, as the assertion of the message of life and civilisation is more important to it than safety and security. It disdains nothing but sloth, inertia and cowardice, and knows that it is this sacred struggle that has led humanity from the cave to the conquest of space. Let the conservatives do their duty, and may liberty live forever.

27 February 1992

Smog in the Cultural Air

As the air we breathe is thick with pollution, so the air of civilisation and culture has become overlain with superstition and chauvinism, and a fear of freedom, adventure and openness to the world. The voice of reason no longer has any weight, creativity has lost its fascination and magic, and differences of opinion and new ideas are no longer embraced. We move from one suffocation to the next, and are nearly paralysed or dying. The sincere efforts exerted by generation after generation to build the individual and society are almost vanishing.

When I look back at my boyhood and youth, I see a time shining with freedom and civilisational and cultural openness. For despite the political atmosphere swinging between democracy and dictatorship, between progressivism and reactionism, between rule of the people and rule of the king, cultural and civilisational openness were held back by nothing. There may have been a reactionary government, but public opinion was with progress and liberty, and it swept away any reactionary views or demands. The loudest voices were those of Taha Hussein, Abbas al-Aqqad, Salama Musa, Ibrahim al-Mazini, Mohamed Husayn Heikal, 'Ali 'Abd al-Razeq, and Mustafa 'Abd al-Razeq, and calls were strong for the liberation of women, for national capitalism, for the people's rule, for science, for industry, for modernity and for the eternal values of our heritage. It was an age of the battle of ideas between traditional and modern poetry, between traditional and modern prose, between contradictory ruling regimes, between atheism and faith, between extremism and freedom. But the battles did not depart from the realm of thought and dialogue – a dialogue took place between the thinkers and their followers among the younger generation, with no place in it for police or terrorism. What has happened today?

The strange thing is that today we enjoy freedom in the political realm that is unprecedented in its strength and continuity, with no watchdog on the side of the government, no censorship and no interference in thought or culture. But after the fount of tolerance between people and certain agencies dried up, they prefer to appeal to brute force rather than to reason and dialogue, while the real appeal in the realm of thought should only be to thought itself. Nothing is gained from violence but the terrorising of thinkers and the obstruction of creative forces, besides the unjust abuse of religion and its reputation on the global level.

Religion has nothing to fear from liberty, and the opposite may be true. Everything that is possible to be said has been said already, and every tendentious or malicious utterance has been carried off in the wind, while religion remains firmly established in people's souls and grows daily stronger and more deeply rooted. Religion has nothing to fear, and we are not lacking in faith, but we do lack the courage to confront life.

5 March 1992

Religious and Secular Debates

There have been successive debates between the supporters of an Islamic state and the supporters of a secular state, and we have welcomed this since it matches the democratic spirit, which prefers dialogue over extremism and terrorism. At the same time, we have found that each group, in its desire for victory over the other, has not limited itself to expounding the advantages of its political vision but has also targeted the weak points of the vision of the other side. So no debate has been free of attacks on modern civilisation or of denouncements of some historic Islamic positions. We feared that the repeated emphasis on the Islamic message would push towards a complete distrust of modern civilisation, and that the secular state supporters would push towards a similar position with regard to Islam itself.

In both groups we see similar characteristics, which should be noted: they both believe in dialogue and reason, they both condemn extremist thought and terrorism, and neither of them can completely reject modern civilisation or disregard Islamic belief. For this reason it has been my hope that the two sides would stop arguing and come together in a broad assembly for a calm, objective discussion in search of points of agreement, in order to work on proposing a constitution that would combine the fixed principles of Islam with modern civilisation. And better still if they could be joined by a selection of our Coptic brethren, since the constitution would apply to all. They will find sources of enlightenment, such as (by way of modest but not exhaustive example) the constitutional proposal presented by Dr Muhammad Hilmi Murad, the dissertation of Dr Kamal Abul-Magd and the book by Professor Hamed Sulayman, *Science in the Path to Islamic Awakening.*

In fact, the differences between the two groups are not as great as many imagine. There is distrust on both sides without any real basis. If the Islamists presented a detailed programme, most of the disagreements would meet in the middle, if not disappear altogether, and if they dropped their accusations about the beliefs of others, the air would be cleared and would be ready for fruitful mutual understanding.

I am well aware that the secularists are calling for the separation of the state from theocratic rule, but nobody can separate the state from the religion itself, unless they want it to be a state without values or morals.

Even if we imagined the establishment of a purely secular rule, any personal-status laws it would pass would certainly be influenced by the spirit of Islam, given that the lawmakers themselves have been born and raised in the embrace of an Islamic culture whose fixed values, as espoused by the people, cannot be challenged.

This is why I hope that the two sides can meet to exchange ideas and work together, away from feelings of enmity and distrust, to pursue an agreement that could save the Islamic awakening from its difficulties.

12 March 1992

Towards a Better System

We have seen in our modern life a strange indifference to the laws of the land, frequently reaching the stage of ignoring them, which spreads chaos and shakes the prestige of the state to its roots. Some laws are openly not applied, and nobody is concerned about their application, and this touches everyone with eyes to see or ears to hear. The laws were made in the first place to regulate relations, control procedures, and establish order and moral behaviour. It has become the custom at the enactment of any new law that it appears above the horizon on a great wave of enthusiasm, appropriate to the circumstances that led to its promulgation, and people reluctantly follow it, in their certainty that it is a passing wave that will soon calm, ebb, and then vanish, for everything to return to how it was before. With the passing days we forget the drama, and the malady once again becomes obtrusive, complaints are heard, and some group or other proposes a law to deal with it, not knowing that the ordinance already exists, but that it has drowned under sleep and negligence.

How are we to breathe life into our laws? And how can we make them last?

Perhaps it is necessary to establish a special agency for the oversight of the implementation of laws (which would not cause us any new burdens, as there are so many underemployed government employees), and branch agencies could be set up on similar lines in the governorates. Their mission would be to oversee the implementation of the laws that are in any case made to serve the population and to reduce their hardships, like the laws on traffic, cleanliness, pollution, food supply and noise, and they would have the authority to put responsible bodies on notice or to raise the matter up to whoever has the power to deal with it.

It is true that the essential guarantee of respect for the law comes from the individual, and though this is not lost automatically as an instinctual action, it needs continual nurturing and public example, and it needs to be addressed at home and in schools. But in order for this to happen, and for it to become our everyday custom, there must be vigilant scrutiny and alert determination, in defence of the dignity of the people and the prestige of the state.

19 March 1992

Violence

Violence has almost become a feature of our life. Yes, no age or society is free of violence, but before now it was not a repeated occurrence day and night. Reports of violence never cease: we hear of it in politics, with stories of bloody assassinations; in families, with children killing parents or parents killing children; in the streets, with bloody fights for reasons justifiable or not, the kidnapping of wives, assaults on women, and armed robbery; and on public transport, where murder is committed openly among the crowds. And of course we may note what takes place in schools between students and their educators, and what happens between married couples.

In fact, violence is no longer exceptional, it is a phenomenon, and indeed it has almost reached the stage that news of it passes without notable excitement, as if it were a regular fixture of daily life. The earthquake was nothing more than the earth and its forces joining in the chain of violence and its battles.[1] When we try to find an explanation for it, we must take into account the negative aspects that so fill our life to overflowing, such as the violence authorities use in their dealings, the economic crisis, the poor services, the unemployment, the dead ends facing our youth and the lack of respect for human rights. Certainly, these factors cannot but have their effect in the creation of the phenomenon of violence. But beyond that, violence shows up in countries that are an example of democracy, respect for human rights, and economic and civilisational balance, which makes violence a global phenomenon, and its explanation becomes more difficult and mysterious.

But it appears that facts are relative, and that the way we look at the advanced societies differs from how they look at themselves. There are negative aspects there too, even if we do not see them that way. There

1 The reference to 'the earthquake' appears to date this article to after the 5.9-magnitude quake of 12 October 1992, which claimed more than five hundred lives in Cairo and left thousands homeless. It is possible that an error was made in dating the piece when it was collated in the published Arabic collection.

are statistics that talk of more than thirty million people living below the poverty line in the United States, the richest country in the world, and millions who suffer from nervous disorders and anxiety, or who are victims of drugs. Add to this that among people in the advanced nations, the sense of what is missing in life is stronger than in ours, so their objection against it is likewise stronger than ours.

In short, our negatives serve as an explanation of the violence in our lives, and our first aim in life must be their extirpation, an aim that is an obligation anyway, regardless of their relation to violence. Violence may even be one of the motivations of revival, as a reaction and as a permanent caution and incitement to reform.

19 March 1992

We Share Your Sorrows

When the incident of al-'Ataba al-Khadra happened, it was much written about and talked about, so those who did not know before could learn something new about what goes on in our society.[1] It was not a rape, which we come across so much in our newspapers these days, but an indecent assault, of the kind that takes place every day in crowded places and on jam-packed buses and that nobody knows about except those who witness it and lower their eyes in great distress and bitterness. The 'Ataba incident became known only because of certain unexpected additional circumstances: the girl's fall to the ground and her screaming, the initiative of the policeman in helping her by opening fire, and the arrest of two of the suspects. This showed that security was not absent, and the fact that members of the public assisted in the arrest of the two suspects showed that the public were not lacking in a positive response. And not to forget the local woman who took off her outer garment to cover the girl, as she lay nearly naked on the ground.

Had it not been for these circumstances, the assault would have passed without anybody knowing about it, as happens so frequently on the buses and in crowded stations, where there are frustrated young men who are sick enough to rub against or sexually assault women by any means and in any manner. It is a problem that may have its roots in other political, economic and social problems, and if we concentrate on this latest manifestation it appears as a crisis of youth, who totter between unemployment (barefaced or veiled) and salaries that fail to allow self-fulfilment in a meaningful life – so there they go, wandering aimlessly in crowded places to satisfy their impulses by illicit means that can lead them to prison or the gallows.

Eradicating this problem will come about only through comprehensive reform and the success of comprehensive development, which will be achieved only in the long term.

---

1 The sexual assault of a young woman among the crowds of al-'Ataba al-Khadra, one of Cairo's busiest squares, caused great consternation and subsequent public discussion and soul-searching.

But there are things that can be done quickly in the short term, such as putting crowded places under constant security surveillance, designating areas for women on buses, strengthening penalties (not as a fulfilment of justice, but as a deterrent), and calling on men of religion, psychologists and sociologists to find appropriate solutions to the sexual frustration of our youth, whose adverse circumstances have condemned them to postpone marriage until their middle age.

In closing, I offer my commiserations to all – for all are the victims of cruel times and conditions.

9 April 1992

Western Civilisation

There are many who distrust western civilisation, a distrust based on reasons that they advertise at every opportunity. In their view it is a foreign civilisation, one that in its dealings with us has not abstained from the sins of war, colonialism, the plundering of resources and the taking of lives. In addition, many of its customs and traditions contradict our fixed values. I wish to discuss this view impartially and objectively.

I will start by saying that western civilisation is not a foreign civilisation. Yes, it was established in strange places among a population of strangers, but historically and realistically it is before all else a human civilisation – human in foundation and humanistic in aim. It is the latest fruiting on the tree of the civilisations that have gone before it, such as the Egyptian, the Assyrian, the Babylonian, the Persian, the Greek, the Roman and the Islamic, from all of which it has benefited, as an incorporation of all the preceding nations that have contributed to it. I do not deny that there are local elements in every civilisation linked to its environment, which may be reviled or rejected by the rest of humankind, but apart from that its aim is humanistic, a project directed at all minds and hearts. The most important example of this is science and its applications, along with a considerable amount of thought, art, politics and social relations. All these are available to humankind for study and acquisition, and to go beyond that in absorption, exchange and innovation – while maintaining our fixed values and rejecting whatever does not blend with them.

It is true that the dark history that the people of this civilisation recorded with us cannot be denied: how much blood they shed, how much they restricted our growth, how much wealth they plundered and how much dignity they degraded; but we must cleanse the past of its wrongs, for we struggled against the oppressors until we freed ourselves of their grip. Thanks to their sciences we established our life on new foundations, and thanks to their medical achievements, millions of lives were saved that were being wiped out by disease every year. And let us remember how we have benefited from their experiments in our agriculture and our industry, in systems of government and in social intercourse. Remembering this may help us in opening a new page with their civilisation and eliminating our distrust of it.

It is time for us to accept reconciliation for the sake of a life befitting this age. Our need for modern civilisation is no less than our need to adhere to our traditional, eternal values.

16 April 1992

The Arab Road

I hope that the Arabs will find the time as soon as possible to choose their destiny in life and the modern vision that this means in thought and work. They need to live their present as befits a people with a glorious past, a people determined that its future will be equal to its past in pride and progress. To do this, we must first succeed in moving beyond our current concerns, after they have been dealt with in a way that assures our attention to the more important issues, those that are crucial for the future. This must happen fast, and to a degree that it will be taken seriously by a populace that loses sleep over the matter of brotherhood, and that is concerned about progress and civilisation. The Libyan problem must not be allowed to drag on or become more complicated, nor must there be any delay in the timing of the resumption of Iraq's reconstruction, and nor should the border problems remain suspended and fractious. Some may count the solution of these problems as a major aim and – if completed – a serious achievement, while in my view it is no more than a matter of cleansing the Arab air of impurities, in preparation for the planned cooperative creation of a comprehensive renaissance. But what are the dimensions of this comprehensive renaissance?

There is a cultural dimension, which must begin with effecting a revolution in the education system, the aim of which would be the creation of citizens who can connect their eternal values with a contemporary attitude to learning and its applications, and a readiness to work in modern life with all its requirements, along with a liberal training of minds that celebrates authenticity, liberation, independence and creativity.

And there is an economic dimension, which is to achieve the integration of the Arab countries from the Atlantic to the Gulf, with the aims of implementing an agricultural revolution and creating an industrial base, of coexistence with the modern age in spirit and practice, and of working with the world as a great nation, capable of giving in exchange for what it takes, and which is indispensable as a productive member of the human family.

Through these two dimensions a kind of political union will be shaped that will suit the Arab countries, far from any sensitivities, claims of leadership, or arousal of division or competition.

Any day that passes without realising a part of this dream must be counted as a day lost in the life of the Arabs.

30 April 1992

Protection

When I was a boy I watched our revolutionary Egyptian people calling for the fall of the British Protectorate, and today I see them in urgent need of national protection. Yes, we have a strong apparatus for the protection of general security, an army capable of protecting our independence, and agencies for fiscal accounting and administrative oversight, but the ordinary citizen proceeds with his hands up and with no support in the streets, on public transport, and in bureaucratic offices – he passes miserable and helpless before the complexities of government departments and their masterful public servants, through a deluge of noise, dirt, aggression, greed, injustice and bigotry.

Good behaviour and kind manners settle in the consciousness of a nation only as the fruit of a long education that accompanies the individual from his earliest beginnings, a fruit that home, school and the media help to anchor. We have this in part, but it is not enough, and far less than is required by our deep-rooted history and the role we aspire to. So we must wait a long time before politeness, conscience and duty become the vocabulary of our sacred life. However, the time of waiting must not be allowed to pass in surrender, pain and dwelling on our sorrows. We have no choice but to seek aid in laws, vigilant scrutiny and preventative penalties. An ombudsman's office should be established and given effective powers, every 'sleeping' law must be woken up, every negligent or idle employee must be motivated, and anyone who infringes on people's rights must be punished.

I have been following the progress of the president around the production centres and new cities, and read his addresses to those in authority about the completion of deficient aspects that he noticed himself or that were drawn to his attention. I wish every visit could be followed by a holding to account of the idle, the careless and the negligent. If this happened, the beneficial effect of a single visit would be extended to cover all places of work, and it would reduce the suffering of the miserable Egyptian people. We really are in need of national protection.

7 May 1992

Playing with Fire

Nuclear weapons stand at the front of the dangers that threaten humanity, along with pollution and the hole in the ozone layer, in addition to their enormous cost, which is being invested in evil and which is consequently not being spent on development in the various countries of the world. For these reasons, the agreement that was reached between the two largest nations to destroy some of these weapons made humankind happy, as we are happy too at the constructive proposals we sometimes hear of in that area aimed at the curtailment of their production or their further reduction. This followed the creation of a good atmosphere for understanding and cooperation between the giant nations. We hope this will be an example to be imitated by all nations in facing their problems and finding just solutions to them.

But what spoils these good hopes, and perhaps threatens their defeat, is the news that small nations are now rushing to acquire or produce nuclear weapons. I mention this in relation to what we have learned about the cooperation between South Africa and Israel in this field, and the race that this will inevitably lead to among countries threatened by them, to possess or produce such weapons or their equivalent in power or destructive capacity.

The acquisition by any small country of this type of weapon – at a time when the hearts of the large nations are beating with their riddance – means upsetting the international balance, disturbing human security and genuinely threatening boundless destruction in a particular area of the planet. The Security Council must look at any endeavour of this kind as a threat to the security and balance of the world, and it must put decisive restrictions in place for the defence of humankind. No nation will be able to step outside the general interests of humanity if it is faced with severe international penalties, like a total economic, social and cultural embargo.

This danger is more frightening than the danger of terrorism or drugs, more urgent than the danger of pollution, and only those who are involved in it in some way could imagine leaving it as it is, or tolerating it. It is a test, and what a test it is: either we adhere to the common cause of humanity, or it is a race to Hell.

14 May 1992

A New Birth in the Embrace of Democracy

The State Council's Parties Court has confirmed the foundation of the Arab Democratic Nasserist Party. The official opinion of the court reported that the party prefaced its programmes with the primary aim of establishing a unified Arab state, that this would come about only by democratic means, and that it rejected violence and armed struggle.

Believers in democracy and those who look forward to the completion of its dimensions and the implementation of anything resembling it are happy at the foundation of any new party, but they may have more than one reason to welcome this new party in particular, for without doubt it broadens the democratic base and the spectrum of parties. And it is a real party, in the sense that it has entered political life not just with a collection of theoretical principles, but with a popular base that, while perhaps not as large as the Nasserists imagine, is not at the vanishing point that their opponents believe. In fact, we come across ardent young Nasserists here and there, in spite of what may be said. In addition, the new party has corrected an imbalance in party life, since it was not logical for all trends to be represented by parties except for the one group that took its name from the leading figure of the Revolution, and that rose out of his victories and defeats and his positive and negative sides, more than the political visions that came after him.

The party's announced programme is based on laudable generosity and development, and its reliance on democracy is a victory for the party and for democracy itself, and a sign of its engagement with the modern age. The same can be said for its condemnation of violence and armed struggle.

We truly welcome the new party, and we hope it will contribute through legitimate party activity to the extension of a political awakening and the spread of a positive spirit that will drive the country forward in its legitimate political fight, and to cooperation in the solution to its problems.

28 May 1992

The Hoped-For Change

Life is change, it is diffusion and growth, and transition from one state to another. Its opposite is death, which is absolute inertia. Moreover, change is not a matter of a passion for new faces: merely changing faces, or some of them, may be distinctly detrimental, a dodging of serious intent, effort and sound practice. But life worthy of the name demands constant change in vision, goal and methods, as it also requires flexibility in performance, adaptation and experimentation. In other words, we should not be seeking just a cabinet reshuffle, since what matters to us is a change of life.

We are now yearning for the fruit of economic reform to reach the ordinary, downtrodden citizen, the residents of the shanty towns, to restore our society's health and well-being and its historic smile.

Many people think, as do we, that the wait for political reform has been too long, hemmed in as it is on all sides by reservations, and that our kind-hearted, deep-rooted Egypt deserves a new constitution, new rights and popular governance that is truly worthy of it.

We are in dire need of a leap forward in production, in order to eliminate unemployment and infuse hope in the life of our youth.

We also need to redouble the attention given to rounding up corruption and the corrupt, and putting the law back on its throne.

We are eager for a more mature politics, which can adopt a comprehensive view to deal with terrorism and bring the strays back to the fold of reason and the true religion.

We certainly look forward to change – but a change of life, not a change of faces.

2 June 1992

A Valuable Youth Experiment

The American University in Cairo has devoted itself to setting up a small-scale model of the United Nations, in which students from universities in a number of countries take part with the aim of kindling their interest in global issues, and providing the opportunity to study them and suggest solutions for them.

This prompted me to give more thought to the activities of the great youth collective that comes under the Higher Council for Youth. It is truly a pleasure to note that through planned policy, our young people have access to training that will build a base for them combining an enlightened mind with a healthy body. In addition to that, we hope they will benefit from the intelligent methods devised by the American University to open a new field for training in national and humanistic vision.

I imagine the experiment could begin with a youth conference, representing the young people of the country, being given one or more domestic issues and one or more global issues, such as unemployment, drugs, racism, terrorism – along with some help, like inviting specialists to give public lectures, organising dedicated symposia, or recommending important resources – and being asked to express their opinions in the end, and share them in a public discussion under the supervision of experts in the various topics.

I perhaps do not need to note the benefits that youth could reap from this experience, but I could mention by way of example:

1. The stimulation of their interest in domestic and global issues in the different media.
2. The emotional and intellectual attachment to the country and the world, bringing them out of their apathy and negativism.
3. The formation of an emotional kernel of national and global loyalty, and the training that comes with that towards the creation of good citizens and citizens of the world.

In addition, there would be the not inconsiderable degree of growth among the youth of social, political and artistic culture, their habituation to independent thinking, and their provision with the skills of debate.

4 June 1992

The Coming Citizen

How do we picture the ordinary citizen, as he ought to be? How do we envision him, without drowning in idealism or being overly indulgent? How do we see him as an ordinary citizen to be reiterated in the millions of young people of the nation?

His formation may – or should – begin in the family, but I will disregard this stage, in which fortune and coincidence play the greatest role, and move ahead to begin with formal education and with one of its most critical stages, which is early schooling.

This is the stage in which the young citizen acquires his first new knowledge. This is important, and one of the foundations of his intellectual formation, but social training at this stage is just as important as factual instruction. This is where the elements of the young citizen's character are shaped by the correct principles of religion and national ideals, and where he gains artistic taste and a love of culture and discovers hidden talents. This is when he experiences higher examples and great models, when he becomes acquainted with the greatest men and women of his history and his time. Thus is completed the building of all his religious, political, moral, artistic and intellectual dimensions, and his life acquires meaning, purpose and examples, accompanied by the greatest thoughts and the noblest emotions.

Educators understand very well what I am talking about, and certainly know that in the past our schools facilitated this for our children to a laudable degree, and that they can now repeat the experiment in a better way, benefitting from earlier experience in the field.

And in order that the process of formation and building in early schooling does not stop, and continues throughout life and grows with time, the broadcast media – radio and television – must reinforce it, in tune with it and in full cultural unity.

We want a nation of citizens healthy in body, mind, taste, morals and beliefs, so that we can have a civilisation that is blessed with these fine human qualities.

8 June 1992

Economic Reform

They talk to us about economic reform with numbers and indicators. But they use a special language understood by the experts and specialists and a handful of intellectuals. Meanwhile, those who are crushed by the crisis neither understand this language nor believe it, and they will never acknowledge reform unless the pressure of life is relieved and their paths run more smoothly.

The experts speak of exchange rate stability and growth rate, of improvement in the balance of trade, and of a rise in private-sector investments, and they promise the introduction of laws concerning banks and deposits, and the development of the financial market.

These are real reforms, but they are put across in an exclusive language, which may address a particular class of citizens, but the ordinary man makes no sense of it and may pay a quarter of his attention to it, unaware of anything but his own crisis in the face of the ghoul of rising prices. In other words, reform deals with the constituent factors of economic life, but it does not reach the people in order to yield its desired conclusive results, and for its effect to be clear on prices and salaries, on increased production, and in the fight against corruption. Without that, the people do not acknowledge or believe in reform. And without it, they will not be able to find the solution to their worries and their problems, regain their balance and the kindness, politeness and integrity for which they are known, or steer clear of extremism and terrorism. Between the reform of economic factors and its desired results the road is not short, and the waiting time is critical. It is a difficult situation that needs every citizen to have their say, if they are able, to alleviate the suffering of the crushed, defend their interests, and counter the negative aspects that impede the course of their lives, while deflecting from them any escalation, aggravation or provocation. It is a situation that requires us to employ constructive criticism, to be objective and sincere, and to rise above personal rancour to become defenders of our national work and our human solidarity in its most sublime sense.

11 June 1992

To the Scholars

It is not right for mediation to cease, and even if one side rejects it for reasons to do with its general responsibility, the other side must persist with it. The march towards good does not brook suspension or postponement, and does not need anyone's permission. It is the duty of the learned towards their religion and their world, and they are urged to the path of good only by the grievous concerns of the righteous people of this nation – concerns like bloodshed, the destruction of property or the convulsion of stability. There is no excuse for anyone who stands back from doing good when he is able, for underhand reasons or through sinking too far into a feud of unforeseen consequences.

The board of scholars that brings together the cream of those who stand for true Islam bears a great responsibility in the circumstances we are experiencing. These are the people best qualified to address the other party, the furthest from suspicion and distrust, and the most knowledgeable about the essence of the disagreements – both reasonable and unreasonable – from time immemorial. The first thing that must be agreed on is a halt to violence, and an announcement to that effect, so that the honourable board can use such an announcement as an acceptable route to engaging with the other side.

A healthy society accommodates all views, in their varying degrees of moderation and extremeness, but debate among them is based on dialogue, reason and respect for human rights, and nothing can demolish its sound edifice but violence and terrorism, which are to be condemned, from whatever direction they come, whether from the authorities or from the population.

So the upholders of true Islam must persevere in their path and must not deviate from their aim, whatever obstacles they face. Their path will not be seriously questioned; rather, it may be asked why the endeavour was so long in coming.

17 June 1992

A Difficult Birth

Does the picture of a world after the Cold War still hold its sparkle? Is it still determined to fulfil its promise to build a world on foundations of international legitimacy, justice and peace? It is true that there have been no shifts in the matter to openly put an end to the hopes that have been set on the establishment of that new world. Indeed, the effort being exerted for the success of the peace conference may be proof that the powers that be in our world are still keeping to the right road.

But there are warnings flying about here and there that at least indicate that the birth of the new world will be difficult, and will demand more devotion and more sacrifices.

As a result of the economic crisis that the United States is suffering, a call has gone out among Americans to put America's interests before all else, even at the cost of the expansion of foreign relations. It is not out of the question that this will be the pivotal point that the presidential election battle will revolve around, and it is clear that this call could inflict deformities on the newborn that could take the world back to the days of suffering, competition, and wars cold and hot.

The crisis has extended to the European Community, where it has whipped up a storm of xenophobia, with Japan being the focus of hostility, having come to represent the evil foe. There are also the disastrous consequences that may come about as a result of the disappearance of the Soviet Union and the formation of the new Commonwealth of Independent States, the accompanying famine that threatens its population, and the disagreements that divide its nations. This could all lead to the presence of dangerous weapons and dangerous experts that the Commonwealth has no need for, the fear being that these weapons and experts will infiltrate many countries of the world, becoming the catalysts for new aggressive ambitions that could present dangers to the world of a kind it has not previously faced, even taking into account the Second World War. And we can include among these warning signs the stance of the West towards Libya, which we hope will end with a solution that will avoid disappointment and bring justice.

All of this means that in order for the new world to be born as we would like it, we will need to make exhausting efforts and great sacrifices. The nations of the world and their peoples will have to rise to a peak that is higher than selfish interests and quick advantage, and we must look at this period of human history with a comprehensive humanistic vision.

18 June 1992

A Dream

It is my right to dream, and the dream of today may become the reality of tomorrow. This dream is not a new one: I shared my view previously in an interview with the esteemed magazine *al-Musawwar,* in 1988, I believe it was. I may not be able to remember the sequence in which I originally presented it, but the content is more important than the form. With apologies in advance for any betrayal of memory, here now are the elements of my dream – or my view:

First, all emergency laws should be scrapped, and there should be unlimited freedom to form political parties.

Second, a committee should be formed, representing all parties and authorities, to begin the process of drafting a new constitution, a referendum to be held on it when the time comes.

Third, the army – in addition to its duty of defending the country – should be tasked with a mission no less serious, which is to protect the constitution from interference, guaranteeing internal freedom and the rotation of authority according to the free will of the people.

Fourth, the president of the Republic should be independent of any party, and his most important function should be the protection of the constitution in his capacity as the symbol of the meeting-point between the people and the army.

Fifth, elections should be proportional, meaning that the whole country should be a single constituency and seats should be assigned to each party according to its share of the vote. This is the safest means to ensure that no vote is wasted, and the best way to safeguard minorities.

Sixth, parties should be given the opportunity to defend their ideals, and allowed equal airtime on television.

Seventh, while all this is going on, the Egyptian administration should continue to promote comprehensive development, under the responsibility of whoever the president of the Republic appoints to the task.

20 June 1992

Below the Poverty Line

During a debate about the budget and the five-year plan, Khaled Muhi al-Din, the president of the Tagammu Party, cited the report of an international body, which said that 40 per cent of Egyptians live below the poverty line. It is very difficult to imagine the wretchedness of this situation in respect to housing, food and clothing, and the deprivation from health, educational and cultural services, indeed the absence of sewerage or clean water. It truly is a wretched situation, and it elucidates the health statistics that we sometimes read concerning anaemia and its spread among children.

This kind of statistic should not exist forty years after a social revolution, a revolution that arose only in protest against poverty, ignorance and disease. After all the agricultural and industrial projects that have been implemented, after the agricultural reforms and the industrial and commercial nationalisations, it was expected that incomes would even out, that class boundaries would melt away, that a minimum standard of living would be available to the general population, that poverty in its usual sense would be circumscribed and that what we call 'below the poverty line' would be wiped out of existence.

What has happened in the land of Egypt to bring us to this unforeseen end?

Inevitably, we must go back to some sorry memories:

The memory that reminds us of democracy, and of our consecration of dictatorship with its unjust and oppressive practices and its disregard for human rights.

The memory of the wars that we invited or were driven to by rash individual decisions, and the setbacks and financial and moral ruin they brought on us.

The memory of the corruption that nested in our administrations and our plans, creating a rich world for the unscrupulous, but hell and suffering for the people.

The memory of the mistakes of the Open-Door Policy, which increased the unscrupulous in wealth and in numbers, and multiplied the suffering of the poor.

Painful statistics and painful memories, but we still have the dedication of those who remain loyal and the will of those who are on the side of civilisation and freedom, so whatever happens, hope can never desert us.

24 June 1992

A Salute to Those Who Bring Happiness

Amitabh Bachchan is the actor who has beguiled our youth and infuriated our wise men. The gist of his story is that he has won the love, admiration and attention of young people everywhere.[1] Meanwhile, our elite leading thinkers see this behaviour as foolish and inane, unbefitting a mature, cultured youth, and see the art that this Indian actor represents as a simple, naive form that derives its attraction from pure entertainment, devoid of any value. Others ask: if young people can have this much positive engagement, how can we explain their unconcern in the face of serious issues and events?

The simple fact of the matter is that this is a man who has succeeded through his work and his talent in gifting happiness to many hearts. He is celebrated by those who have gained happiness through him, and good faith has propelled them to return something of the favour to him – for one good turn deserves another.

It is a healthy and ethical phenomenon, and the greater and more serious things in our lives will not be threatened by the naivety of the entertainment he offers, nor by the unconcern of his audience.

As for entertainment, there are degrees of it. It begins with naive entertainment devoid of any cultural value, which nevertheless is blessed with joy and pleasure. We have all passed through that phase, loved its manifestations and preserved its memories in the dearest part of our hearts. As we move through life there comes the stage of maturity and values, and entertainment is inlaid with enlightenment and thought. So why are the respected critics in such a hurry to impose their tastes on the younger generation, without consideration of their age and the time they live in? The truth is that we have failed our youth in their education, their culture, their work and their living, and then we begrudge them a little innocent happiness and the celebration of those who have freely given it to them.

And as for concern and unconcern, Bachchan has called to these

1 The Hindi action films of Amitabh Bachchan were immensely popular with young audiences in Egypt from the 1970s to the 1990s.

young people's positive side, and it has responded. Perhaps then their positive side might be motivated on the same level in their society if they were befriended by a persuasive and influential person who could embark with strength and determination on a solution to their problems, and who could act as a model, a symbol and a good example for them.

Let us salute those who bring happiness to people in this life full of tribulations and disasters.

25 June 1992

On the Freedom of Thought

Freedom is the fruit of the struggle of the free. It does not come as a result of the existence of a free society, but it is what creates a free society, and it creates it through a bitter and bloody battle that, whether in the distant or the recent past, has not stopped producing martyrs and victims. Did not defiant new ideas come to civilisation only in the Dark Ages and during the Inquisition? And was freethinking anything other than the twin of exposure to open destruction? There is nothing to fear for freedom as long as there are freethinkers, nothing to fear as long as the thinkers carry the torch, do their duty and are not afraid of destiny.

There is no excuse for those who are silent, who retreat, or who hesitate when they are infected by the corruption of the atmosphere, the assault on traditions, the tightening of laws, or the persistence of terrorism, for these – and more – exist, and they can be supported by every sort of myth. There is nothing wrong with criticising every wrongdoing, campaigning against every negative aspect, attacking reactionism wherever it is found – there is nothing wrong with this, and indeed we must not neglect it or be remiss in it: we must consider it one of our unwavering goals. It is required, indeed it is an obligation. But this does not mean that we should postpone freethinking or become lax in it, or begrudge it the necessary sacrifice. Society is not liberated by changing its laws and customs, but its laws and customs change through freethinking, and thanks to its freethinkers.

There can be no progress in science, philosophy or art without free thought – free thought in its true meaning, which is that it follows every path towards truth for the good of humankind and its march forward. We will not be stopped by perverse ideas that arouse excitement, abuse or distraction, and it is not laws that are needed to keep these at bay but sound ideas to respond to them and expose their spurious nature.

To sum up, our society is in need of freedom, whose attainment is within our grasp in spite of everything.

1 July 1992

Tomorrow Is Another Day

How are we to live with the new world?

It is indeed a new world, regardless of its content. After the extinction of the Soviet Union, the old picture has vanished to be replaced by a new picture. The leaders of the new world say that it is based on international legitimacy and the respect for human rights, while some who have lived a long life believe that the old world continues to pursue the same goals but gives expression to them in a new humanistic style.

So I come back to my question: how are we to live with the new world?

We must believe the words of good, for they are a binding covenant, and we must not abandon them unless their truth is revealed to hold another truth. This is better than acting in bad faith, which will only bring us a tangle of errors and problems. Fortunately, all that the politics of the new world asks of the developing nations is democracy, peace, growth and respect for human rights – and these are all goals that we have frequently cherished, without being directed or dictated to. It is certainly also fortunate that these goals do not go against the interests of the strong nations of the new world. This may set the bounds of our political and military roles, but no obstacle can stand in the way of our progress in other areas of civilisation like science and culture, which are more important and more lasting.

We must also broaden our perspective on the world, and bear in mind that it brings together great and small, and that each faction's responsibility must be commensurate with its size and its abilities.

But what if the fine words produce an ugly face?

Certainly we do not possess a deterrent strength, but we do possess the will, the determination and the desire for a decent life and respect for human ideals. And we can unite in a bloc to form a power, and exercise a not inconsiderable passive resistance. We were all colonies once, or under colonial rule, and we had no material strength, but we were victorious over those who had strength and power, and we won our freedom and independence.

I admit that I remain optimistic and hopeful of good to come.

9 July 1992

The Dream Needs Work

In thinking about the new world, we agree and we disagree, we are pessimistic or we are optimistic, and we settle for waiting until the days reveal the truth of it. This is a negative position to take, especially for those who are hoping for a better tomorrow and a more equitable and kinder world. The fact is that the hoped-for world will not endure, will not become a realistic truth, will not be ranked in the established general morality and elevated values unless every authority and every nation leaps to take part in its creation, to promote its philosophy, to work on its behalf and in faith of its ideals.

This will only be attainable through the ratification, acknowledgement and commendation of every positive word said about it by any world leader or major nation, and their declaration before the world and before history that they bear its trust.

And it will not be attainable unless the states that form the United Nations actively engage towards strengthening their organisation and giving it the rights and the authority that will one day make it competent to act as the true global parliament, dedicated to solving the world's problems and determining its fate. They should then follow this by appropriately increasing the number of permanent members of the Security Council, giving more power to the International Court of Justice, and broadening its jurisdiction.

In this line of thought, we welcome the media reports of Dr Boutros Boutros-Ghali's suggestion to establish a peace force, which we hope will represent the nations of the world as far as possible, and in which the Third World should participate to a reasonable degree.[1]

The presence of such a force is essential, even if it is resorted to only in the rare cases when warnings and various political and economic penalties have failed.

---

1 Dr Boutros Boutros-Ghali (1922–2016) was an Egyptian politician who served as secretary-general of the United Nations from 1992 to 1996. The UN peacekeeping role was already well established; what Dr Boutros-Ghali proposed in 1992 was its substantial expansion and strengthening.

We must take this matter seriously, especially as we are about to face important issues such as peace in the Middle East and the elimination of weapons of mass destruction: whoever wants a better, new world must combine intention with work.

16 July 1992

The July Revolution and the Golden Age

We come back again to the July Revolution of 1952. The truth is that we encounter nothing good or bad that does not remind us of it. It had its golden age, which those who lived through it cannot forget, an age that abounded in momentous accomplishments, in dreams achieved, indeed in new dreams created that exceeded the national hopes to form a new nationalism, a pan-Arab nationalism, and participation in the liberation of every enslaved nation.

Then came the 5 June War of 1967 to put an end to the golden age, and the accomplishments collapsed, the dreams evaporated. We came together and found around us nothing but ruins, which were all that was left of the skeletons from whose service, maintenance and development we had been distracted by a chain of wars that destroyed the economy, ruined lives and bloodied our dignity.

What does this sad, heroic epic look like today?

From its very beginning, the Revolution followed two contradictory paths, the path of social reform, reflecting the hopes of the people and their inner cries, and the path of authoritarianism, which was like a continuation of the absolute rule of the king, if not even harsher and more totalitarian, in addition to the crimes of its terrorist security apparatus, which surpassed the Mamluks and the Ottomans in what it did to us. It also became clear that its political ambitions were far greater than its power or its ability, and so – despite wanting to make us the Japan of the Middle East – its golden age was reversed and left us a pile of ruins and sorrows.

There was nothing for the successor of the late leader to do but to save what could be saved and to add a stone here or a wall there to the broken construction.

It was Sadat who revived our spirit in the October War of 1973, restored our occupied land, brought us peace, opened the door to democracy and took steps on the road to the liberation of the economy, though this was unfortunately accompanied by shortcomings in the

Open-Door Policy and a breakdown in morals. Then came Hosni Mubarak, to put in place a radical plan for reconstruction and comprehensive development, and under his regime huge accomplishments have been made, in addition to the firm rooting of democracy, freedom of the press and economic reform; and if millions of citizens have not yet seen relief from their hardships this is not due to a lack of achievements but to the severity of the original dilapidation.

In any case, today is an important date in our history and an opportunity for us to renew the call for our country to overcome all that stands in its way and to reach its deserved station under the umbrella of freedom and progress.

23 July 1992

Survival or Extinction?

Doubtless you remember the Rio de Janeiro Earth Summit.[1] You recall the demands of the poor and the limited response of the rich, and the general disappointment that hit everyone who is concerned about both the short- and the long-term future for the planet and its inhabitants. It is not my intention to repeat things, for everything that can be said has been said, but I want to talk about impressions that cannot be allowed to pass unrecorded.

Overnight, the planet has become one of the important human issues, possibly the most important of all. Intellectuals have been forced to take an interest in it, and it has struck the consciousness of the ordinary person who follows the daily round of the media. This may be enough of a start to bring success to what fell short of success at the conference. I hope it has settled firmly in our minds that if our planet is not given the respect it deserves, it will not give us the life and flowering that we deserve.

Also, some wondered about a new adversary after the collapse of Communism and the disintegration of the Soviet Union. They said the strong do not live without an enemy – there must be a threat in whose confrontation they can build a project of strength, excellence and civilisation. That enemy is now looming over us out of the vastness of nature, threatening us all, though its danger will first befall the weak and the poor. It threatens drought, heat, desertification, pollution, floods and earthquakes, and calls on all of us to work together, to cast aside incidental disagreements, and to change the way we deal with nature from a basis of exploitation, dominion and prodigality to one of cooperation, wisdom and far-sightedness.

Because of all this, I do not think the conference a total failure, as some see it. Relief – even if less than needed – was allocated, and other conferences will be held, because the issue is too important and too critical to be left without follow-up.

---

1 The United Nations Conference on Environment and Development, Rio de Janeiro, 3–14 June 1992.

Perhaps the human race will one day understand that our recent exploration of space was not just a happy scientific success, but it came at a time of necessity!

30 July 1992

Opening the Blocked Road

They talk of terrorism and link it to numerous factors, such as erroneous fatwas, the economic crisis, the political vacuum, totalitarian governance or disregard for human rights. Terrorism may be the bitter fruit of all these phenomena together, or just one of them, according to circumstances and conditions.

But they forget another element that is no less consequential, if not more so, which is the barring of legitimate channels to power, and the frustration and exasperation that this leads to among a rising generation looking for its rights in life, among which – and perhaps at the forefront – is the right to accede to power.

It is true that every new generation looks forward to ruling or governing, as a way to realise their individual identity and their communal dream of changing society. It is every new generation's right to aspire to this; indeed, their duty, loyalty and ambition impose this aspiration on them, and they work to achieve it by any legitimate means. But if the road appears longer than it should, or is artificially lengthened, or is blocked altogether, then there is no hope of a way out. This is when it may occur to some to resort to violence.

I experienced life before the July Revolution of 1952, and I can attest that if the constitution had respected and defined the limits of each entity, our history might have turned out other than it did. The old parties would inevitably have lost their popularity and been replaced by young parties that promised social change. And in my estimation the young generations on both Right and Left would have been heir to the majority in the elections of 1950 and would have gone on to do what the July Revolution did, but in an air of freedom and democracy. This would likely have saved us many fatal mistakes.

Let us look at our reality in the light of the past on the one hand and with an acceptance of human truths on the other, making a road for ourselves that prepares for power, clear of artificial obstacles and the remnants of totalitarianism.

This is why I say: the most ideal solution is democracy, and respect for human rights.

6 August 1992

A Just Freedom

In the recent past, the state swelled to become all things: it was security, defence, education, health, transport, agriculture, industry, culture – everything. And consequently the role of the people dwindled to become nothing.

Everybody was a functionary of the apparatus of the state, and each individual restricted his interest to his own affairs and was otherwise content to observe, though boredom might also turn him away even from that.

Today, things are changing. Zephyrs of democracy pervade the climate, blowing seeds of free agency into souls, and there are signs of a return to the bearing of responsibility and a departure from negativity and idleness.

So we now know the road to deliverance, and what is left for us to do is to clear its surface of obstacles and prepare it not just for walking, but for running ahead. There are obstacles that stubbornly challenge our hopes, such as terrorism, drugs, pollution and corruption, and duty demands that we carry out radical political reform, increase production, overhaul the administration and spread security, safety and stability. Some will wonder: are we to sacrifice social justice?

The role of the state remains substantial, and it will not be confined to security and defence, even in countries with the most deep-rooted democracy. Thus the role of the government goes beyond security and defence, and in our countries, the state will retain control of strategic industries, will remain responsible for education and health, will continue to direct culture and our children's development, will battle the negatives of society and the environment, and in this context will wage war on unemployment and poverty.

Freedom and the respect for human rights will never be a threat to justice, but we will not block freedom and dignity in the name of justice or by resorting to force, tyranny and official terrorism.

13 August 1992

The Wafd School

In the world of politics we live with political leaders and learn from them. I have seen many of them in my time, and each one has given me a gift from their bounty, or more. Today is not the appropriate opportunity to talk about all of them, but it is a historical occasion on which to speak about two significant leaders, Saad Zaghloul and Mustafa al-Nahhas. Both men share certain merits and hold others alone, but together they form a single school of nationalist politics in which I was shaped, in the history of whose struggle I thrived and matured, and in whose two symbolic figures I found the model of all that was noble and good in life.

It may be useful to share something of what I learned in this school, the eternal school of the Wafd Party:

1. In it my heart was infused with the love of Egypt, its people, its land, its air, its heritage, its present and its future.
2. In it I came to believe deeply in Egypt's national unity, and in its Copts and Muslims as one people, one dimension, one past, one present and one starting point.
3. In it we fell in love with independence and made that the focus of our hopes, and we did not hesitate to sacrifice anything dear for its sake.
4. In it we came to believe in the people and in their right to be the source of authority in appointing rulers and removing them, and between this and that point watching them and holding them to account. A people has no dignity if its rights in this are infringed.
5. In it the values of free thought were composed, from which flowed the springs of literature and art.
6. In it we fervently supported the activity of a nationalist capitalism and its honest and legitimate operation.
7. In it our religious faith flourished, based on the love of God and people, and openness to human civilisations.
8. In it we witnessed the first practical application of social justice,

in the treatment of the farmers, the labourers and low-income workers.

9. In it was born that pure, deep love between the people and their two leaders, a love known otherwise only in the tales of lovers and in Sufism.

And finally:

Remember us and we will remember your time / Many a memory has brought near the one who is far
Remember love when it has done with you / It will water the tears and revive the rebuke.[1]

19 August 1992

1 From lines by Abu al-Hasan Mihyar ibn Mirzawayh al-Daylami (d. 1037), a Persian poet who wrote in Arabic.

Days of Steadfast National Unity

How much conditions and circumstances have changed, altering every day from one state to another. Perhaps there remain just single figures of our generation, or tens at the most. Values have retreated and values have advanced, dreams have vanished and hopes have flourished. We have earned the right to view the world from a distance and follow it quietly, employing reserve and sheltering in the sanctuary of wisdom, but when this day of 23 August comes round we remember with profundity and affection the two eternal leaders: Saad Zaghloul and Mustafa al-Nahhas. We take a fleeting stroll back to earlier times, and the past takes us by storm and tears us away from the concerns of the present with an irresistible force and an incontestable desire.

We return to the memory of the two men under whose protection we knew really and truly that we were the source of authority, that we were above the government, and that we brought the rulers from the street to invest them with power. We return to the days of firm and steadfast national unity, which stood up to sly attack and furious blows. We return to the days when we would call for a meeting with the prime minister so that he could hear the opinion of the students on the crisis that had erupted between him and the king, or between him and the British. We return to the time of the chanting that spread like songs in praise of the life of the country, of freedom, of the constitution, and which called for the fall of occupation and oppression. We return to memories of the arguments as they raged in parliament and the press, inflamed with sincerity, with rhetoric and with national feeling. We return to observe the effects of all this on the soul of the labourer, the farmer, the student, the office worker, all of whom without exception were ardently part of it and none of whom was silent. All operated under the shade of an illustrious constitution, a hallowed judiciary, a country of dignity and a population eager for battle.

You two departed leaders: it was thought that you had become history, though of good repute, and that your mission had ended after it had served its purpose. But the world surprised us with new wonders, and the harshest verdict known was handed down against oppression and autocracy, calling forcefully for freedom and respect for human rights, along with social justice.[1] Thus your ideals have come back as a goal, a target and a hope for all who are fighting today or who are looking forward to a better tomorrow.

You two venerable leaders: the separated may meet, having been convinced they would never meet again.

23 August 1992

1 Mahfouz is probably referring here to the removal of King Farouk from power by the Free Officers in the 1952 Revolution.

The National University

There has been disagreement about the national university, but I do not understand how there could be any objection to the founding of a house of learning, especially as the state will not be paying a millieme towards it.[1] The wealthy can open nightclubs if they want to, so how can we prevent them from building a house of learning, even if the primary objective is to provide an opportunity for the education of their own children, who have failed to enter the state universities? Education is in any case the right of every citizen, and there are restrictions only because of the high numbers and the lack of places. In the end what matters is success.

The project has advantages that should be noted, including the fact that it will make available specialisations in higher education that our state universities have unfortunately not managed to touch on. Also, the top 25 per cent of students would be admitted free, which is a victory for the advancement of learning and a victory for the top students of the country. And there is no harm in giving a chance to those who have been cheated of success, those who would anyway have taken that chance by joining foreign universities, paying out huge sums, suffering from being far from home and exposed to various dangers. So why not allow a solution to the problem from the funds of their families? Why should money not be invested in the field of scholarship, as it is in agriculture and industry? And if those among the poor who have failed do not have the same opportunity, the blame must fall on the state, not on the wealthy.

This brings us to another perplexing question: how have we allowed years and years to go by while we have sat content and silent with the deteriorating condition of our universities, which are living behind the times?

We have established thirteen of these backward universities. I believe subsidising an existing university would have been better than building yet another backward one, but we have leaned towards quantity rather

1 A millieme was one-tenth of a piastre, one-thousandth of an Egyptian pound.

than quality. We have fallen behind in the progressive development of our universities, to the extent that some in authority have gone so far as to defend the idea of a national university on the basis of the deterioration of our state universities.

We live in an age that cannot sustain this neglect at all, so let the foundation of a national university plug an ugly gap and spur on the development of our state universities. History will put this favour down to the founder of the national university.

27 August 1992

Sporting Success: The Reality and the Dream

As we went to Barcelona, so we returned from Barcelona.[1]

I will not talk about our reasons for going, as I am fairly certain that this is not worth discussing, because we must in any case have a presence in the world of sport, and a flag must flutter for us. Sport is not only about winning, it is about taking part in a beautiful event. The true sporting spirit is not induced by winning, nor is it defeated by losing: it maintains its glow in all circumstances and conditions.

But we cannot avoid asking the reasons for our total failure. Why did not a single athlete shine? Do not say that competition on an international level is too difficult, or near impossible, because we are not plunging into it for the first time, and we have a history of success in it – and what a history! Sport does not distinguish between one race and another, between one colour and another, or between north and south, and we have won extraordinary, heroic victories in football, weightlifting, swimming, boxing, wrestling and so on, despite belonging to what is today called the Third World. Even before we liberated ourselves from colonial rule, when sport was a generous breathing space on a global level, we proved our worth on the field and demonstrated our hidden abilities. So how did we sink so low in recent times, after our liberation and our advancement in so many dimensions of civilisation?

The matter, in my view, requires no more than love, ambition and training. You must love your sport, have the ambition to win, and train for it. This is what al-Sayyid Nusayr, Mukhtar Husayn, Khidr al-Tuni, Ishaq, 'Amr, Husayn Higazi, al-Suwalim, and many others did.[2] So how

1 Egypt won no medals at the Summer Olympic Games in Barcelona in 1992.

2 Leading Egyptian sportsmen of the 1920s and 1930s. Al-Sayyid Nusayr (1905–74) won gold in boxing at the Amsterdam Olympics in 1928, Mukhtar Husayn (1904–66) was a champion weightlifter, Khidr al-Tuni (1916–56) won gold in weightlifting at the Berlin Olympics of 1936, Husayn Higazi (1891–1961) was captain of the national football team.

did we acquire this consensus of failure? Certainly our athletes are not lacking in love for their sport, or short of ambition to win. What is almost certainly missing is in the training for the job, and in persistence and practice.

Love is required in many different sciences, arts and employments, and ambition is required to reach the highest levels, but there is no patience for hard work and endurance. There is no longer the firm will, the iron determination, the inexhaustible energy. There is always impatience to find the shortest route, the briefest time, and with the least effort. It is the age of connections, of short cuts, of illicit means and of reliance on everything except the self and hard work.

We may face difficulties in renewing ourselves in the arena of work, but the difficulties in sport are less, and we are closer to achieving the defeat of the negatives in this area. So let us be determined once again, and reload our determination with strength and resolve. Because the results at the end are for the industrious.

2 September 1992

The Past and the Present in a Changing World

On Monday 3 August I came across two important headlines in our newspapers.

The first was about the old Islamic quarters of Cairo and the deterioration that their infrastructure and monuments are suffering, and how one of the magnificent historic gates of the city has become a rubbish dump. The second was about the convening of a cultural conference to look at Arab culture in the changing world of tomorrow, and to agree on a charter that the cultural class can adhere to. Thus there came together at the same time a weeping over the ruins and a looking forward to the future. And honestly and truly, all I gained from both headlines was a sense of depression.

I do not know how to defend our historic quarters, as everything has been said about them that can be said. Besides which, I am the son of one such area, who delighted in playing among its friendly spaces at a time when they were swept clean twice a day and sprayed twice with water, all around exuding the glorious fragrance of the past. What is happening to these places today? What has befallen them in the golden age of tourism? Is the language of money and economics adequate in their defence? Or the yearning for memories?

The cultural conference was convened, fine words were spoken as usual, the charter was announced, the party was over, and the curtain came down. What culture? What changing world? Culture is culture; it is production first and last. The world does not stop changing, and culture does not cease. And the charter: would the artists have produced, and would the thinkers have thought, without a charter, if it had not been announced at a conference? Were they wandering about aimlessly until the charter appeared to them with its light? And what power can induce an artist to commit to anything other than what his conscience inspires in him?

I would understand if the cultural class were to come together to present their demands, the most outstanding of which are: revision of the laws covering freedom of thought, removal of the financial and customs obstacles that hinder cultural exchange, strengthening the penalty for forgery, cultural exchange through exhibitions and visits, establishing a foundation at the level of the Arab League for translation into and from Arabic, increasing the hours of TV and radio broadcasting in the cultural realm and establishing a permanent council of Arab ministers of culture, information and education, for the furtherance of culture under its patronage and care.

I believe there are more cultural demands than this, all truly deserving of symposia and conferences.

17 September 1992

Cultural Concerns

Culture is going through a period of poor health – this is what is said every time a conversation revolves around it. And why not? Is there not a general, tangible crisis? How would culture have slipped from its grasp? The state is confronting the crisis with comprehensive development and successive five-year plans, and culture has had its share in this, as demonstrated in promising signs. The first of which that comes to mind is the success of the magazines *Ibda'* (Creativity), *Fusul* (Seasons), and *al-Qahira* (Cairo). But this does not preclude us from mentioning a word about the difficulties of culture, to perhaps summarise some of what is being said. Do there exist general obstacles in the way of culture, for the time being leaving aside the details that apply to each field of culture individually?

Certainly the first to be mentioned is television, for its irresistible attraction and its sweeping popularity, thanks to which it has become the primary source of entertainment, information, spiritual guidance and simplified culture. Television is not a passing negative phenomenon, but a scientific development and a modern fact of life. So no rational person can think of putting limits on it, but we must always strive to make the best of it, and explore ways to skilfully and cleverly work together with it. It brings benefit and advantage to the people through its entertainment, information, guidance and culture. In this it has performed a significant deed for the educated and the illiterate alike, and there remains an opportunity for more. I am certain that what serious culture, as represented by the book, has lost through television, it can make up for through television itself.

There is another obstacle, which is the economic crisis, a situation that must come to an end, just as we must not be remiss in fighting it, and the day we are victorious over it culture will regain a large part of its lost equilibrium. But while we continue to suffer from it, there is no doubt that it is a hulking and burdensome obstacle in the path of the diffusion of culture. Perhaps in the spread of libraries and the renovation of the National Library will be found the means by which we can mitigate the severity of this crisis.

And there is a third obstacle that should not be neglected, which is the effect of extremist views on our youth, in their attack on the arts, literature and thought, and their polarisation in those fields for many young people who have come to loathe culture under their influence. Perhaps it would be useful if the ongoing discussion with these young people included the defence of art, culture and thought.

Nobody who is concerned with the building and formation of good human beings should miss the opportunity to defend culture and to do what he can for it to flourish.

24 September 1992

Daydreams

There is no harm in dreaming a little, so as not to forget amid what something is, what it should be. And also so as not to forget the rights of the populace that have been shelved through force of circumstance. Dreaming is a diversion, but it is not without import, for it is not just within the realm of fantasy to imagine that all the emergency laws have been repealed and that we have revised our constitution to produce a new one that is a mirror of unadulterated democracy and of a living, changing reality, and is more in line with what is happening in the world.

Or that Egyptian, Arab and foreign investments are piling up in an uninterrupted rhythm on top of a deep-rooted stability, taking industry and agriculture in leaps to new levels and bringing an end to many problems, especially unemployment both barefaced and veiled.

Or that the problem of education has been ironed out in the best way, with the building of the necessary schools, the supply of teachers, the transformation of curricula and teaching methods in accordance with the needs of the times, and the best intellectual, emotional, cultural and physical development of our youth, plus the achievement of complete victory over illiteracy.

Or that human rights have become a reality, not just a slogan, practised in the street as in the prisons, at home, in schools, in government institutions and in hospitals, and enjoyed by minorities as by the majority, by women and men, and in thought and in the creative arts.

Or that the Aswan High Dam project has been completed through dealing with its negative aspects, and that we have gained victory in the wars against pollution, drugs and endemic diseases.

Or that Egypt has become a beacon in scientific research, culture, willpower, clarity of genuine religious belief, impartiality and honesty – in short, that we have become a nation favoured by God and content with Him.

Yes, brother, it may be a dream, but today's dream is tomorrow's reality.

10 October 1992

Mood and Violence

Regarding the sad events of Abu Hammad,[1] the governor of the area said: 'Violence is a general mood, and we as responsible agencies must search for a way to cure it.'

But what has made violence a general mood in a people known throughout history for their gentleness and patience?

The truth is, there are many reasons which will not be lost on anybody. Their recent history has been filled with tyranny, terrorism, corruption, defeats, inflation, unemployment, lack of opportunities for youth, injustice, favouritism, poor services, administrative disarray, absence of respect for human rights, extremism and intimidation – and not only from among the population. There may be details that make the picture even more ugly and awful.

And there is another reason, which is that in their historical suffering at the hands of foreign or quasi-foreign rulers who did not have their interests at heart, Egyptians no doubt hoped that after the rulers' children took over,[2] their treatment would change and that an Egyptian might find in government offices, hospitals, schools and prisons what they had never dreamed of before.

These are the reasons that have made us lose patience and driven us to violence, and perhaps the governor knows now that the mission of curing the violence is more critical than can be taken on by him or by his agencies. It needs an overall cure, an integrated plan and exhaustive development. This is what the state is doing and has been concentrating on, especially in the last period. But it needs time, patience, work and effort, so let us 'give to the state what belongs to the state', and think a little about what has arisen between the police and the public, which has almost become a phenomenon, not just a fleeting incident.

The cure is clear, which is to treat people as you would like them

1 Popular riots against the authorities had taken place in Edku and Abu Hammad in the Nile Delta in a spontaneous reaction to police brutality.

2 Mahfouz is probably referring here to the optimism that followed the succession of the unpopular King Fuad by his young son Farouk.

to treat you. But this needs self-discipline, dedication to society and sincere national feeling. The relationship between the police and the public must be based on trust and respect, under an umbrella of respect for human rights. The police must remember that their first duty is to be truly and honestly at the service of the people. We know very well what the police stand for, what their duties are and what their importance is in protecting society and enshrining values and ideals.

For this reason we do not want to hear of someone being mistreated in a police station, let alone being killed in one. We do not want people to believe a false rumour about something that happened in a police station. Your services fill the records, so don't spoil them with a passing rage, or misplaced arrogance.

15 October 1992

A Blessed Movement

The Kuwaiti elections are a great historic event, deriving their significance and importance from the fact that they have taken place in the Arab region, like a revolution against its political traditions. Put simply, the elections were run between the opposition and the supporters of the government, and the opposition won an overwhelming victory, the government suffering a crushing defeat. The result was accepted, and the new cabinet was formed on the basis of it. Thus Kuwait began its new democratic journey with full courage and engagement with the modern age and the new world. The government did not hesitate to acknowledge the facts of the matter, despite the success of the Islamic current, and the country determined to move forward through its reality on its path to the future, without fear of life's exigencies. This reminded me of our first elections in 1924, which the people waded into in the wake of the revolution of 1919, before there was anybody among them who gave themselves the right to falsify votes, misappropriate false trust or establish rule on an illegal basis. I recalled this, and recalled how the prime minister who ran these elections lost them to a man of the people. And I recalled – filled with sorrow – that we have not succeeded in having a free election since then, except in fleeting moments in our life full of tyranny.

This situation in Kuwait obliges us to direct thanks and praise to the Kuwaiti state for its civilised behaviour and its prompt heeding of the call of the modern age.

We warmly applaud the people of Kuwait, of whom the overwhelming majority rushed to the polling stations, affirming their positive attitude, their loyalty and their commitment to national duty, as we salute the Kuwaiti women who demonstrated to demand their right to vote and stand in elections. Anyway, we will follow the government of Kuwait and its chamber of deputies with confidence and interest, and we wish them good fortune and fruitful cooperation in the service of Kuwait and Arab affairs, since the success of this experiment is being closely watched by all the liberals of the Arab world.

22 October 1992

Cultural Independence

I wonder whether the relationship of the state to culture has developed in line with the ongoing transformation from totalitarianism to liberalism in politics and the economy?

In the field of cinema, production was liberalised some time ago, and a few private cinema houses have been opened. Private theatre is more or less subject to the market, while in books there is a balance between the state book authority and private publishing houses, though it should be noted that cultural magazines face unreasonable difficulties, with publication permits unattainable.

Whatever happens, art, writing and thought will sooner or later become independent of the state apparatus. Artistic, literary and intellectual production will follow talent, audience and market in both quantity and quality. They will then develop and settle down, via this battle between higher ideals and commercial demands, in an air of liberalisation and without artificial constraints.

But this does not mean the disappearance of the state, which will still have an effective and active role, whatever degree of independence art may have from it. The state in our countries is the master of the institutes of art and the humanities that have built the study of the arts and literature on a scholarly foundation. The state is responsible for the preservation, restoration and renovation of historic sites and buildings, and it is the state that oversees the awards of encouragement and appreciation that discover new talent and recognise established work. It must appoint the syndicates – including the Writers' Union – to help them fulfil their mission, and it may contribute aid and loans for the building of theatres, cinemas and film studios. Besides this it has a legislative role in promulgating laws for the protection of intellectual and artistic property, for tax exemption, for criminalising piracy and for the removal of impediments to the export and import of the requisites of cultural production. In addition, there is its traditional incumbency of participating in or organising festivals, and even if enlightened businessmen arise to collaborate in these major events, the state will still play an indispensable role. But a free life will not be granted to art, writing and thought until they are independent of the tutelage of the state.

29 October 1992

Between War and Civilisation

War costs humanity more than it can bear, and we have had so much talk of numbers that we are no longer either astonished or frustrated. It is the same whether war is actually carried out or if it is limited to preparation or precaution in an endless race. Add to this what war or preparation for war bring with them in terms of the pollution of the atmosphere and the environment and the spread of ruin, as they thereby employ millions of labouring hands and creative minds to achieve a single final goal, which is to bring about death and destruction. It is estimated – as reported by *Al-Ahram* – that what is spent on this would be enough to cleanse the world of pollution, poverty and many diseases, which would bring a happiness to humanity it cannot dream of in the wretched position it is currently in.

Amazingly, it is said that the expenditure of poor countries on armaments exceeds that of the rich countries, and that it is continuing to increase while the budgets of the rich are tending towards restraint. But our amazement melts away when we know the reason: The great industrialised nations are moving in the direction of rapprochement, while the poor and underdeveloped countries are intent on division and confrontation. This is how things are in the Third World in general, and in the countries of the Middle East in particular. It is as though it has been decided that survival will be the fate of the advanced and the strong; perdition that of the poor and the underdeveloped.

It is for the countries of the Third World to study this information and comprehend its significance, to read their future in the light of these warnings, to review their policies, to settle their differences and to move in the direction of cooperation and long-lasting peace.

Our Arab countries are at the forefront of those who need to grasp this lesson: they have spent enough on war over the past half century to develop all their lands and take them out of the shadows of the Third World and into the light of the developed world. Now they are moving towards establishing peace with Israel, so let us hope that they will then move in the direction of peace and cooperation with each other, so that they may rise once more in a life of progress and civilisation.

5 November 1992

The Struggle

Our problems are all interconnected, and it is no use trying to solve them one by one. They exist together and depend on each other, and they will go away together at the appropriate time, which will be defined by our determination and our ability to confront challenges. We cannot separate the economic crisis from corruption, or the economic crisis and corruption from extremism and bad administration, or all these things together from moral and cultural malaise. Hope is tied to comprehensive development: the development of all spiritual and material activities through successive five-year plans, with a firm commitment to honest work in unceasing and untiring perseverance. The time has come for us to redouble the pace of the rhythm, and to hasten the results and the harvest of the fruits before patience is depleted or we are overtaken by despair.

Perhaps in these times we have only two concerns:

1. To put all the effort we can into encouraging private investment, sparing investors any difficulties, and preparing the beneficial climate that will provide stability, remove obstacles and simplify procedures, and to introduce for this purpose whatever political reforms, legislation and security measures necessity may call for. Let us acknowledge what has been done in this area, though we do not want to stop at any limit. We know best what we are lacking.
2. To achieve the full performance of the government and the public sector. It is true that compassionate reasons and an understanding of reality and its complications call for the tolerance of many behaviours, and the turning of a blind eye to mistakes that could not have been ignored in previous times. So let us resign ourselves to the amounts incurred and the negative effects inflicted on us, but in return the employees must perform their complete and full duty, however much hard work this costs them and however much oversight, monitoring, perseverance and determination it costs us.

We have to show that we are fit for life and worthy of its blessings, that we are able to face challenges and to challenge adversity, in order to fix our small world that is on the point of breakdown, and to restore it to its genuine equilibrium, so that blood will flow through our parched veins and the joy of spiritual, cultural and material riches will return to our lives.

12 November 1992

The Whole Story

The earthquake was an opportunity for a law of nature (or a universal phenomenon) and human laws (or human behaviour) to come together.[1] And it was a chance to compare the two in terms of accuracy, application and results. I am not claiming that contemplating earthquakes will confirm all universal laws when they meet human laws or human behaviour, as an overall judgement would require comprehensive study and global comparisons, so let us be content with looking at the consequences of the meeting of this particular earthquake with our particular laws and behaviour in Egypt.

The earthquake – the outcome of reactions below the surface of the Earth – was a thing of clearly defined results, a masterpiece of precision and perfection. I do not think it reached a degree more or a degree less than was predetermined for it. Likewise its foreordained duration and aftershocks. As was predestined, it shook dwellings, installations, institutions and historic buildings, as well as the hearts and minds of living beings. These are things that in their essence are subject to scientific laws, and when we deal with them they are subject to ethical and human laws and values. Our minds and hearts are nurtured in the fold of divine, social and human directives. It is not an exaggeration to say that the earthquake did not find things or living souls as they should have been. It found that fraud had crept into the construction and core of things, as it had into the minds and hearts of the living. Thus came the consequences that tested us, and it appeared that the earthquake was punishing us for what we had all done. Now, let us note and ponder the following:

1. Suppose we had paid attention to all the warnings we had received about the earthquake, which are said to have reached us from the United Nations, Britain and Germany,

---

1 The earthquake that struck Cairo on 12 October 1992, with a magnitude of 5.8, caused more than five hundred deaths and damaged or destroyed many buildings.

and we had expended every reasonable effort on precautions and preparations...

2. And suppose we had not tolerated a single building infringement...
3. And suppose we had been faithful to our work in construction and the application of the law, and contented ourselves with honest means of earning a living, of which there are plenty...
4. And suppose we had had a civilised, humanistic policy towards old and neglected housing...

Let us suppose all this, which is simple and necessary. Suppose we had done all this, would the earthquake not have passed peacefully, or with minimal losses?

To what extent do we consider ourselves victims of the earthquake?

And to what extent are we victims of ourselves?

19 November 1992

The Other Side of the Coin

The earthquake, as we have said, appears like a punishment. It exposed many of our faults, such as bad administration, lack of respect for the law, fraud, dereliction of duty, disgraceful indifference towards the offenders and weak oversight, accountability and monitoring. The punishment came in deadly and injurious form, bringing loss of property, the collapse of housing, institutions and schools and damage to historic buildings, in addition to terrible panic, deep grief and the depression that has enveloped us like a fog.

This aspect of the discussion must not be lost sight of, but it is not the only aspect: there is also the side of good and hope, and it is not right for us as living beings to let go of hope or undervalue the will of life. Disasters are nothing but trials and dangers that in the end we must embrace and turn into opportunities to arouse ambitions and awaken hidden reserves of power.

These are not meant as words of encouragement, or as daydreams, or as anything beyond that. Certainly, those who have tasted the bitterness of the trial, those whose hearts had their fill of the shakings of the ground, those who felt the breath of death reverberating over their faces – they must strongly and firmly re-examine the administration and how corruption and building violations are dealt with, so that they change their attitude towards negligence, laxity, oversight and accountability.

But what to do about making available the necessary funds for rebuilding everything destroyed by what has happened? Donations are not enough, aid is not sufficient, and it is not out of the question that the plan could be derailed in several ways. Certainly this would be a sorry outcome, but there is no call for despair, for altogether it is no more than a matter of redirecting funds from their original allocation to a new allocation of no less importance.

We will build new schools and restore many schools, we will restore historic buildings, and we will apply a new policy with regard to old housing that is condemned or that has outlived its life expectancy.

For if we do no more than reorganise the administration, clean up corruption and reimpose the sovereignty of the law, we will have gained the greatest consolation and achieved a clear victory.

26 November 1992

A Threat Response Centre

For a long time we have only known threats of a human nature, by which I mean the kind that humans are responsible for, like invasion, colonialism, tyranny and underdevelopment. Of course, we know from history that the first threats facing humankind were natural, like changing weather, storms, wild animals and such things, but people learned how to live with most of them through civilisational advancement; so only the threats that we label human concerned them and polarised their anxiety. But modern civilisation itself has now begun to warn us of natural threats and caution us about the seriousness of their consequences, which could end civilisation or stop its development, and could wipe out the human race itself, to become a thing of the past.

If we want to categorise the threats according to their origin, we can say that there are those that are purely natural, like earthquakes, volcanoes, tornadoes, floods and some serious diseases. And there are others that are also natural but are caused by humankind – that is, as a result of civilisation itself, because our engagement in the struggle of life has made us forget many of the consequences of our actions, including the hole in the ozone layer, pollution, drought, and the epidemics and famine that follow it.

Both types have dire consequences for humankind, indeed for life in general, and result in the terrifying disasters we hear about, such as the widescale destruction of plant life (which may lead to the destruction of all life – plants, animals and humans), the submerging of towns and coasts and the disappearance of considerable portions of continents.

Of course we – all human beings – are demanding that all measures be taken to prevent damaging and sabotaging the environment and pushing it to retaliate in kind. We may even be able to take the first firm and potent steps along that path, which we have no choice but to walk.

But at the same time we must prepare to face any disaster, so that we are not taken unaware, as happened with the recent earthquake and its aftershocks. We must have a permanent response centre to study all possible catastrophic events, and we must have a comprehensive plan, backup preparations, and organisational and human resources.

It is the fate of humanity to live in the face of threats, and to build our culture and civilisation in the midst of this.

2 December 1992

Tourism, Religion and Politics

The drop in tourism can be attributed to two currents that may be working together or each independently of the other. The first is an extremist interpretation of religion, the second is a capricious political will aimed at embarrassing the government, even if it ruins the national economy in the process. In discussing the religious aspect, we may say that two great Islamic thinkers, the mufti and Professor Ghazali,[1] have distanced themselves from it, and the best judgement comes from those who are competent to make it: from both their distinguished positions they have decreed that tourism is religiously lawful and that the life and possessions of the tourist come under the protection of Muslims.

And there may be no harm in supplementing this decisive legal decision with my own view on the subject from a general humanistic perspective, which is that tourists are people who come to our land by choice and through genuine desire. Their visit is a demonstration of their love for Egypt, for which they deserve thanks, and they spend enormous sums in our country, from which we benefit in supporting our revival and progress, for which they also deserve thanks.

Some may object to the customs of the tourists that do not agree with ours or that are incompatible with our tastes – but are we ourselves clear of such bad habits? Even before it became a tourist destination, our country was not free of liquor, drunkenness, gambling, wantonness or licentiousness. There is no way any society can be free of at least some deviancies, which recede or grow according to conditions and circumstances.

I may even add that we have bad habits that the tourists have never heard of before, or that are found only rarely in their countries. Many of their lands do not know – or hardly know – bribery, nor do they know negligence or malingering, nor the fraud in construction that leads to the loss of hundreds of lives in earthquakes and at other times. So it

1 The mufti is the chief Islamic jurist of Egypt. Muhammad al-Ghazali (1917–96) was a renowned Egyptian Islamic scholar and thinker.

should be up to the mufti of the foreign visitors – if they had a mufti – to warn them of *our* bad habits and urge them to be on their guard against them.

The fact is that there is no excuse for attacking tourists, either from the religious standpoint or from the point of view of morals and customs. The only justification left for the crime then is the desire to embarrass the government in order to bring it down and take over authority.

But while the exercising of authority may be a legitimate goal for all citizens of different inclinations, no infringement can be allowed of the sanctity of national public agencies in order to reach that goal. In our political struggle we must be democrats, not terrorists.

10 December 1992

Yahya Hakki

I don't think I knew Yahya Hakki before I read *The Lamp of Umm Hashim*, which afforded me the discovery of a living world of art and beauty, as well as the discovery of one of the giants of literature.[1] I immediately added him to the assembly of immortals of whom I was a student and admirer, which comprised Taha Hussein, Abbas al-Aqqad, Ibrahim al-Mazini, Mohamed Husayn Heikal, and Tawfiq al-Hakim. I so much enjoyed the style, approach, and voice of *The Lamp of Umm Hashim* that I went and asked after the author, learning that he was a member of the diplomatic corps and worked abroad. At the same time I learned that he was one of the pillars of the Egyptian school of the short story, which had begun its experimentation some years previously and which included Mahmoud Taymour and Hussein Fawzy. Unfortunately, I had not begun my literary reading at the time that they were writing: when I began they had already moved on to other careers. I only knew Mahmoud Taymour, who did not cease production as long as he lived and who was not distracted by anything.

I took it as an obligation to read everything that Yahya Hakki wrote, in magazines, newspapers and books, in order to grow in knowledge and taste and to admire his writing's special magic and elegant flavour. We considered his writing a rarity, and did not disagree on its value, but when his articles are added to the scales, we must also acknowledge him among the most prolific of writers. The fact is that he was a school of the short story in himself, and his production attests to his excellence, depth and touches of genius, as his articles attest to his broad erudition and his penetrating critical views, besides his uniquely clear, concise and beautiful style.

Chance had it that Yahya Hakki's work brought him to Egypt, where he was chosen to be the director of the Arts Administration, and the choice fell on the late 'Ali Ahmed Bakthir and myself to work with

1 Yahya Hakki, born in 1905, died on 9 December 1992. He was a renowned and popular Egyptian literary critic and short story writer. The novella *The Lamp of Umm Hashim* is probably his best-known work.

him.[2] Thus time turned its circle, and I found myself in the same administration and under the directorship of the man I had long been looking forward to meeting and conversing with.

From that point on, an intimate friendship and great closeness was established between us, and I came to know the man after I had been dazzled by the artist. Our dialogue continued day after day, as we came to know what we agreed on and what we differed on, but in all cases we were an example of objectivity and impartial thinking. And it was inevitable that alongside the man and the artist I would also know the satirical commentator, who was a serious jester and the master of a humorous spirit, brilliant jokes and unforgettable bons mots. May God encompass you in His grace, you creative artist, you noble man.

13 December 1992

2 'Ali Ahmed Bakthir (1910–69) was an Egyptian poet, playwright and novelist.

How Are We to Confront Terrorism?

Terrorism is a problem that grows more critical day by day, its consequences extending to many areas, as it has come to threaten our security, economy and national unity. It is natural for all citizens to be concerned about how to deal with it and be rid of it, and we cannot ignore it, since there can be no psychological stability if we shut our eyes to it.

At its origin is extremist thinking, which has been found in the history of Islam since its foundation. But extremist thinking in itself is not a problem, for there is no view or doctrine that does not have its moderate and its extremist sides. I recall that throughout my life society has never been free of extremism of either the Right or the Left.

But extremism may turn towards violence, and become terrorism. How and when does extremism turn into terrorism? I hope – right at the outset – that your thoughts are not directed towards one or more foreign countries. Terrorism as a phenomenon cannot be created by a foreign country: the most that such a foreign power can do is to exploit its presence and extend the funds or weapons to it that it needs to function. Thus before anything else we must search for the causes of terrorism here at home. So again, how and when does extremism turn into terrorism?

There are many reasons that may come together to cause it, and its effect may be the greater if they are combined. These include: the economic crisis and the frustration, unemployment and despair that it leads to; corruption and the resulting agitation, rage and loss of confidence in authority and the law; the impossibility of change by legitimate means and the blocking of legitimate routes to power; and the battle between extremists and security forces and the lack of respect for human rights that it reveals, which leads to resentment and revenge.

In setting down the reasons for terrorism, the ways of dealing with it become clear to us, and if they are followed faithfully it will be defeated, becoming just an occasional crime instead of a social phenomenon.

No fair person will deny what the government has done in economic reform or in domestic security while combatting corruption, but its efforts in these areas are less than is needed, just as it has not been as concerned as it should have been with political reform, which covers the other reasons.

You must know, dear readers, that terrorism becomes a phenomenon only when society is in the direst need of treatment, and when that treatment is in the direst need of courage and sacrifice.

17 December 1992

The Path of Life

There must be a total civilisational revival, even if the road is long and filled with obstacles and difficulties. There must be a total civilisational revival, and there must be an iron will strong enough to match the obstacles and difficulties.

It may help to sharpen our resolve and strengthen our determination if we take stock of those obstacles and difficulties, to better estimate the energy we will need in order to achieve our aim and reach our goal.

So what are the obstacles? And what are the difficulties?

There are those that are not of our making, either directly or indirectly, natural universals such as earthquakes. These we face with patience, with faith, and by arming ourselves with whatever instruments of forecast and prediction science can extend to us, and with whatever centres of disaster-preparation we can set up. Beyond that, we must all accept and be content with our destiny.

Then there are the natural disasters that are of our own indirect making, like pollution and the negative side-effects of the Aswan High Dam: we can combat this kind through modern scientific means in the framework of international cooperation. And there are obstacles that are social and natural at the same time, such as the population problem and its increasing gravity year after year. There is a side to this that we can do nothing about, but the other side can be addressed through awareness, and perhaps the best way to achieve success in this is through the spread of education and culture.

The remaining obstacles and difficulties are actually of our making alone, for which we are responsible as a people and as a state. These include the political system, the economy, education, public morality, cultural standards, correct religious instruction, unemployment, drugs, the sovereignty of the law and respect for human rights. The reform of all this requires wisdom and candour on the part of the state, along with flexibility, sincerity, continuous work and a regard and understanding for the new world and the lessons of history. And it requires vigilance, loyalty and seriousness on the part of the people, and the testing of all legitimate paths in the defence of their rights before despair drives them to rebellion or revolution. In all cases, may God be with us.

24 December 1992

A New Year

Happy New Year! And may it be a good one. The start of a new year is an event that calls for optimism and confidence in what is good. In spite of earthquakes, terrorism and scandalous wrongdoings, we must reinforce life and strengthen the instincts of perseverance and triumph in order to derive caveats from life's inconstancies, and lessons and examples from history, and to be able to say – despite earthquakes, terrorism and scandalous wrongdoings: Happy New Year! And may it be a good one.

And why not? Even in the days of hardship and shadows, we have heard a voice bringing tidings of a decrease in inflation and – for the first time – of the growth rate outstripping the increase in population. We have also heard the voice assuring us that our revival depends on peace and good relations with all nations, as well as on science and technology.

And as the new year opens, there also dawn on us new, indispensable hopes:

The hope that a comprehensive, just peace will be achieved in our Arab East, which would allow us to eliminate weapons of mass destruction and be free to pursue development.

The hope that the Arabs will move beyond their mutual disagreements and concentrate on their shared interests.

The hope that cooperation between the states of the Third World will be transformed from the realm of dreams to the realm of realities.

The hope that we can deal with terrorism as we need to, and remove the wrinkles of tension from the face of our political life.

The hope that the new year will be the year of democracy and human rights.

And why not? We have long known bitterness, and we have tasted the poison of wars, despotism, poverty and fanaticism. So it is not so strange that we should look forward to peace, development, democracy and human rights.

7 January 1993

War and International Legitimacy

The latest punitive strike on Iraq excites a whole package of contradictory thoughts, which was not the case during the original war devoted to the liberation of Kuwait. In that war, the Arabs were divided into two camps, one that condemned the invasion and supported the Security Council resolution, looking forward to the birth of a new world, and one that supported the Iraqi decision and rejected and condemned the Security Council resolution. Today there is no Arab with an unambivalent position on the events. True, we are against the assault on Kuwait and against any manipulation of the terms of the ceasefire, but though we may consent to the punitive strike it is with reservations and questions. The Security Council does not preserve the dignity of all its international resolutions with the same standard of vigour or determination. Three countries have been subjected to its resolutions around the same time: it has treated Serbia and Israel gently, not being excessive in its chastisement; but in the case of Iraq it has been an exemplar of firmness and action when it comes to the preservation of international legitimacy, while with the others the situation reminds us of the old world and its politics based on interests and conspiracy. We do not want our hopes to evaporate as we wait for the new world. We do not want the dream of international legitimacy to be squandered after millions of hearts have been filled with optimism.

International legitimacy faces several tests that continue to exist while awaiting solutions:

1. The Palestinians in exile,
2. Bosnia,
3. The global eradication of weapons of mass destruction, without exception or laxity.

In any case, we will know the truth of the Security Council's intentions, whether we agree with them or not.

But the riddle that will remain hard to understand is Saddam Hussein. We are less and less able to comprehend his actions, and our minds take us in all directions. The fact is that the source of this confusion is based on the premise that he is the ruler of a country and that he possesses at least the minimum level of ability and experience to govern. But I no longer believe this: Saddam Hussein and his like may be clever enough to take power if they have the necessary strength, and they then sit cross-legged on the sultan's throne without any real qualifications for the position or the responsibility it entails. This is why we see all kinds of unbelievable behaviour from them that could only be produced by fools or madmen. And we are the more unable to understand them because we imagine them to be worldly, experienced and wise, while in fact their actions are nothing but perverse, and motivated by erroneous calculations produced from empty, tyrannical minds.

19 January 1993

Egypt and Sudan

I am of the generation that considers Egypt and Sudan to be one nation: Egypt is Northern Sudan, and Sudan is Southern Egypt. The words 'Egypt' and 'Sudan' are fixed in my consciousness as a single expression, or as two completely integrated concepts, as we say 'night and day' or 'warp and weft'. Thus the argument over the border hit me as a sudden cruel shock, and then Sudan's complaint to the Security Council appeared as more cruel and more heinous.

Perhaps the first question that crossed my mind was: why did the negotiations between the two sibling countries not end in agreement? And the second question was: if agreement eluded them, where is the Arab League? Is it not reasonable that the Arab League should be the first to be appealed to by its members? It should be up to the Arab League's Secretary-General to study the situation with all the ability and love for Arabs and Arab unity that he is known for. We always hope that the Arab League carries some weight in the eyes of the world, but there is no question that it must carry double that weight in the eyes of its member states. This may make us think once more about the establishment of an Arab court of justice that would have the decisive say in whatever differences might break out between two or more Arab states.

Today we are facing a new world, and it would be the most wretched of situations to face it as separate states or – even more calamitous and bitter – as states in conflict over borders or other issues. I think that what we agree on in economic, cultural and political cooperation is greater and more important than the matters we differ on, so why not depend on the areas where we agree, and leave the differences to be dealt with through the exchange of ideas in good time?

And as a final word: history will not forgive any citizen of Egypt or Sudan who is capable of bringing the two sides together and fails to do so.

26 January 1993

Strength in the Service of Principles

The Security Council recently decided on military intervention in Somalia to save its population from famine and starvation. I have seen crowds of them collapsing in front of empty relief centres as death carries off men, women and children among them.

Some see this intervention as coming too late, after hundreds of thousands of innocent victims have lost their lives, and they wish for a corresponding resolution to protect Bosnia and Herzegovina and strongly punish the oppressive Serbs.

But there are others who look at the resolution with an apprehensive eye, fearing that it is an opening for the stronger countries to gain dominion over smaller states, and a return to colonialism behind new masks and creative pretexts.

It is only fair to say that if this resolution does not become a basis for the United Nations and the Security Council to follow, they will remain empty symbols devoid of any real substance, and the idea of a new world will remain a dream with no hope of coming true.

If the world is truly serious about the defence of the human principles espoused by the United Nations, it must take a determined stand against any negligence of or departure from these principles. Thus it is our hope that the Security Council will retain its independent power, which all the signatory states of the United Nations charter have shared in creating.

To guarantee that there be no deviation or tangled machinations, the basic membership of the Security Council should be broadened, the Third World should be represented on it, and there should be no resort to a military solution except when voted on not just by the Security Council but by the General Assembly as well.

It is not difficult to suggest guarantees to protect against deviation or the arbitrary procedures that the strong states may resort to in their differences with the smaller states, and it may add new powers to the International Court of Justice so that it can be a fair judge among nations.

In summary: we can accept any reality except for the United Nations and its principles to remain a beautiful emblem without power or strength.

28 January 1993

We Want a Pure Awakening

The heart of the Islamic world beats with a religious awakening. The Arabs, the Persians, the Indians and the Africans are tabling similar questions and are looking forward to dreams of the same kind. We welcomed the awakening, and it did not assail us with fear for our recent heritage, the heritage that we have won from the modern age – like democracy, freedom of thought, national unity and respect for human rights. On the contrary, we said that we will derive a new strength from religion with which to embrace the principles of the age. It is a religion with faith and reason, suited to every time and place, even if the names and definitions differ. We could not imagine it denying a modern virtue or impounding an exalted value.

It is a religion that has put all people on an equal footing, that appeals to reason and that calls for reason, a religion that includes the obligations of thought, work and cleanliness, a religion whose measure is in the heart and in how we deal with others. I imagined that what occupies us in the awakening would be what most sublimely concerns humans and humanity, that our thoughts would revolve around and our tongues would be devoted to whatever will bring a person closer to his Lord, improve his world, make him a brother to others, broaden his understanding and increase his knowledge, enlighten his ideas with research and learning and delight his soul with beautiful fine art.

This is how it should have been, but look how it turned out!

The awakening was accompanied by unexpected manifestations like despotism, corruption, defeats, economic crisis, injustice and favouritism. When this happened, the reaction was that the awakening was tarnished in some of its locations by much extremism, and thus the dialogue was altered and the way of thinking changed. Our real concerns were no longer noted in our spontaneous conversation. Talk was more or less restricted to murders, manhunts, torture, the veil and infinite superficialities.

It is a tornado rising, and all the posts are being plucked out. All thought of what is good for us, what will build our nation, develop it, make it beautiful and reap advantage is being silenced.

Let us pray to God that we overcome all the difficulties that have accompanied the awakening, so that our equilibrium returns to us and we to it, and so that we resume our journey under the protection of the Lord of the Worlds.

4 March 1993

The Arabs in the World of Tomorrow

A new world is taking shape hour by hour, and very soon giant economic blocs may be revealed, of the kind that have been established among the European nations and between the United States, Canada and Mexico. And new blocs may be formed; indeed, even the nations that today are tending towards liberation and separation may in the very near future see the wisdom of returning to their blocs in a new manner, or, if they do not see that as working in their best interests, join another established bloc.

I think this has not escaped Arab thinking, or the Arab League. There are two scenarios that can be imagined for the life of the Arab nations:

The first – and this is the dream.– is for all Arab nations to be connected in a great economic integration, to make of them an economic union of influence, which would be the basis of a cooperative revival in culture and scientific research and would announce the entry of the Arab world into the modern age, bringing with it all its qualifications based essentially on economics and science, in addition to the highest values derived from its glorious heritage.

This is the image that we must work towards realising in defence of our existence, our life and our dignity, and from whose path we must remove all hindrances and negativity that might delay or postpone its implementation.

The second – that is, the second scenario – is the regrettable current reality, which is based on division, differences and the bitterness of painful memories. This is an extremely volatile situation, whose eruptions conjure argument, alienation and division.

Our destiny will be decided as a result of the battle between reason and its supporters on the one hand, and volatility and its cohorts on the other.

It may be wise to begin cooperation and integration between nations that are not in dispute with each other, or that are able to erase their mutual contradictions, solve their problems and become oblivious of their bitter memories.

We must make a start, even if with just two, three or four countries.

The success of their cooperation will be a call to others to join in and be convinced by the voice of reason and its wisdom.

19 March 1993

A Return to the New World

We must not make light of what has been said or what is being said about the new world, the post–Cold War world. That President Bush was the first to herald its arrival, and that President Clinton has reinforced this in unequivocal statements, inspires confidence and reassurance.

I cannot deny that many people do not believe what has been said and what is being said, and consider the world built on freedom, peace and justice to be nothing but a cunning political slogan. They have examples to support their argument, and of course I do not deny – for example – that the response to the crisis in Bosnia and Herzegovina did not come close to the response to the crisis in the Gulf. In the Gulf it was characterised by determination, decisiveness, action and strength, while in Bosnia and Herzegovina it appeared weak, languid and slow – words and no deeds, or deeds only after an unbearably long time.

This is what happened when interests trumped principles not supported by interests, and the situation collapsed and hopes were dashed. I do not deny any of this, but we must admit also what was gained in the case, in the mobilising of global opinion, in the sending of a flow of aid and in the imposition of the blockade and embargo. We should not expect the new world to be born perfect. It is enough that it does not swerve from its goal, in order to achieve it in the most perfect form possible, one day not too far distant, through the United Nations.

President Clinton was clear when he talked about:

1. Having a principal role to play in the beginning of peace and its underpinning.
2. Reviewing existing arms sales, to avoid arming any hostile nation.
3. Banning weapons of mass destruction of all kinds.
4. Working together with democracy.
5. Respecting human rights.

I hope the United Nations will become a true force for the protection of the highest human principles and the deterrence of delinquency and delinquents.

8 April 1993

The Role of the Intellectuals

People ask about the role of the intellectuals in the threats that confront us, at the forefront of which is terrorism. In my view, there is no precept particular to intellectuals alone, separate from other sectors of society. Rather, there is one general precept that applies to all, which can perhaps be summarised in the following words: 'Every citizen is required to perform his full duty within the realm of ability available to him.' This precept is right for everyone, whether illiterate, minimally educated, highly educated or specialised in culture and thought. All are required to perform their full duty within the bounds of their ability: the illiterate according to their training, the educated according to their learning, the highly educated according to their learning and cultural level and the intellectuals according to the depth and comprehensiveness of their cultural attainment. All that culture adds to training and learning is that it provides opportunities for the creation of awareness of the social and human dimensions of duty.

After that necessary preface, we can return to the original question about the role of the intellectuals. In fact, their role in the face of threats, especially terrorism, is a link in an integrated chain of national action. This begins at the beginning with the security forces, because if there is a crime there can be no hesitation or delay in confronting it to protect lives, stability and a peaceful existence.

Then comes the role of the state in dealing with the root causes of the phenomenon, through its plans for reform that aim at comprehensive development. Here we should concentrate in particular on battling unemployment, fighting corruption, combatting inflation and political reform. Last but not least comes the role of culture in debating extremism and analysing its thinking, confronting its views and methods, diagnosing it socially and psychologically, and working hard to prescribe the appropriate treatment. The more means of expression that are available to cultural representatives – the press, radio, television, conferences – the more they will be able to convey their message and reach their goals. The role of the intellectuals may even go beyond that, depending on their personal readiness. They participate in practical political and social life, and we should not expect to find just one viewpoint among them all, since they represent all parties and political, social, philosophical and artistic currents, and their views and attitudes will be defined accordingly.

8 April 1993

Suggesting a New Loyalty

I perhaps do not exaggerate if I say that we are a nation of multiple loyalties, and that this heralds a kind of chaos at times, at other times apathy.

The Egypt of 1919 believed in its Egyptianness first and foremost. Its renaissance was founded on national unity, to the famous chant of: 'Religion is for God, the country is for all.' Loyalty was strong, confidently upholding our great popular revolution, and this had no adverse effect on religion, Egypt remaining a wellspring of Islam and Islamic tradition. Arab nationalism, meanwhile, was not as strong here as it was in other Arab countries, and its reflection was limited to certain activities, such as literature and historical memoirs. The Egyptian foundation was strong, and it enfolded both religion and Arabism under its wings without affecting its clarity or strength.

The Egypt of 1952 was overtaken by a tangible change, making Arab nationalism its primary external goal. This was embodied in the union with Syria, and in the Yemen campaign,[1] and the media devoted their propaganda to it, while the educational books in our schools followed or even anticipated it. Two camps were established in the country: the 1919 generation, which held onto its Egyptianness, even when sympathising with the new nationalism; and the generation of the 1952 Revolution, which was loyal to Arabism with heart and soul. This latter trend suffered a lethal blow with the defeat of June 1967.

At that point – and perhaps in reaction to it – a new loyalty appeared, like a sanctuary and a consolation: political Islam. It was the call for religion to regain control of all life, private and public, domestic and external. This led to its demand for the establishment of Islamic rule, and it collided with the existing regime in a clash that is still ongoing and heated.

Alongside this collision stand the three loyalties whose manner of appearance we have indicated: the nationalist Egyptian, the Arab

---

1 The political union between Egypt and Syria lasted from 1958 until 1961. Egypt supported the Republicans in the North Yemen Civil War of 1962–70.

nationalist, and the Islamic. Our real task now may be to form from these three loyalties a greater loyalty that preserves its original constituents but ties them integrally together to make them stronger and more resilient, instead of their strength being squandered in blind struggles.

This is the task of us all, starting with the educators and ending with the politicians.

22 April 1993

A Thorough Review

It is rare to find a heart at peace these days. It is rare to find a person content with his today or hopeful of his tomorrow. Terrorism has certainly hit us hard, but it is not our only problem, and there is a genuine desire for a complete review of everything, arising from a feeling that many things have been overtaken by time and emptied of any meaning. Yes, terrorism is not our only problem. By way of example only: there is still disagreement over political reform and economic reform, and there are still many who interpret the difficulty of economic reform as a shortcoming on the political side.

Can we liberate the economy with hands that were trained and grew and blossomed under totalitarianism? We are asking for investment and its encouragement at a time when complaints are being raised about the obstacles that continue to stand in its path. In addition, our constitution was written for an era that has passed, and there is no constitution for our present time.

Our external world no longer has the clarity it used to have. Arab consensus is in need of lengthy restoration or reconstruction, and the tension that occurred in relations between Egypt and Sudan, or between Egypt and Iran, requires penetrating wisdom and benign efforts.

We need to review everything; we need to read reality correctly; we need to face the facts with courage; we need to build a ship that is fit to face any flood.

There are signs that suggest hope, and some sober writers favour change, while others talk of entente, others still of dialogue and rational mediation. These are pleasing omens, and we hope they lead to success and are widened to include everything else, making room for the righteous of this nation to begin a true renaissance that joins the highest eternal principles with the most modern practices of the age.

29 April 1993

A New Vision

The confrontation of terrorism today stands on two pillars:

1. A new strategy.
2. Popular participation.

Regarding a new strategy, the interior minister has made his decisive position on the departure from legitimacy clear, at the same time presenting a new vision for the battle, one that is committed to a respect for human rights in police stations and prisons, a refusal to target innocent people and a war on corruption and unemployment. This is a new way of confronting terrorism as a security, social and political phenomenon, to be treated with determination and reform and in compliance with human principles, for if it were not this way it would be a battle between terrorists on both sides. We pray to God that the promises will be fulfilled, that security, safety and stability will be assured for the nation, and that further bloodshed will be avoided.

From this starting point, the call for the people to participate begins to have meaning. It is true that it requires people to have courage, and to make sacrifices if necessary, but our people are not short of courage and do not begrudge sacrifice, especially if they are convinced that they are defending their interests, their dignity and their values. They may then hope that their participation in the confrontation with terrorism will be the first step in a greater and more comprehensive participation, that is, in the practice of their consummate political and social rights.

All we ask beyond this is that the actions will match the talk, that the strategy will be flexible enough to follow the reality and its changes and will be adorned with as much wisdom as determination, and that we remember that its true national aim is the achievement of security, safety and stability, and the sparing of Egyptian blood.

6 May 1993

The Price of Peace

Whenever mention is made of our Arab region in the wider world, it comes in the context of contradictory precepts. The region belongs to the Third World, and it is certainly underdeveloped, yet it is a repository of huge wealth; its peoples are bound together under a single nationalistic impulse, yet their many disagreements generate an antagonism otherwise seen only between rival national groups. Meanwhile, its history brings together the greatest philosophies of peace and human brotherhood on the one hand with the rapid march to become today a storehouse of nuclear warheads and biological means of extermination on the other. And while the illiteracy rate in the region is among the highest in the world, we lead the world in expenditure on arms and the acquisition of destructive weaponry.

Thus it was no surprise that our region was the first stop on the tour of the American secretary of state,[1] and that his trip was said to be for the sake of peace and the investigation of the positions of the conflicting parties towards it, and to look into the case of the Palestinians in exile as the greatest obstacle in the way of negotiations today.

It is fortunate that the American administration is continuing its interest in peace in spite of its declared commitment to internal affairs. As for us, peace should be at the forefront of our external concerns, and no less so in our domestic concerns. It is a necessity for development, which is our uppermost priority, and this is no different for development in the region as a whole. We must devote ourselves to regional development, resolve Arab differences and hurry to complete the economic integration that represents comprehensive development for the entire region.

So we hope that there can be a suitable solution for the case of the exiles that will satisfy them in particular and the Arabs in general. This solution must be found so that we can begin peace negotiations at the earliest opportunity. Peace is a necessity for which there can be no alternative or delay. The laws of life do not spare the timid.

12 May 1993

1 Warren Christopher, in office from 20 January 1993 to 17 January 1997.

A Certificate of Good Behaviour

When the new American president met with a group of children in the White House garden,[1] the conversation turned to the problems of childhood old and new – old, when smoking, alcohol, and the like were the dangers; new, when drugs and AIDS were added to them. The president confessed that his grades for good behaviour were weak, which was an alarming admission, the impact of which was lessened by his recollection that the reason was that he talked too much in class. This is a fault less serious than others, and it perhaps explains the number of promises he made in his electoral campaign.

This brings us to the topic of ethics in politics, and reminds us of the general view that morals are for individuals, who are required to follow them in private and in public, but that politics is not subject to the rules of morality and that in the end what matters is the measure of success or failure based on interests, and interests alone. Throughout history, colonialism has been famous for its massacres, its treacherous practice of divide-and-conquer and its betrayal of those living under such a regime, when their weapons are compared to those of their coloniser. The brutality of colonialism became clear in the slave trade. The pledges of the British became renowned for never being honoured, Frederick the Great of Prussia was so well known for violating treaties that he was called 'the fine promise', and Bismarck drew France into the war of 1870 through his proficient lies.[2] Meanwhile, the examples from modern history are still fresh in our memories, the two world wars being the greatest testimony of that. So individuals are judged by their character, politics by its success.

Has this view changed, or are things still the same?

There are many people who take a negative view, many people who see a conspiracy or a plot behind every word or action, many people who distrust any form of politics, even if it conforms with international legitimacy and principles, but the situation has changed from what it

1 Bill Clinton had become president a few months earlier, in January 1993.

2 The Franco-Prussian War, July 1870 to January 1871.

was before. There is no doubt that there exists today a global public opinion, and a global conscience, and any leader, no matter how high his standing, aspires to the shelter of the United Nations and the Security Council. Resolutions may differ from a situation where principles and interests coincide to one where they do not, but pressure, embargo, or the sending of emergency aid are always possible. Besides which, nobody prides themselves any longer on treachery, cruelty or challenging the international will. Indeed, judicial proceedings deter heads of state from their obliquities, and the president of the world's greatest country lost his post because of an accusation that denounced his political behaviour before he came to power.[3]

Let us hope that the situation has changed, and that tomorrow will be better.

20 May 1993

3 Mahfouz may be referring to Richard Nixon here, although the actions that led to his resignation occurred while he was in office, not before.

The Audience and the Play

The theatre is the same, the story is the same, the actors are the same, and the audience is the same. The content is fixed, and the variations are marginal, so the scene as a whole is one, and no notable change occurs in it. The audience follow what is happening on the boards with a heavy, dropping eye, or they do not follow it at all. They may sometimes utter a few words, but mostly retreat into silence. They may wake up once or twice if something worrying happens, or a bloody battle flares up or a natural disaster occurs, when they jump even wider awake, expecting appropriate reactions to the event or the battle, but if their expectation passes without issue they go back to whispering or silence or lethargy.

But what is behind the tale that is being played out on the stage?

In the centre is a ruling regime, with factions to its right and factions to its left.

Some of the factions have had their fill of criticising and demanding change with no result and so have become tired of talking, overcome by feelings of being lost, and no longer differ much from the audience, as though they are just a group of audience members who have taken their seats on the stage instead of in the house.

Then there are factions who express extremist ideas, reinforcing them from time to time with violence. These have succeeded to some extent in attracting attention and waking up the silent members of the audience, but their struggle has gone on in the same way and the back-and-forth conversation between them and the regime has entered a routine cycle, so the audience have returned to silence, drowsiness and the muttering of phrases of irritation and tedium.

In the centre of the stage is the regime, which is undertaking development in production and services and engaging in a continuous battle in defence of stability, working positively and fighting on more than one battleground, while to a large degree also appearing like the victim of a tyrannical bureaucracy, widespread obliquity and a strong fear of full democracy and the demands of the population to decide their own fate.

How long will the situation continue like this?

Perhaps it is the voice of wisdom that every now and then repeats the demand for change – a change of storyline, or at least of director.

27 May 1993

Role Models

Our memory has cheated us; indeed, it has cheated us of purpose and resolve, as our afflictions have come to include the forgetfulness of our glories. There is a strange rift that has separated our past from our present, and dust has been piled up on golden riches, cutting us off, as if we have no heritage. Generation upon generation have been born who do not know their own roots, and have no model to guide them on their paths. This may be among the many reasons we have slid into terrorism, or at least, into losing our way.

We have had unique minds in every field, who attained wonderful achievements that cannot be forgotten. We have had leaders in nationalism and politics, pioneers in natural sciences, engineering, medicine and agriculture, and innovators in religious thought, literature and freedom. Great names, each one of them with their own genius, reverberation and influence on their age and the ages that followed, and all of them deserve to be the subject of productive study in the nationalist agenda of the education system, as well as stars of radio and television programmes. I am only prevented from listing the names by the risk of omitting some and causing offence unintentionally, as others have done intentionally. Also, I am not calling for the revival of their memory only in order to honour them and recognise their contribution, but because there would be ethical and scientific lessons to be had, which would provide examples and role models in all areas of human activity, for the esteem and honour of Egypt, her journey and her history.

There is ample interest in the artists, which is nice and is worthy of thanks, but our interest in other builders of the nation must be no less than that.

22 June 1993

Crime in the Age of Innocence

There are many and varied reasons for crime – including, for example, mental illness and social maladies such as poverty and privation, as well as revenge, honour, love and jealousy. And most crimes can be committed as much by the educated as by the ignorant among the general population, although robberies (and murders through robbery) are most common in the environment of poverty and ignorance. That used to be how it went, but today there is appearing among us a new kind of criminal: criminals who are educated, even from the ranks of the students, where there ought to be innocence, idealism, model behaviour and good examples.

Let us look carefully at the students, symbols of innocence and idealism: how have a number of them turned into gang leaders, cutthroats and rapists? Indeed, how do some of them go so far as to murder their brother, their mother or their father? How does this happen? Of course, I am not saying that they have become a daily phenomenon, but they are no longer a rare exception. It is natural to point to poverty or the need for money, for one reason or another, as causes to focus on for blame, but we must remember that our society has never been free of poverty or the need for money, so we should look for other reasons to understand the corruption that has crept into the life of innocence. I will try to summarise these as follows:

1. Shortcomings in religious, moral and psychological upbringing.
2. The absence of good examples in life.
3. The dead end facing young ambitions.
4. The provocative sight represented by monstrous riches and corruption and their public display.
5. Terrorism and its brutal insinuations.

There is no particular cure for this crime, but its treatment includes the general overall prescription that we call comprehensive development.

29 June 1993

Let Us Make the New World

At first glance it invites gloom: what is happening in Bosnia, what occurred in Somalia, the latest strike received by Iraq – all this invites gloom. The Muslims blame the scales of international justice, and lay bare the evil intentions against Islam and Muslims. Anger is provoked and flares up, but its foaming waves subside into donations here or there and a bitter derision of what was once heralded and named the new world.

The truth is that we have not seen any new international behaviour except that which matches the interest of the strong countries, although perhaps the new features of the new order are not yet finally settled, and perhaps its tomorrow will be better than its today. But is our role restricted to waiting? I feel that the world will welcome whoever intends to participate in it sincerely, whoever considers himself a cell of its body, one of its functions regardless of size, whoever respects its general principles and contributes (in spite of his particular concerns) to its universal symphony, whoever tries to give as much as he takes and proves that he is a civilised part of it that is indispensable, or that could be dispensed with only with regret.

Let us have our particular concerns, but this does not mean that we should stand against the whole, be contrary, or drive in the opposite direction. Particular concerns are a distinct tune that adds to the beauty of the combined melody, but there must be movement towards the spirit of the age:

1. Towards democracy as a mode of government and of life.
2. Towards knowledge as a path and a means of revealing truths and living with them.
3. Towards respect for human rights as a sound climate for mutual understanding and coexistence.

We must do all this and more to contribute to the creation of the new world, and not be content with waiting under the awning of distress.

26 August 1993

When Will We Truly End Terrorism?

Terrorism has so occupied us that it has almost obscured all our other problems. Its ideas are a marvel of absurdity, its methods are unequalled in brutality, and the losses it has brought to our economy are heavy and burdensome and cannot be compensated in the short term. Despite all this, it is not an unsolvable problem. Ibrahim ʻAbd al-Hadi managed to eliminate it,[1] as did President Nasser. It seems these days to be giving up its strongholds, and I do not think it unlikely that it will soon go the way of its antecedents, and that safety and security will be restored.

But I hope that with the end of terrorism we do not consider the matter finished. We must ask ourselves why it keeps coming back. Why, after it has disappeared, does it return to pursue violence and shed blood?

The reality is that there exists a train of Islamic thought of a particular nature, and of more or less known goals, and this tendency has a base among the people that cannot be ignored. It has its representatives, but they do not receive their due recognition, either as an organisation or as a party. So they are excluded from licit activity, and this and its consequent social, political and economic circumstances are reflected in a picture of extremist ideas among some of their young followers, and a hasty rush towards violence again. And we return once more to dealing with violence as it deserves, oblivious of all its surrounding conditions. We consider it an artificial or an imported problem, attacking it with full force until we silence its voice and actions, but only for a time, not for ever, so long as the original issue remains unresolved.

The only solution for this difficulty is democracy, in which every current can enjoy its legitimate rights, putting its message across in detail to the people, and entering a fruitful dialogue with its opponents that will eventually lead to one view or more. And then it is up to the people to judge.

2 September 1993

---

1 Ibrahim ʻAbd al-Hadi was prime minister of Egypt from December 1948 to July 1949.

What Is Proper and What Is Not

What can you say about a nation that possesses all the means for spreading light, while most of its citizens are thrashing about in the dark? The first thing that springs to mind is that they are either incompetent or ignorant in the use of those means, or at the very least do not know the best manner of dealing with them. Or you may think the worst of those responsible for the means and accuse them of ignorance, perhaps of taking advantage with wicked intent, or you may go further still and not rule out conspiracy.

If this is not the case, then please explain to me how it is that we possess such a great number of schools, institutes, universities, mosques, churches, newspapers, magazines, cultural centres and libraries – how, if we possess all of these, can there be a single conscience that is devoid of the clear and pure water of faith? Or a mind without the light of learning and thought? Or a sensitivity with no feeling for beauty in its most wondrous shapes and forms? Indeed, explain to me how it is that we possess all that wealth in the means of upbringing, education and training, while superstitions, fairy tales, ignorance, aberrations and the adherence to trivialities and lies are so widespread among the majority of us?

I will not wade into the details or the evidence, as you have undoubtedly already come across much of it and read some of its nonsense, while commentators have spoken of some of its oddities. I will not go into that, but I will summarise our lamentable position in a few words: we are going through a critical time, such that our souls appear to be threatened with turbidity, our minds to be drowning in darkness and our sensitivities to be befuddled by stupidity.

This is not conceivable or proper when we possess such an ample supply of the means for spreading light.

9 September 1993

When We Resolve to Build the Future

The causes of suffering are many, as it occupies areas in the fields of politics, society and the economy, which are interconnected concerns both at home and abroad, and keeps us preoccupied night and day, tearing at the stability of souls and minds.

But let us, if only for the sake of peace of mind, seek out reasons for hope. This is not a product of daydreams, as its roots extend into reality, hidden within it, waiting only for someone to breathe life into them.

Take, for example, population growth in Egypt, which we count today as an invidious problem that threatens production and development. But how would things be if we could devote ourselves one day to the development of our human resources and prepare them ideally for the modern age, for progress, for construction and for enlightenment? We would reap unexpected riches that we could put to good use to the extent available, and perhaps others in nearby and neighbouring lands could benefit from them too.

Take another example. The deserts that surround us are vast, extensive and forbidding, and water is limited and in great demand. But science is powerful and proficient, and may be able to create a great oak from a little acorn, as they say. Perhaps the future will reveal a boom in Sinai or the Western or Eastern Deserts.

And take a third example, the unused power of the Arabs. Today it is in pieces, united only in elegant rhetoric and lack of cooperation. One day it must become free of the symptoms of malady, and mistrust and resentment will leave it behind, for life to flow into its connections and for everyone to face in the universal direction of economic integration. The giant in name will turn into a giant in fact. And there are similar dreams about Africa, and the Islamic world.

It truly is a rich future, hiding behind a tough present. We only have to recognise the value of time. What a wonderful ally it is for those who respect it – but it does not flatter, and it has no mercy for the complacently idle.

22 September 1993

The Map of Those Who Strive

In our society there are many political parties, and more problems. And it is natural, and to be expected, that differences will arise and opinions will clash around the problems in terms of their diagnosis, treatment and proposed solutions. There is debate around privatisation, there are disagreements over unemployment, and there are numerous views on corruption, but all these go on in an atmosphere of rationality and objectivity, rarely leading to any agitation, and certainly a long way from violence. The exception is the issue of the form of government – whether it should be secular or Islamic – around which the disagreement becomes angry and vehement, sometimes turning to violence and bloodshed. It is no exaggeration to say that this is the primary issue in the schedule of our political life.

It may be useful to take a quick look at the positions of the two sides on this serious issue.

The secularists cleave to a secular government, most of them preferring the democratic framework, in the belief that: 'Religion is for God and the country is for all.' Most of them are believers, some sincerely religious, so they see nothing wrong with acknowledging that Egypt is an Islamic nation and that sharia is the fundamental source of legislation, often stating that 90 per cent of current laws are compatible with Islamic sharia.

Among the Islamists there are extremists, some of them even terrorists, whose view of religion is based on bigotry and excess, even to the point of declaring society infidel – both rulers and ruled. But there are also moderate conservatives, who can best be labelled Salafis, and some are more open-minded, being perhaps the closest to the true spirit of Islam, who respect thought, democracy and national unity, and have the flexibility and enlightenment to face the modern age.

It may be good for the country and its future that the dialogue between the enlightened and the democratic not be interrupted, as it may lead to a unified basis and a common goal.

30 September 1993

Kindly Requested

The beginning of the third term for President Hosni Mubarak …

We congratulate him on his success, and there may be no disagreement about his character, or about the standing he holds in our hearts. The position of the opposition is no more than a political one, which gives voice to the desire for change, the urge for reform and the redoubling of determination in facing reality.

But we cannot present our congratulations and stop there: we cannot let the opportunity pass without once again expressing the desires, wishes and hopes that rage in our breast.

The president begins his new steps after completing two terms that were full of events and experiences. There have been many achievements, without doubt, and there have been serious false steps. We have fluctuated between nobility and courage on the one hand and natural and human disasters on the other, so today we ought to be closer to wisdom, to knowing what is right and to realising our hopes and wishes.

If I gave myself free rein in setting down our requests, I would fill pages and pages. Besides, they have become thoroughly well known through their long repetition and the people's suffering from them. So I will content myself with noting the essence of the issues that I believe will present themselves in the coming period.

The first issue is democracy as a door to every reform.

The second is the economic problem, whose true solution must be linked to the improvement of conditions for the poor and semi-poor.

The third is to define our position in relation to the Islamist current and how to deal with it; this is strongly connected with the first issue.

The fourth concerns a subject that we have almost forgotten about, despite the fact that our existence is tied to it. I mean the completion of the High Dam project: we cannot go on with it in a cycle of action and reaction.[1]

---

1 The Aswan High Dam, completed in 1970, brought major advantages to Egypt in water control and hydroelectric power, but there were disadvantages too, such as

And I have certainly not forgotten urgent matters such as corruption, unemployment and terrorism – but these are all symptoms and results.

7 October 1993

---

land subsidence in the Delta and increased erosion along the north coast, which Mahfouz had addressed in the past (see 'Egypt the Safeguarded', 4 July 1991).

Towards a New Life

It is not stretching optimism too far to believe today that we are about to enter the stage of a comprehensive, just peace.[1] This is a stage long yearned for by many in this part of the world, and by many who have been aware of the dimensions of the tragedy that has struck the region, who were horrified by what its inhabitants have suffered in the material, ethical and civilisational sacrifices they have made, forcing their harsh passage along a fruitless path.

Today the voice of reason is raised high, and the exigencies of reality are respected, as mutual recognition between the Palestinians and the Israelis is accomplished, and the momentum towards the realisation of genuine peace continues to grow.

I am not saying that this will receive total acceptance or complete satisfaction, for the mutual slaughter of almost half a century cannot simply cease with such a happy ending.

On both the Arab and the Israeli sides there are moderates and extremists, right-wingers and left-wingers, so disagreements are inevitable and contrariety is inescapable, but what is important is that the majority are satisfied and in agreement: the rest can be left to time, for it is time that will ensure the revelation of the benefits and advantages of the agreement, which may convince the objectors and bring them round. I consider time the final negotiator, which will have the historic, conclusive say. And it must be understood that true peace begins with mutual relations, as represented in the dialogue of the two civilisations, the meeting of the two cultures, and economic and scientific cooperation. This may bring the development and progress to the region that it deserves.

All Arab nations, regardless of their positions on the new agreements, must review their lives with the same reason and realism, and renew their policies in the light of the new demands of the region and the principles of the new world.

14 October 1993

---

1 The Oslo Accords between the PLO and Israel were signed in Washington, D.C. on 13 September 1993.

The Universality of Arabic Literature

The question is often raised about the universality of Arabic literature and how to reach it, and the connection between it and the Nobel Prize.

The universality of literature means quite simply that it transcends the boundaries of its language and acquires readership and serious expression outside the borders of its homeland, finding admirers in diverse countries, just as it does at home. Universality in this sense is a sublime goal for every literature, which it will only reach if it achieves a substantial degree of depth, inclusivity and humanity, while genuinely preserving its authenticity and its personal perspective. This is a difficult balance, but it is realised every day in every world literature, simplified in the end by the unity of human nature, its congruence of starting point and destiny, and its commonality of hopes, dreams and pains.

This has no definitive connection to any award, as an award may attest to one writer's universality, but tens or hundreds attain universality without a Nobel Prize, and sometimes some are even denied it because its conditions do not apply to them. But universality still needs someone to discover it through good translation and fair publicity, to attract the attention of critics and readers. Most universal writers have found universality this way; only a small number have come to it through the Nobel Prize, and even then the Prize is only a preliminary testimonial, as the final test is settled between the writer and the audience of readers and intellectuals of the world.

Arabic literature does not lack universality, but it is missing the accompanying activity of translation and publicity. I do not doubt that a considerable number of Arab poets and writers deserve universal recognition, including the Nobel Prize, and are awaiting a favourable opportunity.

28 October 1993

The Sun Will Rise Tomorrow

The meeting of any session of the United Nations is an opportunity to hear the voice of the world and the heartbeat of its conscience, when human hopes and demands ring out, calls for justice are raised all around the hall, and constructive suggestions vie with each other about South Africa, Somalia, Bosnia, Third World debt and the ailments of the environment – though the fine words usually do not travel beyond the heart and the tongue. Resolutions are only made in the Security Council, and we are always optimistic, however many mistakes are made or however much inertia prevails over good intentions (though in truth, we are not so over-optimistic as to imagine that the UN has turned into a world parliament, with full parliamentary powers). But we dream of a beginning with steps that are not impossible, such as expanding the membership of the Security Council to include some signs of the Third World, or the Council being supported by a strong armed force to assist it in implementing its just and humanitarian resolutions, to avoid a repetition of the feeble situation that happened in Bosnia.

The world's need for the role of the UN and the Security Council increases day after day, for the world intertwines, interacts and connects, and likewise it becomes apparent each day that its old problems are becoming more complicated and that new ones are turning up. Certainly this is the time for the international body and its security council to work continuously towards discipline, equilibrium and stability.

As I write these words, I can almost see the sarcastic smiles on the lips of the pessimists. But I ask them to compare what happens today with what used to happen, for example comparing the United Nations with the League of Nations, or comparing the liberation of states from colonialism with the politics of plunder, pillage and perfidy.

It is true that we are entering a world full of many hardships and heavy responsibilities, but we enter it under an umbrella of hope and optimism.

4 November 1993

The New Reality

A new reality is being shaped in our region, and there are those among us who greet anything new with distrust and imagined conspiracies and plots. I hear them talking about the isolation, exploitation and marginalisation that are in store for us. We are a people with a long history in politics, administration and dealing with other countries, and we have the experience and the functionaries sufficient to support us in any confrontation. We can distinguish between what is beneficial and what is detrimental, and weigh our interests against the interests of others. We can trade in politics without forfeit, in economics without being devoured and in culture without losing our authenticity. We were already heading towards solving problems and attaining peace, and now peace is being realised day by day, heralding a new world of action and interaction. So let us progress with all courage and self-confidence, looking forward to a better world.

But we cannot progress without full preparation, some on our part, some on the part of our Arab brothers.

For our part, as far as possible, we must put in place democracy, respect for human rights and the rule of law, and the purging of corruption, through which we hope to eliminate terrorism and the state of emergency with all its notorious laws. Yes, we cannot progress until we provide our ancient land with true stability and a civilised face.

As for our Arab brothers, it is time for them to rise above their disagreements, whatever sacrifices it may cost them, so that the opportunity is there for them to participate, in their full strength and will.

A new reality is being shaped, which provokes fear. Entering it requires us to change and renew what is in our selves.

11 November 1993

Freedom and Justice

The left has returned to power in Poland and Greece, and it appears that the democratic tide is receding in the face of the socialist tide. So was the revolution against socialism an incidental outburst, after which the people regained their equilibrium and returned to their senses?

In fact, we must not forget the effect of the economic crisis in the new situation, which, if it indicates anything, shows that people hate and dread hunger, not that they love communism. It may be that this reversion would not have happened if the democrats had been more successful in their economic project.

Even so, the old communism has not come back, and democracy has not come to a halt, or yielded. The communists won thanks to democracy, not by coercion or by force, and they will rule in its shade and under its oversight. There will be no tyranny or oppression, no suppression of freedom, no attrition of human rights; the revolving door of authority will remain open, with the people's word supreme.

So democracy is still standing, and the new communism is a democratic communism, which is attempting to bring together the justice of socialism with the freedom of democracy. This system may be what is being revealed by the new world order. Are we now to think that neoliberalism, so deep-rooted in its firmest strongholds, has been influenced by socialism, and that its governments are undertaking to provide their people with major services in health and education?

West and East are exchanging advantages to the benefit of their populations, and every day brings more certainty that humanity cannot do without two great values: freedom and social justice.

18 November 1993

Respect

There is much talk of how the West regards Islam and the Muslims, concluding with the often repeated view that Islam is the proposed enemy and the next challenge to western civilisation.

Why should this be so?

The historical legacy plays a large role, as there are those who believe that the Crusades will never end.

Then there is the question of perceived terrorism.[1]

And last but not least, civilisational underdevelopment has a large part to play.

What do we think of these reasons?

I do not think that the historical legacy remains in time's memory any longer than it should. History witnesses the melting away of old enmities that had come between nations and peoples, and their disappearance from sight in the face of new interests and the call of renewed life.

As for terrorism, so many countries of the world suffer from it, and it is carried out there more strongly and terribly than it is in the Islamic nations, though without affecting their reputation and standing.

In underdevelopment we could find an excuse for the West, if they were to focus on us with an uncomfortably close look: some Islamic countries govern in a manner far from the spirit of the age, with human rights disregarded and treated with hostility, and administrations characterised by weakness and corruption, in addition to their backwardness in science and culture.

But it is the Muslims who should be held to account for such a condition, not Islam, which is a religion of consultation, which has respect for humanity, and which holds freedom, justice, learning and work sacred.

Better than grumbling and remonstrating with the West, better than this would be to critique and correct ourselves, and correct

---

1 This paragraph was apparently missing from the published Arabic text and has been reconstructed by the translator.

our world. Then we would receive respect without complaint or propaganda.

25 November 1993

The Principal Enemy

It is very good that we are thinking about our present and our future, and it is very good that we are calling upon everybody to do the same – even though it is every citizen's duty to do so without being called upon, and it is not right to interpret the call as allowing us to put off attending to a problem, since problems are interconnected and development must be comprehensive. Just as the overhaul of the education system is as essential as life itself, the issue of pollution is of a seriousness that similarly cannot be ignored. The foundation of any revival on firm democratic grounds is a matter of the utmost importance, and we believe in it with total faith.

So let the call have the aim of accentuating the significance of and throwing a light on a truly important subject that impinges on more than one problem and affects our present and our future more than any doubt or disagreement does. I am talking about frustration or, if you like, hopelessness – the killer disease of every soul, the blind mover behind innumerable evils and crimes beyond count. It is a disaster if it strikes anybody, but it is doubly disastrous if it infiltrates the soul of our youth, where it will live to spread darkness, futility, crime, malice and mental imbalance. We must fight hopelessness with all means, whatever sacrifices it may cost us.

Unemployment may be its primary nest, but it is not the only one. It may be born in a deficient, depressing school, in a disorganised workplace, in a salary that achieves no goal, in the painful feeling of partiality or a lack of equal opportunities, or in the futility of the rule of law in the absence of respect for human rights.

Fight hopelessness in its nests or wherever it is to be found. It is we who plant it, and it is we who reap it.

2 December 1993

Priorities

In truth, it is meaningless to look into priorities. It would have meaning if it were possible to advance one issue and delay another in order to complete the first. But which issue in our life can we postpone, even by an hour? This is why comprehensive development is imperative. However, this does not prevent us from being able to weigh up the different issues in terms of importance or value, in the light of the higher civilisational ideal that we aspire to. On this basis, I can talk about priorities, presenting a personal point of view.

The first item I would place on the list is education, or the dream of the perfect school, the perfect teacher, the free, innovative curriculum, training in all its forms – religious, national, cultural, artistic and sporting – in short, the factory that would produce for us the ideal model of the Arab–Egyptian person, combining eternal values with living modernity.

Second on the list is scientific research, and the preparation of the proper climate for it, the setting up of whatever equipment it needs, and the provision of the means of recognition and encouragement for the researchers, all in view of science being the basis of every issue, from the economy to sport.

Third on the list is administration, considering proper administration to be the foundation for the success of any governmental or civic undertaking.

I do not wish to further weigh up any of the remaining issues. They can all be looked at in the same way and evaluated on the same scale.

Finally, I would like to say that the reform of education, scientific research and administration is futile unless the planning is based on the foundation of a democracy that arises from freedom and the respect for human rights.

9 December 1993

The Flood Once More

This is a single world in spite of its disagreements, its contradictions and its differing stages of development. It is made a single world through the means of communication that carry the dialogue of its peoples and communities, of its problems, its hopes and its pains, hiding from no one the astonishing progress of the advanced areas or the distressing underdevelopment of the areas that lag behind. So the optimists are justified in their optimism, as the pessimists may be excused their pessimism. Meanwhile, life moves on along its path without averting its gaze from the goals of success and victory.

While we frequently remark injustice, outrage, aggression and selfishness, we should also remark aid and loans, the free sharing of experience and knowledge and the defence of human rights with the heart, the tongue and sometimes the arm.

But the Third World has to believe that its role is greater than simply waiting with its hand outstretched, importuning those who have scientific learning and experience.

It has more than just large populations and raw materials. It has been shown capable of sacrifice and forfeit, because it possesses willpower and high ideals and is supported by a heritage that sanctifies values, learning and work. It must kindle the noblest of what is in its spirit, to then advance on the path of infinite life.

And it must understand that it is living in an age of a new flood, and that only those who grow in faith, learning and work, and who are determined to build a better existence, will be saved on the ark. And woe betide those who fall behind.

11 December 1993

From Self-Sacrifice to Reason

The new Arab renaissance is passing through two phases, the phase of liberation and the phase of construction, and the two are inextricably linked together. Construction began in the liberation phase, just as the construction phase contains remnants of the liberation phase that have not yet been filtered out. We can cast a little light if we say that the liberation phase comprises liberation from colonialism, internal enslavement and outdated ideas and habits. And the construction phase comprises civil innovation in its diverse aspects – in industry, agriculture, science and culture – and in general the Arabs have proved that they are at the required level to fulfill their primary mission.

They have staged many political, social and intellectual revolutions, lost countless martyrs and victims and borne oppression and tyranny. The Arab freedom fighter became the symbol of this heroic phase, embodying sacrifice in its clearest expression, and the banner of this noble cause was carried by thousands of young people and tens of commanders and leaders. This was the phase of liberation in the full meaning of the word, as it was the phase of the freedom fighter in the exalted meaning of that phrase.

But the construction phase requires a different human quality, which has perhaps drawn its eternal self-sacrificing spirit from the fight for freedom on the path of higher values, though it is building a foundation on the institutions of sound education, on endeavour, perseverance and patience, and in the broad love for truth, the passion for discovering the unknown, the quality of science and scientific research and the sanctity of production and labour.

Today the thinking, inquiring, productive Arab must occupy the place of the freedom-fighting Arab who undertook the work of liberation and prepared the way.

It is the age of reason – and praise be to Him who blessed and distinguished us with reason.

23 December 1993

On Culture

What I hear about the state of culture in Egypt is not pleasing. It is repeated and confirmed almost unanimously, and it seems to apply to literature, theatre, cinema and music. So I have the right to believe what is said, and to wonder about the reasons for it: are there reasons to explain the decline of culture?

I mentioned the state of education some time ago.[1] We no longer have proper schools or proper teachers, classes are overcrowded, and instruction has practically disappeared. There is no library or magazine or activity conducive to revealing talents. We no longer provide the right atmosphere for the discovery of creative personalities on the one hand or the training of intellectuals on the other. We have struck down creativity and taste, so the field has been emptied of beauty and splendour, and it has collapsed into drought. This is why we follow news of the revolution in education with the greatest interest and anticipation.

I have also mentioned the influence of television and its mastery over minds and hearts.[2] It hunts down numerous book lovers, adding them to the millions of television lovers, as it also hunts down many writers, who then turn from literature to the service of this magical apparatus, enjoying whatever fame or fortune wafts their way. Of course, we do not deny the achievements of television and its services, but we cannot ignore the deep effect it is having on art.

And I have mentioned the harmful effects of the economic crisis, unemployment and extremist ideas, all of which declare themselves the enemy of culture.

The picture as we see it is gloomy, but it does not call for despondency. It is connected to the plans for comprehensive development and to the challenges that we face. We must endure the distress a little, but the new life is coming, there is no doubt about that.

30 December 1993

---

1 See 'Towards a Modern Education', 1 August 1991.

2 See 'Cultural Concerns', 24 September 1992.

Catastrophes on the Scales

In many catastrophes, and in their aftermath, it becomes apparent to us as we follow the news that the accident had been expected to happen and that the responsible agencies had already warned people about it, asking them to vacate their homes or leave the area that is under threat.[1] But no one takes any notice, nor does the responsible agency take any measures to enforce what the general good requires.

What is the explanation for this?

If we attempt a close investigation of the reasons, this may help to change things in the future, avoiding such catastrophes and lessening their sorry consequences.

One of the main negative reasons here is that moving house, or relocating from one area to another, is not an option for the great majority of people. Residential accommodation is in short supply, and the housing crisis is well known and on record, so people prefer to stay in a home that is threatened with collapse rather than wander in the streets without one.

Another reason is our natural tendency to be fatalistic, our comfort in that, our absolute submission to destiny, and our stubborn belief that what is written is stronger than the cautions of the cautioners or the predictions of the predictors. And the responsible specialists themselves may not be free of this tendency, as they issue their orders but do not care that these orders evaporate into thin air.

Then, of course, all the warnings come as a result of scientific assessments, and we are still not accustomed to awarding science its due sanctity, so only a few believe them while the majority do not assign them the seriousness or concern they deserve.

I have no doubt that the relevant official agency would not treat the matter with such disregard if it held any true respect or genuine patriotic love for the citizens as human beings. And we will not forget that

1 Mahfouz seems to be talking here about the sadly common occurrence of sudden building collapses, rather than natural disasters.

the government is responsible, first and last, for the housing problem, and for the protection of lives.

6 January 1994

A Hymn to the New Year

What can we say about the past year, if we give credit to both what is said and what happened? I mean I would like to summarise it relying on the official statements, which are issued by the authorities and which we are supposed – indeed, obliged – to trust; and relying also on reality and what we have seen, which are facts that cannot be denied or ignored.

We believe in the good intentions that the state harbours towards democracy, trusting that it is eager for the appropriate time to bring it to full perfection.

We believe that our economy has progressed, that the steps to its reform have earned the appreciation of the world, and that 1995 will be the year of harvest and prosperity.

We do not doubt that a revolutionary movement is taking place in the arena of education, and we wish it success with all our hearts. And we believe that the government has taken a firm hold on terrorism and that it will put an end to it after tearing away all its secrets.

And we believe everything that has been said about our achievements in all fields of production and services. But it is also inevitable that we surrender to what is foretold by events.

Because the great majority of Egyptians are suffering bitterly from life and its various hardships, such as rising prices, pollution of air, water and food, overcrowding, transport, mistreatment in hospitals and government offices, lack of security, continuing terrorist attacks, the shocking news of corruption and unemployment and the atrocious injustices reported by the victims of patronage.

What a year! Or what an age – one that has gathered together the finest intentions and achievements on the one hand with the most appalling violations of human rights on the other.

Whatever the situation, let us welcome the new year in anticipation of good things to come, and may God Almighty not allow them to be thwarted.

13 January 1994

The Letters and the Ministers

Do you read the letters page of *Al-Ahram*? Do you follow what people write to the press? I think it is a very successful portal, and hardly a reader passes over it, so honest and straightforward is it and so profound are the messages that it conveys to our hearts and minds. It is a mirror that reflects our life as a whole, focusing specifically on the hardships and difficulties faced by the citizen: the negligence and carelessness, the oppression and cruelty, the indifference in places of work and leisure, on the road, in the school, in the hospital, on the buses and trains, in the government offices, in the police stations – all of it beyond counting, beyond the belief of any mind, unpalatable to any taste and unacceptable by any civilised standard. It is a most astonishing thing that conduct and behaviour have tumbled to this level in a country that prides itself on its association with civilisation for a period of seven thousand years, while the reader takes nothing from what he reads but grief, distress and sorrow, hardly ever moving beyond that to find a very rare positive point. Indeed, I almost fear that the matter is minimised by its daily repetition, and that our tragedies are becoming normal events that we pass through with no noticeable reaction.

I wonder whether the relevant ministers read this daily insight? Today we no longer have a bureau for injustices, so all that is left is for the ministers to start their daily work by looking specifically through the letters pages, as this may be a starting point for reform in all areas, and may delineate the first steps in straightening all that is crooked, simplifying all that is complicated and applying the laws, so that reverence and respect are restored to the state.

We could measure the success of the ministers – especially those responsible for services – by the disappearance of complaints and the scarcity of anyone complaining.

20 January 1994

Sorrow and Anger

The intellectual and creative community is right to be sad and angry. They are right not because a question about culture was put in front of the People's Assembly, but because this questioning has reopened many wounds that do not heal, and has returned the tragedy of the whole field of culture to the focus of awareness and memory.

The fact is that the questioning did not surprise us at all. All it has done is to present an old issue about the relationship of literature and thought to religion on the one hand and to ethics on the other. It is an old issue that is set in motion at every occasion, or even without occasion, and it is not possible for a single, final view on it to be determined. So it is not the questioning that has saddened and angered the intellectuals, but it has pushed them to confront their tense reality, and to recall what has happened in their world: the serious accusations that have been made, the seizure of not a few books, the embarrassment of some among them, and the spread of fabrications and poorly formed opinions through the various media – in addition to the extremist opinions that have declared literature and art to be forbidden by religion, even if their form has no connection to religion or ethics. This strangling circle is completed by the general cultural decline imposed by the economic and social crises.

With all this, the reasons for sorrow and anger are plentiful, and everybody should review everything connected to their noble activity.

The dialogue both among ourselves and between us and the state should revolve around the following points, and any new ones that may be suggested:

1. The role of schools in cultural training.
2. The role of television.
3. Removing the taxes on paper and the requisites for printing, and the liberation of book export from any restrictions.
4. That in the case of disagreements, discussion should take the place of legal action.

5. An increase in the budgets for cultural magazines, to help them to revive and compete.
6. Taking care of the Mass Culture Committee, so that it can promote its message in the most perfect manner.

23 January 1994

Thought, Creativity and Freedom

Thinkers and creative artists hope that that there will be a climate of freedom for them to think and create without restriction or circumspection.[1] If what they produce meets with satisfaction and acceptance, their wish will have been fulfilled; if otherwise, they do not mind criticism and discussion, but without exposure to accusation, censorship or prosecution.

But reality contradicts hopes, for the society they live in is controlled by laws that cannot be ignored, including the criminalisation of any impingement on the sacredness of religions or the sanctity of ethics. In the case of any violation, a ruling may be sought from the justice system, which will issue its judgement as it sees fit. But the supervisory agencies can do no more than issue an opinion or institute proceedings, to which they resort in order to defend religion and ethics, not to attack thought and art, as indicated by the fact that they also have their thinkers and creators. If the law were changed, the whole intellectual and creative conflict would take place in a clear atmosphere of discussion and the pitting of one argument against another.

The path is clear for the thinkers and creators: all they must do is to think and create without touching on anything that is sacred or forbidden, so they will face no threat or constraint. And if their thought does lead them into dangerous areas, they must then decide which is preferable: to sacrifice their ideas, or to sacrifice their security and safety – in this, each is master of his own decision, and responsible for his own fate.

Freedom is not gifted or granted, nor is it won through insults, accusing the innocent, or delusions of intrigue – but history always attests that its price has been high, and its martyrs have been many.

3 February 1994

---

1 At the time this article was written, a Cairo University assistant professor, Nasr Hamed Abu Zayd, was on trial for apostasy, having written a thesis that challenged mainstream views on the Qur'an.

The World at Your Fingertips

You will be able to invite the world and everything in it into your sitting room, and this will cost you no more than the push of a button on the television, something you could only previously imagine in the world of magic and demons. You will find the whole world standing within your sight and hearing. Without any effort, you will receive information, spectacle, customs and traditions, ideas and opinions and art in all its shapes and forms. The world will be blended in a single melting-pot, and no watchdog, law, regime or regulation will impede it. One of the inevitable results of this unrestricted opening up is that we will know the facts without falsification or distortion, and that we will come across different points of view on one idea. We will see the harmony of people as well as their differences and their contradictions. The rising star of a unified humanity will be proclaimed.

If we make ourselves fit to receive this future revolution, we will derive pure benefit from it, but if we receive it without grounding or preparation, we will find as much bad in it as good.

We must raise our young people to be open-minded and independent in their judgements, and to think before they accept or reject anything. This way, we will be able to face any new views or thoughts without fear of the negative effects of weak thinking or dazzled enchantment.

We must raise them in the embrace of the highest values, so that they are not carried away by cheap temptations or common pleasures.

And finally we must elevate our intellectual and artistic cultural output, for success in the coming world will only be awarded to the truest, the finest, the most lasting. Fear of life is no longer a feasible attitude – fortitude, courage and self-confidence are essential.

10 February 1994

Identity

The preservation of identity springs from a love of self, of country, of history and of memories of life and generations. There is nothing wrong with an attachment to identity, but it is not right that such attachment should extend to turning it into something sacred. There may be nothing – with the exception of religion – that is sacred about identity, for it is altogether composed of elements that can be developed, changed or renewed, even deleted or added, as may be required by advancement or progress along humanity's long road towards the consummate life.

The defence of identity for no more reason than that it is our identity is invalid, just as the denial of identity for no more reason than being dazzled by the identity of another civilisation is also invalid. Both positions are unreasonable and inauthentic and will lead to nothing but disorder and error, which means only clinging to what brings harm and no benefit, or to what is more harmful than beneficial.

This conclusion is confirmed by a presentation of the elements of which identity is composed, that is: customs, traditions, ideas and tastes. The assessment of these elements – whether as they stand or in comparison with their counterparts in other cultures – must be built on what they comprise of good or bad, or what they bring of benefit or harm, or what supports them of sincerity or beauty. Based on this continuing debate, we will end up either maintaining our identity and rejecting everything that is foreign, or being influenced by others – and there is no harm in this case in favouring entire elements over those we already have. The important thing is that we act with independence of thought and freedom of choice. Interaction will reveal a new identity that will not take long to become a legacy, and the identity of fathers and forefathers.

We must face the age of the great global village with courage and self-confidence.

17 February 1994

Comprehensive Peace

If we want to be free to build, reconstruct and advance, we must start out on ground that is blessed with stability and peace. So let 1994 be the year of comprehensive peace – between Arabs and Israelis, between Arabs and Arabs, and between Egyptians and Egyptians.

The climate of Arab–Israeli peace inspires optimism, in spite of slow progress at times, or stumbling at others. It is apparent that the two sides are persevering in their goal of an unswerving end from which there can be no going back, and they have also come to believe in the necessity of peace and its advantages.

As for Arab–Arab peace, it is impossible to imagine that it can be any more difficult than peace between the Arabs and Israel. Any residues from the past can be dissolved in the channel of time, there can be understanding over borders, and the Gulf War can be brought closer to an agreement that will reassure hearts and ease consciences. I am not belittling serious matters, but any disagreement appears trivial in light of the demands of the future and what we must make of ourselves in order to catch the train of modernity.

And as for peace among Egyptians, the least we ask of ourselves is to be as concerned about our own peace as we are about that of others. We have made – and are still making – continuous efforts to mediate for good and to bring viewpoints closer, and our task is no less than to maintain this laudable enthusiasm as we mend our differences and disputes. Let us exchange views instead of exchanging bullets.

Let 1994 be the year of comprehensive peace, to free us up for the greater struggle – by which I mean building, reconstruction and advancement.

3 March 1994

The Required Mission

How do we raise our productive potential to the highest level of both quality and quantity?

The answer has to be sincere and clear. It will not happen unless we change the way things are, and there is no longer time for half measures, as we are entering into both the Middle Eastern market and GATT.[1] The motivation needed will be at our disposal only under the following conditions:

1. The achievement of stability and security, whatever this costs us in flexibility and sacrifice.
2. Raising wages to the appropriate – even if minimum – level, so that the labourer or office worker can do without a second job and is able to resist any kind of dishonest activity, and uphold the principle of reward and penalty with precision and honesty.
3. Making full use of science and its applications and studies, investing in the national scientific experience, and turning to foreign experience for help when necessary.
4. Liberating and renovating administration, paying attention to the recommendations of the financial and administrative oversight agencies, in a return to the control, respect and sovereignty of the law.
5. The establishment of dealing in total fairness: outlawing favouritism, nepotism and everything that infringes on a person's rights or pushes him to despair and frustration.
6. Taking account of genuine excellence when distributing dividends and incentives.
7. Encouraging investment through the removal of all obstacles in its path and providing the atmosphere that can exist only under the shade of full democracy.

6 March 1994

1 GATT: The General Agreement on Tariffs and Trade, predecessor to the World Trade Organisation.

A Dialogue with Violence

Why do some turn to the use of violence in their dealings with others or with society?

The first thought that comes to mind is mental or psychological illness, and whatever hereditary causes or social circumstances lie behind it.

Then there is the violence that results from power, which the strong boy or strong youth, proud of his muscles, resorts to in confrontation with others. The authorities may also do this in countries where the rights of citizens are undervalued.

And there is violence that may be exerted unintentionally, as when thieves are cornered, having been trapped with no way of escape.

Of course, we must not forget the violence that is inspired by traditions, such as the blood feud, or rage over honour. We should also not forget the criminal violence of war, which reaps millions of victims. And there is political violence, which usually arises with the loss of hope of reaching one's goal through legitimate channels, a feeling that is formed in the face of dead ends, when aims seem to be far beyond reach, or when dealing with an enemy so superior in strength that it is not an even match.

And there are circumstances that, even if they do not lead directly or definitively to violence, create an atmosphere that invites or induces it and a mental state that is in sympathy with it – such as, for example, unemployment, the inability of the young to realise their legitimate claims, the spread of nepotism, the lack of equal opportunities, the diffusion of corruption and contempt for human rights.

In any case, the closer a society comes to the sound conduct of its affairs, the further it moves away from violence in all its shapes and forms.

17 March 1994

A Dialogue with Corruption

No society is free of corruption. There is a human instinct that leads to hostility, killing, pillage and all kinds of harm, though when we turn to life in a society we are vouchsafed the distinction between the righteous and the corrupt, between good and evil, and can enact laws for reward and punishment. But whatever means of education or upbringing we are granted, whatever good examples or religion or values we are exposed to, a part of us will remain the victim of unruly passions and latent impulses.

This is why we find corruption in every land, whether underdeveloped or advanced, dictatorship or democracy, even if the degree of resistance to corruption differs between one country and another. The advanced nation is blessed with a superior education system, good role models in every field, a high standard of living and a healthier and more secure psychological climate, and all this tends to strengthen correct conduct and resist evil and corruption.

Likewise the democratic country: there is ample freedom and oversight, monitoring and opposition, respect for human rights and sanctity of the law and its supremacy over all, as well as equal opportunities and whatever else reinforces integrity, keeps corruption in check and chases down the corrupt.

What happens in the authoritarian society is the complete opposite: the leaders elevate themselves above the law; natural impulses find a climate free from fear, responsibility and scrutiny, in which the most heinous offences can be safely committed; the prerogatives of the rulers extend to their followers, relatives, friends and attendants; and values and principles vanish, as hopes are extinguished.

Fortunately, we know what is good and we know its path, as we also know the value of honesty in our work.

24 March 1994

The Voice of Progress

Extremist thinking goes back a long way in our country, rejecting everything new that comes from the West. Modern thinking also has a not inconsiderable history, working to build a nation of the modern age, taking from the West a model for guidance. And while extremist thinking claims to be the true representative of religion, modern thinking asserts that it is the real representative of true religion.

History shows that the relationship between the two ways of thinking is an antithetical one: whenever one of them gains strength, it raises its voice and spreads its influence, and vice versa.

Government under modern thinking has always differed in its degree of modernity from one period to another, and likewise its periods of rule have risen and fallen. The high points have included the achievements of the 1919 Revolution, the advances of the early Nasser era, and the October victory of 1973 and the liberation of the homeland. Among the low points have been the Cairo Fire of 1952 and the subsequent collapse of the monarchy, the June defeat of 1967, the ill-conceived Open-Door policy, the economic crisis and corruption.

At every upturn the voice of the extremists dies away, and at every downturn it rises and turns to violence.

So the successful confrontation of violence will come about only through holistic action. Security and counter-argument are certainly both necessary, but they are of no use on their own, and holistic action is essential, with all force and perseverance – action that includes political, economic, social and cultural reform together. It is a matter of freedom and justice, building and renovation, and the purging of corruption and negativity. And it is a question of looking forward to the future with minds enlightened by learning and hearts filled with faith.

2 April 1994

Do Not Lose Hope

Do not lose hope. I say this inspired by knowledge and faith, not by way of preaching. I am not unaware of what you are not unaware of, and what keeps you awake at night keeps me awake at night too. Nevertheless, I tell you: do not lose hope. I am not unaware of the news of corruption, debt, underproduction, overpopulation, administrative decline, terrorism and political reactionism. Nor am I unaware of the news of pollution, the hole in the ozone layer, drought, earthquakes, famine, tribal disagreements, the oppression of minorities, the massacre in Bosnia, weapons of mass destruction and divisions among the Arabs. My breast rages with all this, yet I tell you: do not lose hope.

I keep in mind at the same time that humanity has reached a peak of civilisation never before dreamed of: knowledge accumulates, discoveries compete with one another, values proliferate in different forms, and journeys into space multiply and excite the greatest wonder. Human relations are improving and a familial conscience is being born, its impulses spreading support, kindness and respect for human rights. And do not forget the extraordinary advances in the field of health, nor the beauty and pleasure of creative artistry or the contemplation and wisdom that are in the air. Look at this constant movement towards progress: it is flowing, and it is affirming its flow in the confrontation of the negativities that obstruct the channel of life – and perhaps if it were not for these imperfections, movement would cease. In ancient times, our forefathers faced drought and were threatened with death, so they came to the Nile, discovered agriculture, and erected the first edifice of civilisation in our known history.

So do not lose hope. Evil is not there to push you to despair, it is there to urge you to sharpen your thinking and your will, and to prepare for the perpetual revolution.

2 April 1994

The Chart of Culture

We used to have a cultural chart in our childhood and youth, and it was split into two main divisions. We called one of them the innovators and the other the conservatives. Each division in its turn was split into two classes, the extreme and the moderate. Thus the chart could be read as follows:

1. Extreme innovators, who advocated an unrestrained and unconditional leap into the embrace of western civilisation. They took Kemalist Turkey as their model and ideal.
2. Moderate innovators, who took pride in tradition and promoted its outstanding features, but were open to global cultures, especially western culture, without their self-confidence being shaken. They extolled the wonders of tradition, while critiquing it maturely.
3. Extreme conservatives, who invoked the time of our venerable forefathers in thought, feeling and conduct, and closed their windows in the face of the West.
4. Moderate conservatives, who were in overall agreement with the moderate innovators, perhaps the important difference between the two groups being that one established a traditional foundation, then opened up to the world, while the other established a civil foundation, then turned towards tradition.

The chart today may not have changed substantially, even if the names are different. The innovator and the conservative have disappeared and been replaced by the leftist and the secularist on the one hand, and the two orders of Islamists on the other.

In addition, there is another factor that has an important effect, which is the general climate. In the old days there was a climate of tolerance, so the sound of discussion rang out, while altercation disappeared under the influence of the revolution that created this climate, the 1919 Revolution of liberation and freedom.

Today, the climate is pervaded by intransigence and fanaticism, and is characterised by violence. There is depression, and accusations and confiscations abound as a result of the revolution that created this climate. The 1952 Revolution, which came by force, imposed its principles by force, and deferred the application of freedom in the belief that it was not compatible with the justice it had implemented.

Thus we see that the problem of culture is not a purely cultural problem, but primarily a political one, and that the only way to restore equilibrium is through full democracy and respect for human rights.

7 April 1994

The Reader and the Writer

The correct definition of a writer is not that he is one who writes; it is more correct to say that he is one who is read. So long as he has not yet reached his readers, he is an aspiring writer, no more, whatever his own opinion of himself, or his friends' opinions. And if the critics recognise him before any reader turns to him, this is an individual judgement and a forecast, but he only becomes a writer when his readers certify that he exists. I know there may be a writer who is ahead of his time, as they say, and whose acceptance is delayed, but he remains an aspiring writer until time delivers his readers and they confirm his real existence.

The fact is that all writers write for the audience that their nature guides them to. The pronouncement of some that they do not care about an audience is incorrect and unethical. Like anything else, literature is a social function that has its significance because it is a message addressed to an audience. If a writer says 'I write first and foremost for my own satisfaction', this in my view translates as: 'I write for some audience or other, firstly through my own satisfaction, not in pursuit of an audience at any price.'

Every writer must present the best of what he has, to the best of his ability and proficiency, and care as much about the communication of his message as he does about how he expresses it, without sacrificing any of the principles of art and creativity, and through his pursuit and endeavour reach the audience that is decreed for him. The kind and level of that audience will be the true guide to the kind and level of the writer.

Some writers please the elite, some please ordinary people and some please both, but in all cases it is the audience that certifies the writer's existence and defines his worth.

14 April 1994

A Conspiracy against Islam

Talk of conspiracies that are hatched night and day against Islam and Muslims is well known and regularly passed on. It has been repeated so frequently that it is practically learned by heart, and I do not intend to debate it. I submit to it, if only out of respect for the majority, for the majority has an undeniable right to be respected.

But I am pointing out – in addition to what has been said before – a conspiracy that has not had its share of light and attention: the conspiracy (or conspiracies) woven by Muslims themselves against Islam and Muslims. There is terrorism and there are terrorists who are extremist Muslims: if they are convinced of their extreme ideas, that is their right, and it is their right also to spread those ideas through any legitimate channel, but they go beyond extremism into violence and terrorism. They do not hide their nature, and pride themselves on being terrorists, on devoting their lives to bringing terror to Muslim society, which they regard as irreligious, and on putting an end to its symbols and institutions; their rage even carrying them so far as to kill innocent men, women and children. So whether intentional or unintentional, this is a conspiracy that weakens the cohesion and progress of the Islamic world and spreads anxiety and frustration among its citizenries.

Then there are the rich Muslims, the wealthy, whose fortunes around the world are quite considerable. They could have been a source of appeal for the Islamic world in its material advancement and its economic and scientific ascendancy, but they forget the brotherhood of Islam and invest their wealth in the international market, begrudging their own feeble countries all but the crumbs. It is said that they spend 80 dollars abroad for every one dollar they spend at home. So whether intentional or unintentional, this is another conspiracy.

If this is how we treat ourselves, we do not have the right to blame outsiders.

11 May 1994

In the Press

The press reports the presence of 160 billion Egyptian pounds in Egyptian banks, as some have rightly estimated. The investment of this enormous amount of cash would be sufficient to bring about the desired welfare of the country and its citizens. Why is this wealth piled up without being invested? We must ask ourselves this question and ponder it, in order to know the barriers and impediments, and to really and truly prepare the way for moving forward. If we do not, we will be committing a folly the like of which history has never seen before. We have the money and the human resources, we are not short of the learning and the expertise, and we see nothing wrong if necessary in appealing for help from foreign expertise, so when will we venture upon the serious work, and put our trust in God?

Then there is the talk that arises from time to time about our need for a national project to bring our disparate parts together, unify our goals and fill our souls with the spirit of determination. We seek the help of a national project to put an end to negativity, indifference, idleness, corruption and all the flaws that hinder our march. How often have I said it: the national project exists, and it is called comprehensive development. We are carrying it out plan after plan, but our moderate pace satisfies no one, and the truth is that what we lack is not the national project but the elimination of the flaws and the shortcomings in it. So let us search for a different cure, in order to be aware of the national project that is on the table and to serve it with the care and attention it deserves. We may find the needed cure in democracy, in administrative reorganisation, in judicious dealings based on reward and punishment, in determination in the pursuit of corruption, in the sovereignty of the law, in respect for human rights and in the application of the principle of equality in citizens' rights and responsibilities. If we do this, we will regain our spirit of zeal, action and struggle, and we will devote ourselves with all vigour to dealing with our national project. Indeed, we will consider any honest work a national project and a goal for victory and eminence.

12 May 1994

A Difficult Birth!

Ask any Arab: which is better for the Arabs, to disagree for reasons simple or complicated, or for all the reasons for disagreement among them to be removed?

Ask any Arab: which is preferable for the Arabs, to face the world divided and squabbling, or to face it as a body in agreement at least on motivations and goals?

Ask any Arab: which is more useful to the Arabs, to develop their countries only through their own effort and endeavour, or to develop them through investing their financial surpluses in their economic integration?

I do not think you will receive a single negative answer.

Then ask him: why has this not happened, in spite of its abundant contemporary and historical incentives? He will talk to you about borders, about certain historical failings, and about the painful memories of hostile invasion. We are not ignorant of human nature, and we can find an explanation for every weakness, nor do we want to exaggerate idealism and the quest for perfection. But we are asking that the voice of reason be listened to, just as we listen to the call of instinct. We must admit that we are in need of a few doses of honest objectivity.

We must examine ourselves critically time and again. We must elevate our future above the whirlpool of disagreements and resentments, and believe completely that there is no life for us without cooperation and bloc-formation – economic, scientific and cultural groupings and cooperation, before political. Not because the political side is unimportant but in order to start with what we can agree on without division. Even if we cannot begin with total cooperation, let us start with the cooperation that is possible within the available boundaries.

In any case, we must begin. And perhaps the first obligation of the Arab League in this historic time is to work on solving problems and removing the reasons for disagreement, to clear the field for the desired bloc-formation. The Arab League must be the path to true agglomeration.

19 May 1994

Morals

Frequently we exchange complaints about the deterioration in our public and private morals, a deterioration that nobody can ignore or dismiss the seriousness of. And frequently we explain this with a limited reason, according to the circumstances of the conversation, or by way of simplification: the reason is the economic crisis, or unemployment or even the cinema or television. But the phenomenon of human behaviour is much more complicated. It is interconnected with many social phenomena. I will not go into the mental and psychological reasons, as these are pathological conditions whose treatment is in the hands of medical science before all else. What matters to me here is to enumerate the social reasons, because on the one hand they are the main ones, while on the other hand just noting them is an indication of how we may free ourselves from them.

Our morals today are the bitter fruit of several factors, of which I present to you a few:

1. Authoritarian rule has terrified people with its severity, until fear has nested in their hearts and humiliation in their souls, making hypocrisy and duplicity the code of life.
2. One of the results of authoritarianism is the absolute dependence on confidantes in preference over experts, which foils the value of learning and work and leads to an increase in sycophancy, wrongdoing, special relationships, sharp practice and recklessness.
3. The economic crisis and its consequences of inflation and unemployment have devastated those with limited income and others among the poor, have drawn many into all kinds of obliquity and contempt for the bonds of intimacy that in the past were almost sacred, and have been the motivation behind many thefts, murders, rapes and drug crimes.
4. Contempt for the sanctity of the law – its public flouting, laxity in its application and negligence in implementing its judgements.

The cure may need time, and talking and preaching will serve no purpose. There must be comprehensive development, which must include political, economic, educational and cultural reform.

2 June 1994

Essential Qualities

Those who hold positions of leadership in the community need three qualities at least: national pride, good morals and knowledge and expertise. From national pride they draw love, zeal and fidelity. From good morals: the principles and values that govern and direct honest work. From knowledge and expertise: thought, planning, procedure and goals. It is not rare to find these qualities combined in many individuals, especially when well selected and free from self-interest.

Indeed, success can be achieved with two of the three, but there is no hope of that with anything less. Thus what is the use of national pride alone if a person is denied the two blessings of morals and knowledge? What benefit are morals alone without the support of knowledge or national pride? And what good do we expect of knowledge if an individual's conscience is without national pride or morals?

Meanwhile, if a person in authority is lacking or deficient in knowledge and expertise but has his full share of national pride and morals, he can compensate for his shortcoming through consultation and turning to scholars and experts for help.

Or if his national loyalty is weak but he still has knowledge and morals, it is possible that morals will push him to perform his duty, while knowledge and expertise will assist in his view and vision. There are unscrupulous people in authority, with no conscience or morality, yet even these, if they have sufficient national pride, knowledge and expertise, can be useful and can provide not inconsiderable services – even if their behaviour shows no sign of integrity or honesty, they fill their positions until their deviation is uncovered and they are removed.

This is why the choice of competent people is a matter of crucial importance, for they may build a revival, or they may lead us into decline and collapse. And this is why democracy has excelled over all forms of government in providing opportunities for choice and in the strength of its structures for monitoring, oversight, accountability and dialogue.

3 June 1994

The Near Future

It may be unfeasible – even from a non-specialist standpoint – for the follower of public life to picture the scientific aspect of tomorrow's world, as this requires a comprehensive look at the sciences, bringing together the achievements that are made every year with the subjects being researched, in order to build a picture on an objective foundation. But it must be granted that it will bring advances that exceed all imagination, on both the theoretical and the applied levels, and that these advances will have their effect on everything, from under the planet's surface to deep space, on rocks, on plants, on animals and on humanity.

So much knowledge will be accumulated that it will be beyond encompassing. Life will become complicated in behaviour, relationships and dealings with material things, whether in factories, in amenities or in everyday life. This is why the US secretary of labor said that the twenty-first century will be the century of the privileged citizen, capable of positive engagement with scientific progress in all fields. The only alternative is confusion, losing our way and faltering in life. It is the age of science: every day it gains new ground, and life grows in grandeur and complexity.

Science is extending its arms to embrace everything from the bathroom to the laboratory, in transportation, institutions and entertainment. It is the age of science, scientists, and a privileged public that has gained the ability – even if at a minimal level – to engage with a scientific world. We have read recently that some experts have warned England about falling into the abyss of the Third World, the main reason cited being the migration of creative scientific minds abroad, where they find a better climate for work and recognition. And this is a warning to us too of the result of the brain drain, drawing our attention to the importance of scientific innovation if we want to escape the clutches of the Third World.

Those who are thinking about the overhaul of the education system in our countries must take this point into consideration – that is, scientific studies and the scientific curriculum, and the formation of free minds capable of thought and invention. Of course, the objectives of education are broader than this, but science is actually what ties them to the modern age. In the near future we may witness humanity divided into two types: the scientific and the primitive.

5 June 1994

Secrets of Life

Grievance does not exist without cause. Behind it there is generally a defect in the body, the mind or the spirit, or in a person's relations with others, or with society as a whole, or even with the universe itself. The causes of grievance are limitless, and absolutely no individual, group or nation is innocent of it, though it may differ or vary according to circumstances and conditions, with dissimilarities in values, civilisation and learning. It is not a bad natural disposition, especially if distinguished by objectivity and viewed positively. Indeed, it may be the main motivator that drives us to search for a better life, whether at the level of the individual, society or humankind. What we sometimes imagine to be a time of life free from grievance is a delusion, just as the belief in the existence of higher worlds devoid of it is also a delusion. There is no time that is free from it, even the happy childhood – we escape to our childhood from a harsh and cruel reality, forgetting the pains, fears and troubles we suffered then. Likewise, we sometimes think that this or that advanced nation has attained perfection and rid itself of any cause for grievance, but why does its youth rebel? Why does its suicide rate rise? Why are there violent uprisings, and even revolutions?

We can find an explanation for this in an eternal truth, which is that humankind never stops imagining and dreaming. We live in a reality in which we deal with its good and its bad, dreaming of and looking forward to what is better, and it is in between reality and dream that grievance and the causes of rebellion and revolution erupt, and we achieve new progress on an endless road.

Human life is a continuous dispute between contentment and discontent, a dispute that usually ends in progress. But progress is not a definitive outcome unless supported by free will and firm struggle, which is why history has known both survival and extinction. To everyone their fate according to their ardour.

9 June 1994

Love of the Homeland

Love of the homeland and its people is a common and well-known emotion, and some even believe it is innate, as instincts are. But it may not exist, and national allegiance may be weak to the point of absence. The truth is that this emotion grows and blooms with good upbringing, as it grows and blooms in the sound atmosphere of a wholesome, healthy society.

It is patriotic upbringing that pours love for country and zeal for its heritage and glories into our hearts, aided in this by the study of history and certain cultural activities. The mission is continued by the media in various print, audio and visual forms. But this comprehensive education is of no use on its own unless it is backed up by action – action that sets love in motion, so that its reward will be love in return for love, fidelity for fidelity and loyalty for loyalty.

The society that provides its members with the essential services in education, health care, ease of transportation, clean spaces and appropriate housing is different from the society that provides some of these things but not others, or the society that provides them all but in a sorry, disappointing state. Naturally, love will differ between one and the other.

And the society that makes job opportunities available, and envelopes this with truth and justice, differs from the impotent society, or the one that denies itself the principle of equal opportunities and is influenced in its choices by kinship, friendship, politics or religion. The first will win love and appreciation, while the second will yield rage and rebellion.

The society in which human rights and the highest values are respected is one whose members will enjoy spiritual and mental well-being, while that which exploits its members, maltreats them and makes a mockery of its laws will taste its own medicine.

God aid you in the creation of a righteous nation that will be a sanctuary and a place for love.

12 June 1994

The Noble Thief

The noble thief is a popular legend, based around a hero of the people who is constructed from truth and fiction, like Robin Hood or Adham al-Sharqawi.[1] On the level of reality, he is a thief, a highwayman and a killer, though he chooses his victims from among the rich and those of rank and authority and shares his booty and spoils with the poor and disadvantaged. He has generally been found in periods of oppression, tyranny and subjugation, when rulers act despotically and place no value on people's lives, plundering wealth and property through any means, whether licit or illicit. Because of this, the people forgive the noble thief his transgressions, shower him with love and devotion, and give him protection wherever he happens to be. He may be a thief but he steals from those who steal from them, and he may be a killer but he kills those who play with their lives, and in the end he is not sparing in his generosity with them. If he comes to the end of his preordained destiny, and is arrested and executed, they weep and grieve for him from the depths of their hearts, and celebrate him in ballads that are sung for generations. This is all different to the ordinary thief, the ordinary killer, the ordinary highwayman, who are loathed and despised, and who the people help the police to catch or corner.

Then time brings the true heroes of the people, represented in their national and community leaders, who direct them by good example, rare courage and high values towards better conduct and lives. But even then, the general public does not forget its old champion, the noble thief, the hero of bad times and stubborn oppression.

16 June 1994

---

1 Adham al-Sharqawi (1898–1921) became a folk hero in Egypt following his attacks on the British occupiers of the country and on feudalistic land-owners.

The Future of the Nation

Look at the youth, and you see the nation of the future and beyond. Their sentiments, their conduct, their way of thinking will shape the sentiments, conduct and way of thinking of the nation. There are many institutions that work together in the formation of our youth and their preparation for life, such as family, schools and media and cultural organisations. Specialised in this field is the Higher Council for Youth, as the state is also considered responsible through its general policies for furnishing them with work opportunities and providing fair channels for entering employment and establishing themselves.

Families, schools, media and cultural organisations and the Higher Council – each in their special way and within their capability – provide education in all its varieties (religious, national, cultural, artistic), as well as preparing and qualifying the young for practical modern life. They must not fall short in equipping them with what they need for the building of their character in all its human and national dimensions and for their preparation for life in the modern age. Any shortcoming in this matter will bring frustration to youth and loss and delay to the nation. And girls must receive the same attention as boys: the role of girls in building civilisation is no less serious than the role of boys, and even exceeds it when you take into consideration the consequences of motherhood and family life.

Then comes the role of the state in creating job opportunities for the new generations and distributing them on a fair and scrupulous basis, while preserving respect for human rights. The state's success in this will constitute the boundary between indifference and loyalty, between rebellion and devotion, between violence and peace.

23 June 1994

An Old Comic Song

I still recall a comic song I memorised as a child, which went:

If you don't have an uncle / Or very much money
Your promotion is hopeless / In this age of rascals

And included the words:

This life is like a platter / Of bread, rice, and broth in the mosque
Around it are the watchmen and their captain / Who gives to his kin and makes a mess
And yells at the wretched reader of Qur'an

I can't recall the lyricist or the composer for certain, but at the same time I have never known a more eloquent description of the manner of life that is followed in our land and embraced by everybody, submitted to by all as if it were a sacred religion. It is the faith of every party, of every age, of every type. There is no difference between a liberal age and a totalitarian one, and it has been like that since the Eloquent Peasant first raised his voice in complaint.[1] We have always consisted of two classes: one of grace and one of grief. The first comprises those with the right connections, wealth, or position, while the second comprises the general public. To the first could be added some of the friends of the connected, or some of the bodyguards, the entourage, or the servants. The division of the spoils depends on privilege, power and connections, and the class of grace wins all the boons: the best positions, the easements in all fields, the exceptional services and the rosy settlements with the law and regulations. For the class of grief, all that is left for them is toil, hardship, misfortune, disease, affliction, unemployment and the slums.

Deliverance appears to be a long way off and out of reach, but it

---

1 *The Eloquent Peasant* is an Ancient Egyptian literary composition from the nineteenth century BCE, in which a poor peasant appeals for justice.

is very far from that. All we need is an equitable justice system that makes no exceptions for anybody, and in order to have that justice system there must be built a free and fair state.

7 July 1994

Terrorism and Its Kin

Perhaps the simplest definition of terrorism is the use of illicit force in order to achieve a certain aim. If this definition is correct, then terrorism as we commonly understand it is not the only kind to be practised in our society: everything that is achieved by force, not by law or through legitimate means, is a form of terrorism. And force means not only bullets and bombs – there is also the force of influence, nepotism, party affiliation, family, faction and religion. So it can be said that any force that is used in violation of legitimacy or that oversteps the law is terrorism, and we must recognise it as such and place it on the same side of the scales as the terrorism that we hunt down morning and evening.

Power can be attained as the result of legitimate effort, or as the fruit of terrorist violence. Appointment to a position in the public sector can be according to educational achievement or through a fair recruitment examination, or it can depend on the force of influence and connections – that is, through terrorism. Business deals may depend on the laws of the market, or they may be controlled by influence and bribery, or by other means of economic terrorism. Services work the same way: look at what happens in the street, in the hospitals, on buses and trains and in government offices – is everyone treated according to a fixed and comprehensive system that does not distinguish between one person and another? Or are some warmly welcomed with open arms while the torment of unaccountable suffering is poured over others?

After this preamble, I invite all readers to ponder what happens in our society, and to judge for themselves: is it a society of law and legitimacy, or is it one of terrorism?

I think you will agree with me that the first steps on the ladder to civilisation are for society to be transformed from one based on natural impulses and force to one that lives under the shade of the law and legitimacy, so that it can realise freedom and justice.

14 July 1994

The Demands of the Young Generation

While we are demanding that the youth be the pillar of the present and the hope of the future – our share in civilisation is a sacred trust in their hands, and we pray fervently that they are up to the responsibility of that trust – at the same time, in return, we cannot ignore their own demands. So what are the demands of the young generation?

The first thing they ask for is an education that will qualify them to operate in modern life, with a trade or profession, or a field in which to do something creative or exercise a unique talent.

They demand instruction that is worthy of building all aspects of their character – religious, moral, national, humanitarian, artistic, sporting – to be healthy in body, and to be prepared in spirit for wisdom and maturity.

Then they ask for work opportunities in line with what they have been promised, so that they can be fulfilled and serve their society. Salaries must be sufficient, accommodation must be available and their path must be clear of obstacles that might disappoint and frustrate them.

They demand security and stability under the shade of the sovereignty of law, and for all to be equal in front of the law in rights and responsibilities, without artificial distinction for social, political, religious or other reasons. Hard work must be the foundation for success, and success must be the measure in recruitment to a position or promotion to a higher rank. They will give back to work their worth and to the nation their commitment, feeling that they live in a civilised society, not simply in an agglomeration of individuals ruled by violence, injustice and self-interest.

These are first principles, which will bring in their wake the protection of minds and talents, and attention to centres of scientific research. The encouragement of outstanding performers and the announcement of their achievements are what will confirm trust, love and respect between them and their fellow citizens, propelling them to further diligence and excellence.

21 July 1994

The Work Ethic

The work ethic is what makes work an exalted social and human value. It is what has made the working citizens of the advanced nations prime examples of diligence and abundant commitment. The work ethic is shaped by two important factors: the education of the new generation and the treatment of the mature workforce. Education provides us with the experience of the educators, the treasures of tradition and effective strength, while how workers are treated at recruitment, promotion, or in the distribution of incentives connects the work to the effort exerted.

The work ethic in our country has been subject to scourges and maladies, as it has long been the policy to appoint graduates to jobs in the public sector whether they are needed or not; incentives and salary increases have been handed out in a bureaucratic manner, not on the basis of the worker's contribution or importance; and relatives have been chosen for significant positions and superior ranks, with preference given to trusted intimates over experts. This is how the young have found their fate decided and their future defined for reasons that have nothing to do with diligence, endeavour or true productivity, so their work ethic and their confidence in the way forward have begun to weaken and dwindle, and duplicity has grown stronger and more forceful. The sickness has even spread among students, starting in the age of innocence, so that attention is now concentrated on the leaving certificate, and away from the acquisition of learning. We have entered ailing times of mass cheating and attacks on invigilators. Importance is no longer attached to anything except the certificate as a licence to employment, without the need for learning or experience: the alternative dubious means guarantee everything needed.

The loss of the work ethic turns the worker into a time-server, wastes the forces of production, and leads to many causes of misery.

We must restore the work ethic, and the way to do this is clear: sound education is conceivable, and the treatment of people based on diligence, endeavour and good performance is not impossible. This is an absolute necessity if we are to enter the new world.

28 July 1994

The Message and the Preachers

I have written on several occasions in the past about the message of Islam and those who preach it. I have praised the great mission they carry out in the life of the Islamic community as the nurturers of its religious sentiment and the voice that is heard in its mosques throughout towns and villages. It is true that because of the nature of their message they have the greatest effect on people, and rapidly penetrate their hearts, and it is certainly within their capability to participate in the shaping of generations and to arouse them from their slumber. Because of this, I called for a rise in their preparedness to the highest scholarly and cultural levels, so that they become competent to bear the responsibility in this exceedingly complex age, the so-called age of science, communication and information.

We must not forget what has happened to us on account of the spread of the extremist ideas that have hurt Islam and its followers, and the spread of those ideas should not make us at any point review our obligations towards religion and to the preachers. True Islam cannot be defeated by extremism when it holds the mosques, the media, the right and the truth.

We must prepare those who preach Islam, and provide them with the means for good work. They are the tongue of religious enlightenment, and they must always be in all places at all times.

Our expectation from the preachers is that we will understand Islam in its meaning, its precepts and its ethics, and that their lessons will go on to include the principle of consultation, or the democracy of political Islam as it ought to be understood today and in the future.

We expect them to tell us about social justice in Islam, and the sacred value that Islam places on freedom, thought, work and production.

And about the human rights that were set down by Islam, as well as about the rights that it did not set down but can accept.

God be praised, they will not lack for sources ancient or modern, nor will they lack the sincere desire for the advancement of the Islamic community in the modern age.

4 August 1994

The Working Spirit

We must work with all resolve and serious intent to boost the working spirit to the highest possible level. We must employ all our strengths, manifest and latent, for the sake of asserting our presence in the new world without delay, negligence or laxity. We have many of the means for gaining success – we have the education and instruction, the research and training centres, the scholars and experts. It is up to us to make the best use of this wealth, to extract the best possibilities from it, and to make religion, learning and national feeling our driving strengths and guiding beacons.

At the same time we must learn from the mistakes of the past, which were harmful to the love and sanctity of work, to the respect for earnest diligence and to the rightful devotion to national allegiance. We must learn from the mistakes that countervailed the value of work and endeavour, and weakened the feelings of loyalty to the nation.

For this reason, it is essential that we make the following a reality:

First: equality before the law in rights and responsibilities, and putting an end to any exceptions in that area, bringing severe punishment to whoever commits this crime against the nation.

Second: equal opportunities, and everybody to be recompensed according to their competence, diligence and moral character.

Third: the linking of appointments, promotions, bonuses, awards and incentives to production, first and foremost.

Fourth: relying in our administration and production on research and training centres, and benefiting further from the information age.

In a word: we must build our society on learning, justice and freedom, and draw from our heritage everything that supports, strengthens and guides that.

11 August 1994

Fear of Freedom

How many contradictory voices there are, though they all arise out of sincerity and honesty. Those who are happy with the age of GATT and the Middle Eastern market are sincere and honest. Those who fear this age and expect it to bring harm and damage are sincere and honest. Those who welcome and promote normalisation are sincere and honest.[1] And those who reject it and call for a boycott are sincere and honest.

What is behind this contradiction, and how can it be explained?

Perhaps it is the fear of freedom and a lack of self-confidence.

We lived a long period of time under the authority of totalitarian rule, and we have not yet been liberated from its control, as we should have been. Totalitarian rulers eliminate thought and free will, and hold the individual captive under the shade of power in order to perform all general responsibilities in his place, leaving him able to conduct only his own affairs, and even this he does within limits and with caution. So this individual does not feel he is responsible, or could ever be responsible, having lost his self-confidence through placing his trust in the apparatus of power.

Suddenly these people who have been subject to totalitarian rule find themselves within sight of a new world that is built, contrary to their own totalitarian world, on freedom, competition and self-reliance, and in which there is no room for blind trust, only for efficiency, innovation, proficiency, fairness and production.

So they are afraid, they are pessimistic, and they anticipate the worst – how can they operate outside protection, monopoly and bureaucracy? Words of warning trip from their tongues about defeat, ruin and damage.

We have proved our competence in the not too distant past, and those of us who have emigrated abroad also prove their competence in other countries every day. We possess both heritage and modernity,

---

1 In spite of Egypt's peace treaty with Israel of 1978, the normalisation of relations was still at the time of writing (and is still now) a contentious issue.

which justifies optimism, invites hope, and derides the spirit of hesitation and defeat.

18 August 1994

Between Freedom of Thought and Freedom of Expression

Freedom in the creative field means freedom of thought on the one hand and freedom of expression on the other. It is the right of the creative community to demand complete freedom in their activities, just as it is the right of the conservative community to demand adherence to religion and morals. The issue is an old one, and it seems to endure without a final verdict. And attitudes towards it vary from one time to another, from one place to another and from one culture to another. I witnessed an age that was a good example of tolerance and open-mindedness and that held discussions and only rarely made judgements, but our current time is being taken over by intransigence, with a proliferation of suspicion and distrust.

My view is that both sides are right and that sometimes collision is unavoidable, and that progress itself is achieved only through conflict.

It is my hope that thought will attain absolute freedom, and that disagreements over it will be restricted to informed and objective discussion, because any infringement on the freedom of thought will impede and hold back truth and progress. The legitimacy of these hopes is supported by the fact that true thought occurs in the circles of the most reasonable people, of whom there is no fear that they will be blinded by falsehoods.

In the case of expression, the situation is different. Thoughtful artistic expression gives voice to the human experiment and its intellectual, emotional and instinctual aspects, and its sphere of interaction is much wider than that of thought alone. In addition, there are many who know their way to the mass means of expression, so their effect will reach even the illiterate. For this reason, they should maintain modesty, decency and taste, and it would certainly do no harm to do so.

1 September 1994

Tomorrow Is Another Day

Our modern life beckons to us with two new worlds: these are the world of the Middle Eastern market and the world of GATT.

As usual, everything good or bad that can be said about these two worlds has been said. For some they are the road to deliverance, for others the road to perdition. What is apparent is that heading towards the two worlds is irrevocable and inevitable, and thus we have settled on this choice – and I do not think we have chosen self-destruction.

The post-Cold War world is one in which struggle is based on free competition, and which depends at its core on the will to live and work, on knowledge and experience, and on the proper climate for a forward-looking human life. In such a world the status of every nation is determined according to the potential it has and the effort it exerts.

It is not right that our self-confidence should disappear to the extent of surrendering to defeatism. We possess material and human resources and spiritual values, and we have long dealings with knowledge and expertise.

All this qualifies us for a role in the region, and consequently in the world.

But we must look again at our souls and blow new life into them to prepare them for true success in that global struggle. I say – and I do not tire of saying again and again – that we cannot focus on work while we are preoccupied with the fight against terrorism, while we are drowning in corruption, while we are content for democracy and the respect for human rights to be marginal notes of no benefit or utility, nor while we surrender to bureaucracy and emergency laws.

We must be liberated from every nightmarish shackle before we knock at the doors of the new world.

8 September 1994

The Sovereignty of the Law

The law in our country must enjoy strength, reverence, sovereignty and justice. All people must be equal before it, and it must not distinguish between high and low. Its application must know no kind of exception, and there must be punishment for everybody who violates it, from which no person may escape. There must be fair judges to apply the law, and honest custodians to oversee, monitor and execute it. We must be able to feel that the law is our ruler and our recourse, and the first and last arbiter between right and wrong.

The law is the basis of any society, and without it – or in its neglect – any society becomes no more than an agglomeration, far from civilisation in its true sense. It is no coincidence that the law enjoys all prerogatives in a democratic system where criticism, oversight and the rotation of power thrive. It is also no coincidence that the law is subject to contempt in totalitarian regimes, in which the ruler finds himself above it. The law is a solid foundation for a civilised society.

If a society is not free of corruption, terrorism, unemployment, or economic, political or social crises, this perhaps does not preclude it from being a civilised society, but I doubt if it deserves that description if the law in it is sidelined or weakened or invaded by corruption.

It has been said that justice is the foundation of God's world, and justice when translated is nothing but law.

15 September 1994

The People's Dream

Our people have long aspired to freedom and justice. In 1919 they launched their popular revolution, setting out to liberate themselves politically and economically from foreign control and fight against royal despotism at home, imagining that they would realise their dream of attaining freedom and justice. But a long time went by, there were bitter trials, the population grew and the problems multiplied and became more complicated – yet the old dream of freedom and justice still beguiled our hearts.

Then came the revolution of 1952, which brought huge advances in social affairs, while postponing freedom for the time being. Time passed, and positive steps followed one after another, but battles and wars occurred, debts mounted up and a difficult, harsh era reigned – and again the dream of freedom and justice beguiled our hearts.

The state does what it can to make the dream come true, and there have been many achievements and innovations in the economy and in politics, but millions of toiling and exhausted people have still not benefited from the fruit of the efforts exerted.

And one group of people have renounced any human effort or humane trend, having found only disappointment and deceit in both, and have pounced like wild beasts to kill and destroy.

It is a terrible race that requires the state to do more than its utmost to purge itself and to loose its latent strengths in work, reconstruction and development.

There is no security except in the realisation of the old dream, eternally renewed: the dream of freedom and justice.

22 September 1994

The Patriotic Value

I had heard and read much about the low level of patriotism among the younger generations. Even so, I was very disturbed when a young man confronted me, saying: 'I find no sense in your call to loyalty to the country. Why should I be loyal to the country? What benefit has the country promised me, that I should be loyal to it?' Hearing of something is not the same as seeing it for oneself. I am of a generation that considers patriotism truly an instinct, a natural impulse, and which is insulted to find it a topic of discussion or ridicule. I wonder what has corrupted this instinct in some people? Do ideologies – like pan-Arabism or leftism, for example – have an effect? They may not be without effect, but they do not erase love for country from hearts forever, so we must search further for the causes.

The reason is not that people are divided into rich and poor, healthy and sick, educated and illiterate, or even employed and unemployed. All this may be present, and people come to understand the reasons and do what they can to fight against it without their natural love for their country vanishing from their hearts. But it is different if the youth feel that their country does not spread its love and care to all its children with equality and fairness. Perhaps it does not treat them equally in wealth or in many natural advantages, but it deals with them equally before the law, applies the same treatment to them, and provides them with the same opportunities. If young people are aware of this justice, they may endure their bad luck for the time being and may await their opportunity without curse or rancour. But if the scales of justice (which is the foundation of God's world) are out of balance, you will come across someone saying: 'What benefit has the country promised me, that I should be loyal to it?'

And at every step, we are missing this justice: we miss it in the street, in public services, in hospitals, in selections for public sector jobs, in the filling of higher vacancies – there is so much discrimination in everything that we have killed off patriotic values, as we have killed off the work ethic. And without these two values there is no society, only a collection of profiteers, artful dodgers and people without hope.

We must restore the value to work and to patriotism, and this requires of us no more than the sovereignty and sanctity of the law and its application with absolute justice, and an understanding that the breach of this is a great crime against society, to be punished by imprisonment for life.

29 September 1994

Universal Defence

What has been published about the preparation of a plan for the defence of the planet against the dangers of the universe that threaten it is one of the most extraordinary things I have come across. For example, there is Halley's Comet, which approaches Earth on its cycle every 76 years, raising fears about the possibility of it crashing into us, and the disastrous consequences for life on the planet. And there are the meteors that are travelling towards us at speed and almost impossible to see, for they burn up and disappear in the atmosphere. The terrible effect of these meteors has been discovered on the surface of the moon, and similar ones could fall on Earth.

This means that our planet is floating in space among many dangers that surround it and the life that flourishes on it. But those who are accustomed to dealing with science and its applications are not standing before this threat with their hands tied. They are working to put in place a global plan for the planet's defence, a plan that involves the participation of advanced nations like the United States, Europe, Russia and Japan, and includes the construction of space stations for observation and early warning, as well as ideas for blowing up or knocking off course any bodies that carry danger, using nuclear bombs.

This enterprising scientific spirit deserves salutation and admiration, and a doubling of humankind's hopes in science and its services. All we wish in addition to this is that we act to stave off the harm of humans on humans living on Earth itself, so that the saying of the Prophet will be true of us: 'If you show mercy to those on the earth, He who is in the heaven will show mercy to you.'

6 October 1994

Good Morning to the World

Let us take a look at a newspaper or two. It does not much matter which, if you are to know the events that are making history at home and abroad, and especially if you focus on the essential issues.

The news of achievements dominates the front page. Reforms surge like the Flood of 'Arim in all aspects of production and services.[1] True, the opposition papers present a contrasting, stagnant picture, devoid of life, and heaving with ills, delay and disappointment, but we are merely documenting, not entering into the heart of the disagreement. Turning to crises, there is an economic crisis and there is inflation and all that they bring in the way of unemployment and every shade and form of corruption, and the outside world is also suffering from an economic crisis and unemployment, and has more than enough instances of corruption.

As for terrorism, do not be shy to speak of it, whether local or global, whether religious, racist, or nationalist. Even drug kings have become masters in the terrorism of their opponents.

There are bloody political issues, which you find in Yemen, Sudan and Afghanistan, reaching their peak in Bosnia, Somalia and Rwanda.

And then there are the discarded poor of the Third World, as well as of the advanced world, where millions live below the poverty line. Details of the statistics are not known, nor is the frightening future of poverty on Earth.

It is a world replete with offensive things, and it is rare to come across something pleasing. Perhaps happy news proliferates – barely – in only one area, which is science. In the overall darkness, lights gleam in the research centres, where there is always growing knowledge, the discovery of new truths, and the vigorous battle against diseases and epidemics.

Open your newspaper, and do not despair of taking in what is better and brighter.

12 October 1994

1 The Flood of 'Arim was a disastrous historical flood that is mentioned in the Qur'an (34:16), caused by the breach of the Dam of 'Arim in ancient Yemen.

From Enlightenment to Comprehensive Reform[1]

Public opinion has been alerted by a repentant terrorist to the importance of books, whether in the recruitment of young people to extremism or in their rescue from extremist ideas, according to the kind of book and the vision it presents. There is nothing new in this, as we have long known about books and cassette tapes that make the call to extremism, just as we know about books of enlightenment, both secular and religious.

The discussion has been very animated about the role of family, schools and the media, but what is not in doubt is that the role of ideas is of the greatest importance in confronting terrorism, equal in importance to the security response mounted by the security forces with all strength, courage and sacrifice. But we must not lose sight of the role of poverty, unemployment, corruption and everything that casts youth into the claws of hopelessness and frustration.

People respond to extremist books only if they are psychologically and socially prepared to do so, and those who are in good psychological and social health will not lean towards extremist views: even if they embrace them as ideas in rare circumstances, they will not turn with them to violence and terrorism, and expose their peaceful, healthy lives to ruin. But extremist ideas and calls to terrorism may find an echo in souls that are exhausted by poverty, despair and feelings of injustice. This is why the preachers of terrorism have found easy prey in the slum areas and in impoverished, deprived surroundings.

Terrorism is a dangerous disease, and its treatment must be comprehensive, through security, through ideas, through reform and through politics. We are not asking for anything exceptional: a sound society based on freedom and justice is the aim of every sound nation.

20 October 1994

---

1 [Note in the Arabic edition:] Our great writer wrote this article a few days before the criminal attack he suffered [on 14 October 1994].

Pathological Tensions[1]

Where is the discussion that ends as objectively and quietly and with as much respect for the other view as it began?

The literary, political and philosophical discussions that I am able to follow are marked by the overwhelming stamp of vehemence and violence, transforming in no time from discussion to battle. Meetings turn from the topic at hand to the personal, and accusations fly in the air according to circumstances and conditions, from ignorance, backwardness and blinkered horizons to blind imitation, hubris and the departure from honest values. And the matter may not be without innuendo and insinuations of a threat to honour, conscience or national loyalty, while the original cause of disagreement can languish in a neglected corner, or be overlooked as something insignificant, usually no more than a footnote.

The fact is that minds have begun to close in the face of discussion, and cannot bear other opinions. They are not characterised by any kind of understanding or tolerance, as if anyone with an opinion sees himself as an authority that should be above every power, above every view, and as if it is not right for anyone who encounters this authority – whether at close quarters or at a distance – to walk free without severe punishment.

The climate of terrorism has gained ground in literature, thought and debate, even if the means and aims differ. This is why many are passionate about freedom, not as a general human value but as a means to establishing their state and their doctrines – otherwise they are completely prepared to overthrow it and put it in chains.

We have been truly damaged by our long acquaintance with totalitarian regimes, and we are in need of a profound spiritual salvation.

27 October 1994

---

1 [Note in the Arabic edition:] Our great writer also wrote this article a few days before the criminal attack he suffered [on 14 October 1994].